THE
TRAVEL
BOOK

Malcolm Croft

Illustrated by Maggie Li

CONTENTS

Asia

Oceania

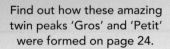

Find out how these amazing twin peaks 'Gros' and 'Petit' were formed on page 24.

Discover where more than half the world's mountain gorillas live on page 121.

Do you know what ingredients you'll need to make this dish? Find out on page 101.

THE TRAVEL BOOK

Discover the crazy sport of *kiiking* on page 52.

You might not realize it yet, but you're holding the world in your hands right now. Yes, this book is your ticket to a round-the-world journey through every country on the planet.

There are wild rainforests and tropical islands, busy cities and soaring mountains, wild animals, incredible architecture, tasty treats and a whole lot of amazing people waiting to be discovered.

So, what are you waiting for? Turn the page and begin your journey around the world!

THE COUNTRY CARDS

At the top of each page you'll find a pair of cards. They're color coded to tell you which continent you're in, but there's also a lot of information packed onto each one.

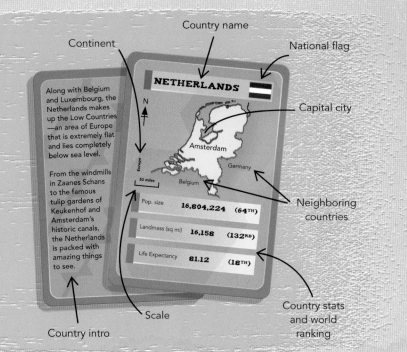

Continent

Country name

National flag

NETHERLANDS

N

Along with Belgium and Luxembourg, the Netherlands makes up the Low Countries —an area of Europe that is extremely flat and lies completely below sea level.

From the windmills in Zaanes Schans to the famous tulip gardens of Keukenhof and Amsterdam's historic canals, the Netherlands is packed with amazing things to see.

Amsterdam

Capital city

Germany

50 miles

Belgium

Neighboring countries

Pop. size	16,804,224	(64TH)
Landmass (sq mi)	16,158	(132RD)
Life Expectancy	81.12	(18TH)

Country stats and world ranking

Scale

Country intro

CANADA

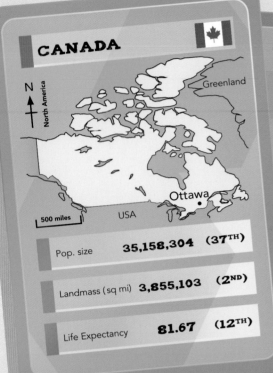

🍁

N
North America

Greenland

Ottawa

USA

500 miles

Pop. size	35,158,304	(37TH)
Landmass (sq mi)	3,855,103	(2ND)
Life Expectancy	81.67	(12TH)

Maple syrup, ice hockey, prisons for polar bears—you name it, Canada has it!

The second largest country in the world, Canada is roughly the same size as Europe! It also happens to have one of the happiest populations on the planet too. Welcome to Canada!

A LAND OF LAKES

Canada is home to around two million lakes! In winter, at Moraine Lake in Alberta, the water becomes so clean and clear that it mirrors the sky.

Which country do Monarch butterflies migrate to each year?

GO TO PAGE 8

THE MIGHTY THOR

Mount Thor, made of pure granite is Canada's most treasured mountainous peak. Located on Baffin Island, northern Canada, Mount Thor has the world's greatest vertical drop—a 4,100-ft. (1,250-m) view that goes straight down. It is three times the height of the Empire State Building in New York!

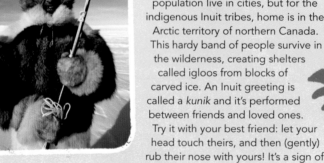

Mount Thor's drop
4,100FT.
(1,250M)

Burj Khalifa, Dubai
2,716FT.
(828M)

Empire State Building, NY
1,250FT.
(381M)

HOME IS WHERE THE IGLOO IS

Today, 80 percent of Canada's population live in cities, but for the indigenous Inuit tribes, home is in the Arctic territory of northern Canada. This hardy band of people survive in the wilderness, creating shelters called igloos from blocks of carved ice. An Inuit greeting is called a *kunik* and it's performed between friends and loved ones. Try it with your best friend: let your head touch theirs, and then (gently) rub their nose with yours! It's a sign of respect and affection.

FALLING FOR NIAGARA!

Niagara Falls is Canada's most famous natural landmark. This incredible water feature is actually three giant waterfalls in one. In 1859, a French tightrope walker named Charles Blondin crossed over the top of the falls several times on a tightrope. As if that weren't crazy enough, the daredevil also completed this feat while blindfolded, carrying someone on his back and, on one occasion, cooking and eating an omelet halfway across!

Sasquatch

HERE BE MONSTERS!

Cryptozoologists (scientists who study beasts that may not exist) claim that Canada is a hotspot for monsters. Examples of such mysterious beasts found here include the Sasquatch—a super-sized hairy creature—and a number of lake monsters, such as Ogopogo in Lake Okanagan and the Qalupalik—a scary Inuit legend.

Ogopogo

Can you think of another lake with a famous mythical monster hiding in it?

GO TO PAGE 42

HOME OF THE BURGER

The world's favorite fast food was created in America over 100 years ago. Today, more than 40 billion burgers are eaten in America each year!

ONE WORLD TRADE CENTER

Built on the site of the Twin Towers —the two huge office buildings that were destroyed on September 11, 2001—the mega-skyscraper One World Trade Center opened in November 2014 at a height of 1776 ft. (541 m). The number 1776 is important to America —it was the year the Declaration of Independence was signed.

UNITED STATES

After the American Revolutionary War ended in 1783, the new nation claimed independence from Great Britain and the United States of America was born. Over the next century, the country divided itself up into territories, known as states, and there are now 50 of these. Here are the five biggest, with all their letters mixed up. Can you unscramble the names?

1. Laaaks
2. Xetsa
3. Norialifac
4. Tanmona
5. Mex cionwe

Answers: 1. Alaska, 2. Texas, 3. California, 4. Montana, 5. New Mexico

The Chinese name for the United States of America is *Meiguo*, which literally means "beautiful country." And how right they are! America isn't only beautiful . . . it's also very big, right down to its buffalos, buildings and, beef burgers!

Divided up into 50 unique states, America is like lots of countries rolled into one.

U.S.A.

Canada

North America

N

500 miles

Washington, D.C.

Pop. size	316,128,839 (3RD)
Landmass (sq mi)	3,794,100 (3RD)
Life Expectancy	79.56 (33RD)

THE FIRST AMERICANS

The land we now know as "America" was once populated by many separate native tribes. The Apache Indians, who for thousands of years lived in the country's south-western deserts around the states of Arizona, New Mexico, and Texas, still exist today. Apache tribes live on their own reservations—land that belongs solely to them—but they must obey American laws.

Apache Indian

GROUNDHOG DAY

Every February 2, the people of Punxsutawney, Pennsylvania, gather around to observe a groundhog (a type of land beaver, also known as a whistle-pig!) called Phil emerge from his burrow. Upon waking, if Phil sees his shadow, there will be six more weeks of winter. If not, locals can expect an early spring. This amazing custom dates back to 1886, making Phil over 130 years old!

RACE TO THE MOON

In the 1960s, America and Russia were in a race to be the first nations to send men to the Moon. In July, 1969, America achieved this remarkable feat. Taking three days, astronauts Neil Armstrong, Buzz Aldrin and Michael Collins travelled 238,855 mi. (384,000 km) and descended to the lunar surface. The first footage of this historic moment was beamed down from the Moon back to planet Earth, where the world was watching.

WHAT A RUSH!

Four of America's most famous presidents are carved into the side of Mount Rushmore in South Dakota. The faces of George Washington, Thomas Jefferson, Theodore Roosevelt, and Abraham Lincoln are over 60 ft. (18 m) high—the same size as a six-storey building! Sculpting began in 1927 and took over 14 years to complete. It is said that George Washington's giant nose can get quite runny when it's cold!

CUDDLY TOY

The teddy bear was named after President Theodore "Teddy" Roosevelt, after he refused to shoot a black bear on a hunting trip. The president hated his nickname, but the teddy bear is still one of the world's most loved toys.

MEXICO

(map showing USA, Mexico City, North America, 200 miles scale)

Pop. size	122,322,399	(11TH)
Landmass (sq mi)	758,449	(13TH)
Life Expectancy	75.43	(74TH)

From semi-deserts to tropical forests and volcanic mountains, Mexico is a country as up and down as its brutal history.

It's chock-full of lost civilizations and heaving modern cities, local traditions and colorful customs. Say *hola* to Mexico!

BEFORE THE SPANISH

Mexico, like much of Central and South America, was once home to many great, but now lost, civilizations. From 1150 BC to AD 1519 Mexico was the central location of six ancient civilizations: Olmec, Teotihuacán, Maya, Zapotec, Toltec and Aztec.

THE SPANISH INVASION

When 508 Spanish soldiers, 11 ships and 16 horses came ashore in Mexico in March, 1519, led by Hernán Cortés, a Spanish conquistador (conqueror), they managed to overthrow an entire civilization of 25 million people. This Aztec civilization, the last native empire to inhabit these lands, had never seen horses before and believed Cortés to be a god.

CHICHÉN ITZÁ

Chichén Itzá was a large city built by the Mayan people around the year 600. The ruins of this lost city largely remain, including the incredible Kukulkan Pyramid, which is one of the new seven Wonders of the World.

DINOSAUR KILLER

You might have heard that a massive asteroid killed off all the dinosaurs 65 million years ago, but what many people don't know is that it was Mexico where the asteroid crash-landed! This super-charged space rock smashed into the Yucatán Peninsula—leaving a crater 110 mi. (175 km) and 12 mi. (20 km) deep, and triggering the extinction of all the poor dinos!

MONARCH AIRWAYS

The monarch butterfly migration is one of nature's greatest spectacles. Each year, as many as one billion beautiful monarch butterflies make the journey from eastern Canada to the forests of western central Mexico, a journey that spans more than 2,500 mi. (4,000 km)!

DAY OF THE DEAD

Día de Muertos, or "Day of the Dead," is a grand festival that Mexicans celebrate every November. During the Day of the Dead, deceased relatives are believed to return home where they're honored with flowers and food. Colorful sugar skulls decorate tombstones and houses, and people stay in graveyards celebrating all night long.

CAVE OF CRYSTALS

Mexico's Cave of Crystals, located 984 ft. (300 m) below ground, is the hottest cave in the world, regularly recording temperatures of 111°F (44°C). The crystals are the largest natural crystals to be found on Earth, and can weigh up to 50 tons—that's heavier than six elephants!

TEQUILA!

The iconic national drink of Mexico is tequila. This very alcoholic drink is made from a type of cactus, which grows around the town of Tequila.

THE ROAD TO MAYAN RUINS

Belize was once the thriving centre of the Mayan civilization, and the country is filled with the ruins of ancient temples, towns, and cities. There are still many treasured Mayan sites that have yet to be discovered.

MOVING CAPITAL

Belize's capital city moved to Belmopan after a hurricane nearly destroyed Belize City in 1961.

Known to locals as "the Jewel," Belize is home to one of the largest coral reefs in the world, as well as Belmopan, one of the world's smallest capital cities.

Belize is a country so paradise-perfect, with so much packed in, that you won't quite *Belize* your eyes when you realize it's the same size as Wales!

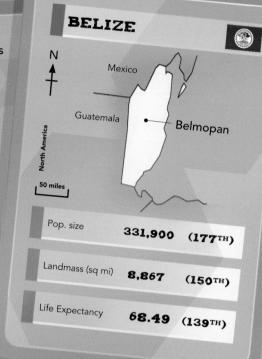

BELIZE

N

Mexico

Guatemala

Belmopan

North America

50 miles

Pop. size	331,900	(177TH)
Landmass (sq mi)	8,867	(150TH)
Life Expectancy	68.49	(139TH)

A BIG BLUE HOLE

The Great Blue Hole is a large sinkhole located near Ambergris Caye, Belize. The diameter of the sinkhole is 984 ft. (300 m) and it's 406 ft. (124 m) deep. This Blue Hole was declared one of the best places to scuba dive by legendary ocean explorer Jacques-Yves Cousteau.

NOT-SO-LOVELY LION…

Belize's beautiful coral reefs are under threat from one of their inhabitants—the red lionfish. With poisonous spines and a huge appetite, the lionfish are munching their way through the reef's wildlife. Environmental groups in Belize are encouraging local chefs to cook the venomous-but-tasty beasties, to bring down the numbers and save the reef!

BELIZE'S BIG CATS

The Cockscomb Basin Wildlife Sanctuary, in south-central Belize, is the world's number one place to visit if you want to get up close and furry with a jaguar—the only big cat species found in the Americas. It's the world's only jaguar sanctuary.

FIRST NAMES COME LAST

Residents of Belize take their local traditions seriously. So don't rush to call anybody by their first name until you know them, as it's considered rude.

Red lionfish

Jaguar

EL SISIMITO— LEGEND OF BELIZE

One thing you are allowed to call by its first name (if you're ever unlucky enough to meet it) is the mythical El Sisimito—a huge hairy creature with a taste for human flesh. He has no knees and his feet face backward, which means whenever you see his footprints, it looks like they're going away from you—but actually the beast is coming right for you!

Watch out! El Sisimito is coming!

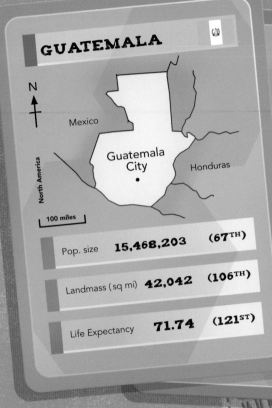

GUATEMALA

N

Mexico

Guatemala City

Honduras

North America

100 miles

Pop. size	**15,468,203**	(67TH)
Landmass (sq mi)	**42,042**	(106TH)
Life Expectancy	**71.74**	(121ST)

Sandwiched between Mexico and Honduras, Guatemala is known as the "Land of the Trees."

It's a landscape full to the top with mountains and thick rainforests —a great place to hide the ruins of ancient cities and temples!

TIKAL TEMPLE
Flourishing more than 1,200 years ago, the ancient city of Tikal was once the capital of the Mayan civilization. More than half of all Guatemalans are descendants of the indigenous Mayan peoples.

END OF THE WORLD?
The Mayan calendar, which has 18 months of 20 days, dates back 2,500 years, and it's still used in some communities in Guatemala today. It was thought that when this calendar ended its cycle, on December 21, 2012, the world would end!

Mayan calendar

A LAND OF INVENTIONS
Guatemala has given the world many amazing inventions. From the list below, take a guess at which three are Guatemalan originals.

Blue denim

Briefcases

Scissors

Instant coffee

Chocolate bars

Calculators

The number "0"

Bungee jumping

CHICHICASTENANGO!
A word that's worth repeating— Chichicastenango!—is the famous Guatemalan street market where many of the country's distinct groups of peoples, such as Mam, Ixil, and Kaqchikel, sell their colorful textiles and goods and speak in their own unique dialects.

WORRY DOLLS
Known as *muñecas quitapenas*, Guatemalan worry dolls are teeny-tiny colorful dolls that children keep to help them sleep. The child whispers their worries to the doll before bedtime. Mom and dad then remove the doll during the night, magically making the trouble disappear along with it.

Quetzal

ALMOST EXTINCT
Guatemala's quetzal bird is one of the country's national icons. It's also, sadly, declining in numbers. The quetzal's feathers were once so important that they were used as currency. In fact, Guatemala's currency is now called the Quetzal, in honor of this great bird!

Answers: Instant coffee, chocolate bars, the number "0".

MARIA LUISA CAKE

The country's national cake, this tasty sponge is soaked in orange marmalade and topped with powdered sugar.

TAZUMAL

Tazumal is the site of the most famous and best-preserved Mayan ruins in El Salvador. The name Tazumal translates as, "the place where people were burned." A statue of the Aztec god, Xipe Totec, was discovered here in perfect condition, having survived almost 3,000 years!

SAUCY!

Worcestershire sauce is usually thought of as a very English condiment, but Salvadorans go crazy for it, slurping up more than 450 tons of the spicy sauce every year!

The heart of Central America and "Land of the Volcanoes," El Salvador may be the smallest country in Central America, but it is the most densely populated.

It is loved for its famous surf spots, still-steaming volcanoes, and coffee—*que chivo!*—"how cool!"

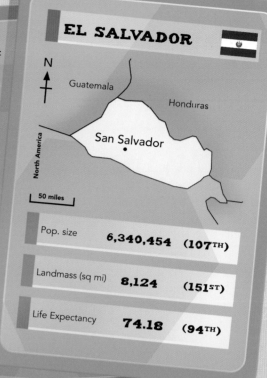

EL SALVADOR

N
Guatemala
Honduras
North America
San Salvador
50 miles

Pop. size	**6,340,454**	**(107TH)**
Landmass (sq mi)	**8,124**	**(151ST)**
Life Expectancy	**74.18**	**(94TH)**

TASTY TORTILLAS

A popular dish in El Salvador is the *pupusa*—a thick corn tortilla that's filled with a delicious mixture of cheese, spicy pork, and refried beans and then fried on a griddle. They're a scrumptious street snack.

NATIONAL SPORT

Soccer is El Salvador's national sport. The country's home ground is Central America's largest stadium, Estadio Cuscatlán. Opened in 1976, the stadium can seat over 50,000 soccer-mad fans.

SURF'S UP!

The surfing at Punta Roca—El Salvador's most popular beach—is famous all over the world. The best time to go is between March and May, when the waves can get as high as 12 ft. (3.5 m)—that's as tall as an elephant!

"45-MINUTE" COUNTRY

El Salvador is so small that locals sometimes call it "the 45-minute country," because you can drive to any of its destinations within 45 minutes. Off you go then!

45 MINUTES!

HONDURAS

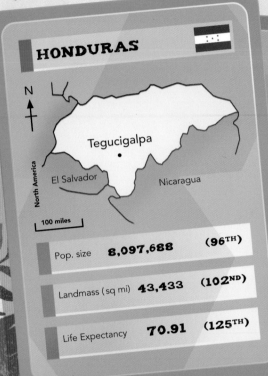

N

North America

Tegucigalpa

El Salvador   Nicaragua

100 miles

Pop. size	8,097,688	(96TH)
Landmass (sq mi)	43,433	(102ND)
Life Expectancy	70.91	(125TH)

With a history that dates back over 3,000 years, the name Honduras means "depths" in English.

According to legend, when Columbus first landed on the country's shores after a bad storm, he apparently exclaimed, in Spanish, "Thank God we've left these depths!" ... the word stuck!

CHATTY PARROTS

Scarlet macaw parrots were considered sacred by Mayan culture and are now Honduras' national bird. These colorful parrots can mimic human speech, the only animals on Earth to do so.

Scarlet macaw

THE GATES OF HELL

The longest river in Honduras, the Patuca River, is known for the infamous white-water rapids known as El Portal del Infierno (The Gates of Hell) a dangerous section of fast-flowing water.

THE ACROPOLIS

Containing giant stone faces, a 98 ft. (30 m) high staircase, more than 2,200 Mayan petroglyphs, and amazing sculptures of jaguars, the city of Copán is one of the world's most important Mayan ruin sites.

DWARF FORESTS

Honduras is famous for its Cusuco National Park. This mammoth reserve is divided into four different kinds of forests, including cloud forests (trees that grow on mountain slopes) and dwarf forests—a place where no tree grows higher than 10 ft. (3 m)!

FISH FALLING FROM THE SKY!

Known as the Lluvia de Peces (Rain of Fish,) every year the small town of Yoro witnesses a phenomenon where fish start falling from the sky! To celebrate this strange occurrence, local townspeople now hold an annual festival.

NICARAGUA GOES TO WAR

Between 1806 and 1821, many Latin American nations began to stand up and revolt against their tyrannical parent nation, Spain. In order to rule themselves, the Nicaraguan people gained independence from Spain after the Mexican War of Independence ended. September 15, 1821 is now celebrated as Independence Day and is a national holiday in Nicaragua.

CANARY CATHEDRAL

The most recognizable landmark in the colorful city of Granada is its striking yellow cathedral. This beautiful building was first constructed in 1583, but has been repeatedly destroyed and rebuilt.

Slightly smaller than the state of New York, Nicaragua is the largest country in Central America and often referred to as the "land of lakes and volcanoes."

It is one of the few places on Earth that has two ocean coasts on opposite sides of the country. This means you can take a morning swim in the Atlantic and an evening dip in the Pacific!

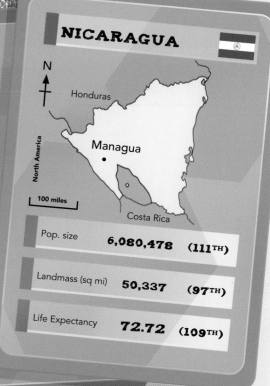

NICARAGUA

Honduras

Managua

North America

100 miles

Costa Rica

Pop. size	6,080,478	(111TH)
Landmass (sq mi)	50,337	(97TH)
Life Expectancy	72.72	(109TH)

OLD HISTORY

In 1522, the Spanish conquered Nicaragua. Upon settling, the Spanish invaders found three established tribes roaming the land, the Niquirano, the Chorotegano, and the Chontal, each with their own culture and language. Chief Nicarao of the Niquiramo tribe allowed his tribe to get close to their Spanish conquerors, thus creating the Mestizos, the most common ethnic mix in Nicaragua today.

VOLCANOES

Nicaragua has hundreds of volcanic islands and 19 active volcanoes, many of which could erupt at a second's notice! The country is also home to the world's only dual volcano. This type of volcano is fed underground by two separate magma flows, which means it can erupt twice in one eruption.

AN ASHY THRILL RIDE

If you're a bit of a daredevil, then head straight for the dark gray slopes of Nicaragua's Cerro Negro peak. Here you'll find the birthplace of volcano boarding—surely the world's coolest extreme sport. Hop on a sled, and whizz down the side of the volcano, getting covered in dust and ash as you go!

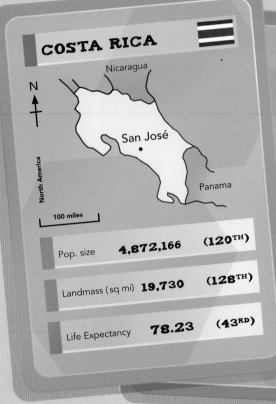

COSTA RICA

Nicaragua

San José

North America

Panama

100 miles

Pop. size	**4,872,166**	**(120TH)**
Landmass (sq mi)	**19,730**	**(128TH)**
Life Expectancy	**78.23**	**(43RD)**

Revered as a jungle paradise, Costa Rica is one of the world's happiest nations.

Home to sloths, orchids, ghost crabs, and cowboys known as gauchos, this beautiful country has more than 745 mi. (1,200 km) of coastline—roughly the same length as Britain!

PURA VIDA

When two locals meet, or say goodbye, the customary and affectionate phrase *pura vida* is often spoken, accompanied with a thumbs up, naturally! The saying means "pure life."

TICOS AND TICAS

In Costa Rica, men and woman are known as *ticos* and *ticas*. But if you want to call someone a "dude" then the word *mae* is what you need!

Tica

Tico

SLOTHS GALORE

The world-famous sanctuary at Penshurst has some unusual residents—sloths! These cute creatures are known for being slooooow. They hang upside down from tree branches, and move at a top speed of 16 ft. (5 m) per minute. On the ground, they're even slower. Yawn!

TREASURE ISLAND

Located 341 mi. (550 km) off the Costa Rican coast lies the elusive Cocos Island. This is the inspiration for many works of famous English fiction, including Isla Nublar in *Jurassic Park* and Robert Louis Stevenson's *Treasure Island*. Legend speaks of 200 treasure chests full of jewels, gold crowns, and hundreds of gold and silver bars buried on the island, known as the Treasure of Lima.

NO ARMY

In 1948, after the end of the Costa Rican Civil War, President José Figueres Ferrer abolished the army of Costa Rica. Since then, the country has lived in peace.

NATIONAL ANTHEM

Costa Rica is a very proud nation. Every morning, all of the country's radio stations play the national anthem at 7 A.M., a simple reminder to everybody who listens that you should always be proud of your home.

EAST AND WEST

You may have to get up early in the morning, but in Panama it's worth it. The sun rises over the Pacific Ocean and sets over the Atlantic Ocean. Wow!

Prudhoe Bay, Alaska

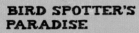

Stripecheeked woodpecker

BIRD SPOTTER'S PARADISE

With 940 species flying in the skies above, it's official: Panama has more bird species than the USA and Canada combined.

PANAMA CITY

Panama City is the only capital in the world that has a rainforest in it! Metropolitan Park is home to many species of plants and animals, including capuchin monkeys.

Known as the "crossroads of the world," Panama is the nation that connects North and South America.

Thousands of ships may sail through its famous canal every day, but to the residents who live here, the country has so much more to offer than just the canal and Panama hats.

PANAMA

Costa Rica

North America

Panama City

Colombia

100 miles

N

Pop. size	3,864,170	(130TH)
Landmass (sq mi)	29,119	(118TH)
Life Expectancy	78.3	(42ND)

Darién Gap

THE PAN-AMERICAN HIGHWAY

If it weren't for the Darién Gap—an untameable section of tropical forest in northern Panama—the Pan-American Highway would connect the lowest tip of South America, in Argentina, to the very top of North America, in Alaska.

Capuchin monkey

KABOOM!

30,000

Tons of dynamite were used to build the Panama Canal. This famous waterway joins up the Atlantic and Pacific Oceans, and stops ships having to travel all the way around South America.

Ushuaia, Argentina

SAY IT OUT LOUD!

"A man a plan a canal panama" is a famous type of what?

A) Acronym

B) Palindrome

C) Anagram

Answer: B—it's a palindrome, which means it's spelled exactly the same way forward and backward!

BAHAMAS

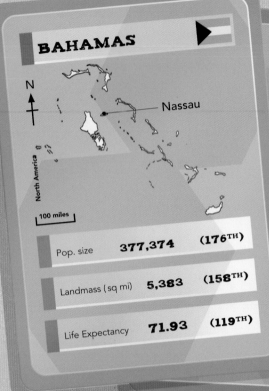

N

North America

Nassau

100 miles

Pop. size	377,374	(176TH)
Landmass (sq mi)	5,383	(158TH)
Life Expectancy	71.93	(119TH)

Named *Baja Mar* (meaning "shallow seas"), the luxurious islands of the Bahamas are only 50 mi. (80 km) away from Miami, Florida.

They are an exotic brew of American and Caribbean influences, unlike any other found in the aquamarine oceans of the Caribbean Sea.

NEW WORLD

The New World began in the Bahamas—it was the first country that European explorer Christopher Columbus saw through his telescope during his first voyage in 1492. It is now thought that while the Americas may have been new and exciting to Columbus, there were in fact 50 million people already living there.

JOIN THE DOTS

The Bahamas is not a massive lump of a country—far from it! Instead it is 3,100 islands and cayes. If you spent a day on each one it would take you eight years to see the whole of the Bahamas!

PINK SAND

The Bahamas is famed for its white-sand beaches. But it is the beach at Harbor Island that sticks out like a sore thumb—the sand is pink! How does that happen? Take a guess:

A) The famous pink flamingos' feathers fall off and dye the sand

B) The red shells of *foraminifera*—a single-celled marine animal that lives in waters around the island—mix with the white sand

C) It's red poop from the red snapper fish that turns the sand pink!

Answer: B

WAHOO!

The Bahamas is famous for its fishing, predominantly for tuna, barracuda, shark, snapper, and grouper. But one of the most prized catches is the wahoo fish. These slippery and silvery monsters can be up to 8 ft. (2.5 m) long and have razor-sharp teeth.

FREAK WEATHER!

Despite being an iconic tropical paradise, it once snowed in the Bahamas. On January 19, 1977, an unexpected cold front descended from southern Florida, U.S.A. and brought cold weather all the way to the Bahamas. On that day—and for the only time in recorded history!—snow fell in the Bahamas.

Wahoo fish

FLAMINGO-AGOGO

The national bird of the Bahamas is the flamingo. If you want to see 80,000 flamingos in one go, head to Inagua Island, the largest breeding colony of this bird in the world. Flamingos get their pink feathers from their diet, which consists mainly of shrimp and algae.

KING OF PIRATES

The Bahamas' (and the world's) most famous pirate, Blackbeard, was actually an Englishman called Edward Teach. His legendary pirate ship, *Queen Anne's Revenge*, had 40 cannons on it! Before battles, Blackbeard would strap several pistols to his chest and put on a large black captain's hat. He would then put slow-burning fuses in his hair and beard, so a cloud of smoke disguised him brilliantly from his intended captors.

← **Blackbeard**

RAKE 'N' SCRAPE

One of the most popular forms of music in the Bahamas, along with calypso, is rake 'n' scrape. This form of music is created by percussion instruments made out of saws, hammers, ratchets, cans . . . and anything else you can bang and scratch loudly!

El Cocodrilo

CROCODILE SMILE

Imagine you're a bird, flying high above the island. If you were to look down on Cuba you'd find that it resembles a reptile. Cubans often refer to their land as *El Cocodrilo*—"the crocodile."

Bee hummingbird

5 ZUNZUNCITO
Mellisuga helenae

CORREOS 1964

Cuba

THAT HUMMING SOUND

The bee hummingbird, the world's smallest bird, lives in Cuba—and nowhere else on the planet. It is 1.9 in. (5 cm) long, which is only this long:

Actual size!

cm 0 1 2 3 4 5

Cuba is the largest country in the Caribbean and has a rich and fascinating history.

From its cigars to its home-cooked ajiaco stew, from its sweaty salsa dancing to its world-renowned Havana culture, Cuba is a place to be seen, heard, and enjoyed!

CUBA

N

Havana

North America

100 miles

Jamaica

Pop. size	11,265,629	(77TH)
Landmass (sq mi)	42,426	(105TH)
Life Expectancy	78.22	(44TH)

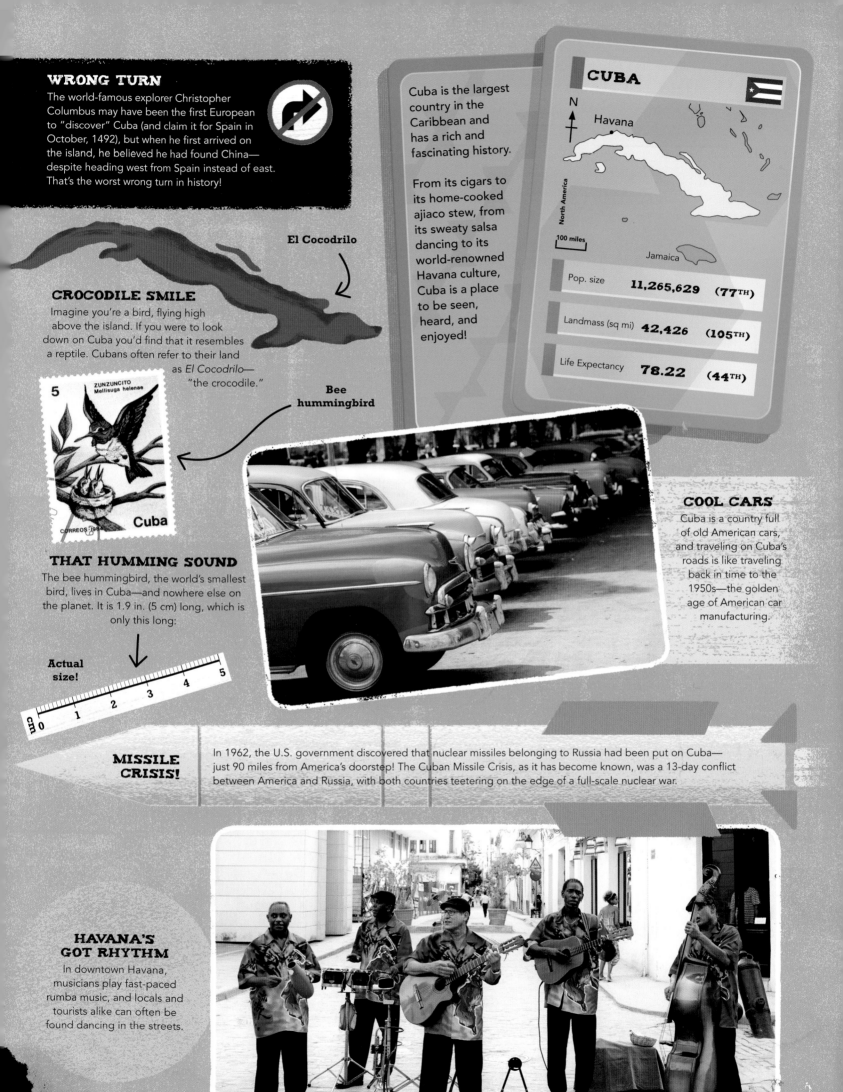

COOL CARS

Cuba is a country full of old American cars, and traveling on Cuba's roads is like traveling back in time to the 1950s—the golden age of American car manufacturing.

MISSILE CRISIS!

In 1962, the U.S. government discovered that nuclear missiles belonging to Russia had been put on Cuba—just 90 miles from America's doorstep! The Cuban Missile Crisis, as it has become known, was a 13-day conflict between America and Russia, with both countries teetering on the edge of a full-scale nuclear war.

HAVANA'S GOT RHYTHM

In downtown Havana, musicians play fast-paced rumba music, and locals and tourists alike can often be found dancing in the streets.

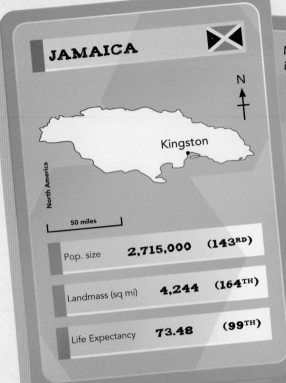

JAMAICA

Kingston

North America

50 miles

Pop. size	2,715,000	(143RD)
Landmass (sq mi)	4,244	(164TH)
Life Expectancy	73.48	(99TH)

No other country in the Caribbean proudly boasts of its African roots as much as Jamaica.

After becoming the first Caribbean country to gain independence in 1962, the island is known for its laid-back and relaxed attitude, its reggae music, and its Rastafarians.

JUNKANOO

Before the abolition of slavery, African slaves were given three days off at Christmas, which they celebrated by wearing colorful masks and singing and dancing up and down the streets. Centuries later, this celebration, now known as Junkanoo, is still going strong and is one of the Caribbean's most festive festivals!

THE MOST RELIGIOUS

Jamaica could be called the world's most religious nation, with more churches per square mile than anywhere else on Earth.

THE NAME'S BOND

Everybody knows the world's most famous secret agent, James Bond, is British. But his creator, Ian Fleming, wrote his James Bond spy thrillers in Jamaica.

ARECACEAE

Also known as coconut palm trees, the Arecaceae species of tree lines the beaches and roads of pretty much every Caribbean nation, including Jamaica. However, these symbols are not native to the lands. They were imported, along with sugar canes and mangoes, many centuries ago when the Europeans first started sailing over.

Jamaican Olympic bobsleigh team

COOL RUNNINGS

Jamaica became the first tropical country to enter a Winter Olympic event—the bobsleigh. They didn't win, but it was the thought that counted!

REGGAE

Jamaica is famous for its reggae music. Bob Marley, the Jamaican singer with his famous dreadlock hairstyle, made reggae music internationally famous in the 1970s. Reggae music combines calypso, jazz, rhythm and blues, and ska together in a laid-back but upbeat musical style.

BOLT OF LIGHTNING

Currently the world's fastest man, Usain Bolt is a Jamaican sprinter . . . and proud of it. In the 2012 London Olympics, he became the only man to hold the 100 meter and 200 meter world records and the first person ever to win six gold medals in the sprinting events.

WORD ASSOCIATION

The words "hammock," "hurricane," "tobacco," "barbecue," and "canoe" all derive from the Taíno language, spoken by the people who origi... in Jamaica.

HOW ARE YOU?

Haitians, the native people of Haiti, have had a mixed history, full of tragedy and triumph. It's no wonder that a reply to "How are you?" evokes a sinister, but honest response—"*M pa pli mal*" ("No worse than before").

M pa pli mal!

DO YOU DO VODOU?

A fusion of West African and Catholic teachings, Vodou (also known as Voodoo) is the main religious belief on the island. Vodou teaches believers of a supreme being called *Bondye* and individual spirits, called *Loa*. Male priests are called *Houngan* and female priests are known as *Mambo*.

Haiti was the first nation to witness a slave revolt, which went on to produce the world's first black independent republic—over two centuries ago!

The country is still rebuilding itself after 2010's catastrophic earthquake, but its people are determined, and slowly but surely, things are looking up.

HAITI

North America

N

50 miles

Port-au-Prince

Dominican Republic

Pop. size	10,347,461	(87TH)
Landmass (sq mi)	10,714	(146TH)
Life Expectancy	63.18	(166TH)

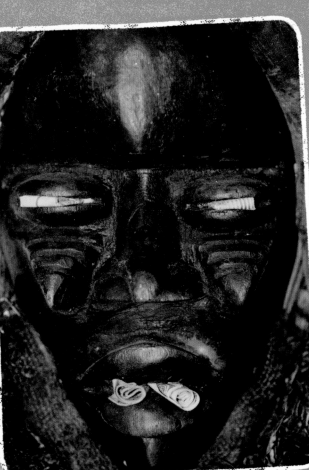

TOUSSAINT L'OUVERTURE

Haitian hero, Toussaint L'Ouverture—also known as The Black Napoleon—was the leader of the Haitian Revolution, 1791–1804. This first-of-a-kind revolution was a slave revolt against Haiti's French colonial masters. It led to the elimination of slavery and the founding of the Republic of Haiti—the first country to be run by previously enslaved people.

TAP-TAP

Watch out for tap-taps on Haiti's roads. These colorfully painted buses serve as share taxis that travel all around the island. The translation of tap-tap is "quick, quick!"

Tap-tap!

THE DAY THE WORLD SHOOK

On 12 January 2010, Haiti hit the world's headlines when it experienced an earthquake that measured 7.0 on the Richter Scale, killing over 230,000 people. The impact the earthquake had on the country will be felt for several decades to come.

DOMINICAN REPUBLIC

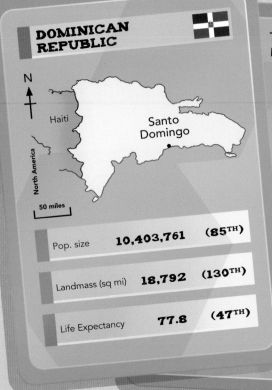

N

Haiti

Santo Domingo

North America

50 miles

Pop. size	10,403,761	(85TH)
Landmass (sq mi)	18,792	(130TH)
Life Expectancy	77.8	(47TH)

The Dominican Republic was the first country to have a European settlement in the Americas after it was "discovered" by Christopher Columbus in 1492.

Known as "the bread basket of the Caribbean" (for all the natural treats it contains!), DR shares the island of Hispaniola with Haiti.

ENDLESS SUMMER

If you fancy year-long sunshine, and sun-scorched sand, then the Dominican Republic is the place to live. It experiences what many believe is an "endless summer."

TAÍNO INDIANS

Before Columbus and his crew came ashore on Hispaniola, millions of native Arawak Indians, known as Taíno, occupied the land, and had done for thousands of years! The Taíno Indians welcomed Columbus on his arrival and showered him with peaceful and generous hospitality. In return, Columbus took control of the tribes and plundered them of their natural resources, including gold (found in Hispaniola's rivers), parrots and exotic spices that he sent back to Spain.

JURASSIC BUG

For fans of *Jurassic Park* and *Jurassic World*, The Amber Museum (in Puerto Plata) houses the famous amber stone with a prehistoric mosquito preserved inside. This piece of amber was the inspiration behind the bestselling book *Jurassic Park* and it was actually used in the blockbuster film version.

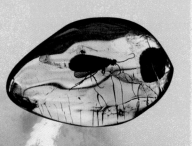

DANCE WITH ME

The world-renowned merengue is a dance that was created in the Dominican Republic, and is the official dance and music of the nation. Why not try it out, with the dance moves shown here—expect to get sweaty!

START

2 1 4 3 Man

Woman 2 1 4 3

START

. . . repeat

SLIPPERY WHEN WET

The Rio Damajagua Falls, located in the hills of the North Corridor mountain range is, in fact, 27 separate waterfalls all cascading together, falling into limestone pools. These form amazing natural waterslides that visitors can shoot, slip, and slide down!

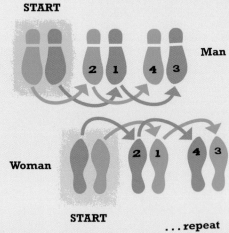

Humpback whale

BIG BABIES

The warm waters of Samaná become home to hundreds of huge humpback whales who travel to the Dominican Republic each year to give birth. The whale calves can weigh more than 1 ton when they're born—that's as much as a small car!

SEE THE LIGHT

In the 14th to 17th centuries, religion was an important part of everyday island life, even if it was the enforced Christian beliefs of the European invaders. The oldest cathedral in the Americas can be found in Santo Domingo—building began in 1512. The first stone of the cathedral was laid by Diego Columbus, Christopher Columbus's son.

A NATION IS BORN

In September 1983, after centuries of British colonial rule, Saint Kitts and Nevis became an independent nation. While the nation remains a sovereign realm of Britain, with Queen Elizabeth remaining as head of state, the U.K.'s government no longer rules the country.

16

SEPTEMBER

LIAMUIGA

Saint Kitts was first sighted by Christopher Columbus (him again!) on his second New World voyage in 1493. Before Columbus, Saint Kitts was originally known as *Liamuiga*, or "fertile land."

NATIONAL HERO

The first Premier of Saint Kitts and Nevis was Robert Bradshaw, an activist who is regarded as being responsible for leading the two islands' independence from Britain. After his death, Bradshaw was awarded the title of First National Hero and he is honored annually on National Heroes Day—his birthday!

GOAT WATER STEW

Should you find yourself shipwrecked on these remote islands, why not eat yourself happy with Saint Kitts and Nevis' most famous dish—goat water stew? Just mix together goat meat, breadfruit, green papaya and dumplings with chopped tomatoes and *voilà*!

RECIPE

1. Goat
2. Breadfruit
3. Green papaya
4. Dumplings
5. Tomatoes

The joining together of two islands, Saint Kitts and Nevis, formed the smallest country in the Americas.

Life here isn't very busy, which is convenient, because when the scenery looks this tranquil, you don't really want to do much except sit back and relax . . .

SAINT KITTS AND NEVIS

N

North America

Basseterre

10 miles

Pop. size	**54,191**	**(195TH)**
Landmass (sq mi)	**101**	**(196TH)**
Life Expectancy	**75.29**	**(75TH)**

CULTURAMA

Every year on the island of Nevis, a festival called the Culturama Festival occurs to celebrate the emancipation of slaves in the 1830s, as well the colorful calypso culture. Two of the most important events are the Calypso King competition and the Miss Culture Queen competition.

Calypso King

Miss Culture Queen

NOT SO SWEET

Sugar cane was once the most important business on Saint Kitts and Nevis, but most of the factories have closed down, and the sugar cane plantations have been abandoned. The atmospheric ruins of sugar mills and factories are dotted all over the islands.

MOKO JUMBIES!

Moko Jumbies are an important part of calypso culture and are often seen performing during parades at local festivals and celebrations. But what on Earth are they? Take your pick.

A) Traditional stilt-walkers?

B) Clowns with very small shoes?

C) People dressed as colorful ghosts?

Answer: A

ANTIGUA AND BARBUDA

N ↑

North America

St. John's
(Antigua)

10 miles

Pop. size	**89,985**	**(191ST)**
Landmass (sq mi)	**171**	**(190TH)**
Life Expectancy	**76.12**	**(66TH)**

The two island nations of Antigua and Barbuda are the definition of Beauty and the Beast: opposites that very much attract.

Antigua is a heaving throng of industry and business, and Barbuda, a reclusive haven, known to many as the "Land of 365 Beaches." Let's see what they have to offer . . .

BOGGY PEAK

Until 2009, Antigua and Barbuda's highest point was known as Boggy Peak. The name changed to Mount Obama on August 4, in honor of the 44th President of the United States—Barack Obama.

HIDE AND FLEET

Admiral Horatio Lord Nelson fell in love with Antigua and Barbuda, but not because of the beaches. With an unbroken wall of coral reef, many natural harbors and high lookout points, Antigua was the perfect place to hide his naval fleet.

Man of War bird

MAN OF WAR

A tourist attraction near Barbuda is Man of War Island. Don't let the name fool you, this peaceful haven is home to a frigate seabird colony. Man of War birds, as they are known locally, have a huge red chest and cannot walk or swim, so they survive solely by stealing fish from other birds or by grabbing them out of the water.

WHAT'S IN A NAME?

The word "Antigua" comes from the Spanish language to mean "ancient." The local West Indies residents have another name for their island, which means "our own." Can you guess it from the list below? (One is real, three are made up!)

A) Waladli
B) Woolbombing
C) Figgyribbit
D) Wallating

Answer: A

SHIPWRECKED

Antigua has 127 documented shipwrecks lying off its shores. The most well known is *The Andes*. This massive ship caught fire and sank in Deep Bay in July 1905, though the bow of the ship sticks out of the water! The wreck is now a playground for coral and fish.

DUCANA RECIPE

Ducana is the local Antiguan speciality that all the locals love. Mix together a solid chunk of grated sweet potato with coconut and spices and then steam in a banana leaf!

LAZY SUNDAY

It's that clever chap Christopher Columbus again. He named Dominica for the day he "discovered" it in 1493—*Dominica* is Latin for "Sunday."

Sisserou Parrot

Despite its remote location in the Caribbean Sea, sandwiched between Guadeloupe and Martinique, Dominica is renowned for its tropical rainforest that occupies over 60 percent of the island.

A hiker's and diver's paradise, Dominica is bursting with wildlife and crazy feats of nature.

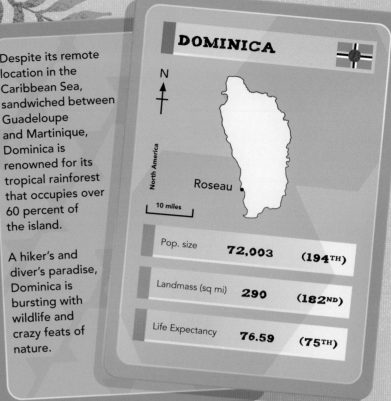

DOMINICA

N

North America

Roseau

10 miles

Pop. size	72,003	(194TH)
Landmass (sq mi)	290	(182ND)
Life Expectancy	76.59	(75TH)

SISSEROU PARROT

The national bird, the Sisserou parrot (as seen on the flag) is the largest of all Amazon parrots and thrives in trees along Dominica's hundreds of rivers. This parrot can only be found in Dominica and it is an endangered species.

THE LAKE THAT BOILS

Hidden deep in the Morne Trois Pitons National Park is Boiling Lake —yes, it really is a lake that boils! This eerie lake is a cauldron of bubbling gray-blue water covered in cloud vapor. The water is warmed by the gases that escape from the molten lava, which flows many miles below.

THE BEACH THAT FIZZES

If you've ever wanted to spot whales and dolphins swimming in the wild, then there is no place like Champagne Beach, a place where the water fizzes due to the volcanic hot springs that bubble underneath the water.

WELCOME TO MASSACRE!

Dominica's smallest town, with only 1,200 inhabitants, is named Massacre after the brutal slaying of native Caribbean Indians here by British troops in 1674.

SAINT LUCIA

N

North America

Castries

10 miles

Pop. size	**89,985**	**(185TH)**
Landmass (sq mi)	**238**	**(186TH)**
Life Expectancy	**77.41**	**(50TH)**

This idyllic and peaceful island nation comes out top as the Caribbean's best getaway spot for foreigners.

The island attracts 350,000 people a year, which means that the Saint Lucian population is constantly outnumbered 2:1. Let's find out why...

THE ONE AND ONLY

Saint Lucia holds a unique position as the only country in this book (and the world!), that is, well, can you guess?

A) The only country in the world named after a woman

B) The first country to grow bananas

C) The last country to get the Internet

Answer: A

JUNGLE BIKING

Two words that go together well! Saint Lucia is one of the few places in the world where you can get on your bike and get lost in incredible rainforests and nature reserves.

DRIVE-IN VOLCANO

Saint Lucia is the only island in the world that can boast a drive-in volcano. Strap on your seatbelt, drive to the edge of the volcano, and watch black water erupt from the sulphur springs. Remember to hold your nose though, the springs give off a stench stronger than dozens of rotten eggs!

TWIN PEAKS, GROS AND PETIT

Saint Lucia's the Pitons are two mountainous peaks that rise out of the Caribbean Sea. The pitons, named Gros and Petit, are known as volcanic plugs, because they were created when the nearby volcano erupted and created a bottle-neck of lava, which then cooled and formed conical shapes.

ENTRANCE TO SULPHUR SPRINGS PARK

THE CARIBBEAN'S ONLY DRIVE-IN VOLCANO

FATHER OF THE NATION

Sir John Compton is known as Saint Lucia's "Father of the Nation." He was the country's first leader under British rule, between 1964–79, and then its first Prime Minister after independence came in 1979. He served as Prime Minister three times between 1979 and 2007.

TUG OF WAR

So popular was Saint Lucia with the British and the French, that between 1660 and 1814 a dozen wars were waged between the two countries, with Saint Lucia changing hands back and forth 14 times!

PIRATES OF THE CARIBBEAN

Several locations of the billion-dollar movie franchise *Pirates of the Caribbean* can be found in and around Saint Vincent and the Grenadines. The island that Captain Jack Sparrow was famously marooned on (twice!)—Rumrunner's Isle—was in fact, Petit Tabac, one of the country's smallest islands, and part of the Tobago Cays.

Lying 100 mi. (160 km) west of Barbados, Saint Vincent and the Grenadines are a string of islands.

They may live close together—they are all within 9 mi. (14 km) of each other—but they are quite different in geography and personality.

SAINT VINCENT AND THE GRENADINES

N

Kingstown

North America

20 miles

Pop. size	109,373	(186TH)
Landmass (sq mi)	150	(192ND)
Life Expectancy	74.86	(85TH)

TREATY OF PARIS, 1763

Though more of a trick than a treat, the Treaty of Paris was signed in 1763 and, in a flick of the wrist, Saint Vincent and the Grenadines belonged to the British. The islands only gained independence in 1979.

HOW DOES YOUR GARDEN GROW?

The botanic gardens in Saint Vincent have been carefully looked after since 1765. Many of the plants were brought over from neighboring countries on ships, and some sailed from as far away as Tahiti!

The Botanic Gardens have over 500 different species of plant!

THIRTY-TWO ISLANDS

The Grenadines is made up of 32 islands. Each island has its own distinct personality, and some are very bizarrely-named: All Awash Island, Rabbit Island, Young Island, Mustique, Pigeon Island, Catholic Island, Isle à Quatre, and The Pillories, for example. Only nine of the 32 islands are inhabited.

MAYREAU

The smallest island in The Grenadines is Mayreau. It has a population of just 250 people. Over the years thousands of couples have got married on the island, but if you do so, there is just one rule: you must stay on the island for 72 hours.

12 11 10 9 8 7 6 5 4 3 2 1

72 hours! That's six times around the clockface.

WE'VE BEEN HERE 3 DAYS!

BARBADOS

N

• Bridgetown

North America

5 miles

Pop. size	284,644	(180TH)
Landmass (sq mi)	166	(191ST)
Life Expectancy	74.99	(82ND)

Barbados has many nicknames—from "The Bearded Island" (because the white sea spray gives the island a beard) to "Pork Chop Island" (because it's shaped like one!).

Regardless of what you call it, this tiny island is four times smaller than London and it is the perfect place to see the world's most exotic mammal —the beach bum!

FLY, FISH, FLY!

The unique species of flying fish are famously connected with Barbados' tropical waters. This remarkable fish can glide through the air for distances of up to 131 ft. (40 m)! Before take-off, the fish swims quickly towards the surface, bursting into the air at speeds of 34 mph (55 km/h). The fish then spreads out its pectoral fins and uses them as wings!

Bajan flying fish

RIHANNA

The American pop phenomenon Rihanna is actually from Barbados. The singer moved away from her homeland at the age of 16 to pursue her music career.

NELSON'S COLUMN

This statue of Lord Nelson, erected in Bridgetown's Trafalgar Square on March 22 1813, is older than the statue of the same name in London's Trafalgar Square.

Admiral Lord Nelson

NELSON

INDENTURED SERVANTS

The first slaves in Barbados were white people—though they weren't called slaves, they were called Indentured Servants. These "unlucky" people were, for various reasons, deemed enemies of the British monarchy and sent to Barbados to work. This practice was so common during the 1640s, that the phrase "to be Barbado'ed," was invented.

BAJAN / BRITISH

Barbadian culture is a blend of West African and British. While English is the official language of the country, spoken on TV and by the authorities, it is the Bajan dialect that is an iconic part of the native culture. The Bajan dialect is renowned for its use of glottal stops—"I didn't do that" becomes "I ain' do dat!"

THE SUN ALWAYS SHINES

Barbados receives over 3,000 hours of bright, cloudless sunshine every year—making it one of the sunniest places on Earth. Do the math: how many hours of sunshine is that per day?

SOUP BOWL

Located on the east coast of the country, the Soup Bowl at Bathsheba derives its name from the foamy surf that crashes against the coastline. It lures many of the world's professional surfers and is the site of many local and international surfing championships.

OIL DOWN

The national dish of Grenada is a belt-loosening one-pot meal of salted meat, chicken, dumplings, and breadfruit in a coconut flavoured stew. To be accompanied by a fruity beverage called *mauby*—a bittersweet drink made from the squashed bark of mauby trees!

OLD SPICE

Over one-third of all the world's nutmeg comes from Grenada, making it the second largest producer after Indonesia. Nutmeg has many health-giving properties and has been highly sought after since ancient times.

Nutmeg

Known as the "Island of Spice," the volcanic and fertile nation of Grenada is responsible for some of the Caribbean's best beaches and coolest calypso music.

Despite Hurricane Ivan damaging 90 percent of the country's homes in 2004, the island continues to be a jewel in the Caribbean crown.

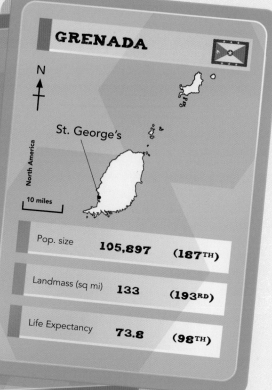

GRENADA

N

St. George's

North America

10 miles

Pop. size	**105,897**	**(187TH)**
Landmass (sq mi)	**133**	**(193RD)**
Life Expectancy	**73.8**	**(98TH)**

328 FT.

below sea level!

BIANCA C SHIPWRECK

In 1961, this massive 600-ft. (180-m) long Italian cruise ship was anchored at Grenada port when a fire broke out in the engine room. Within minutes, the whole ship was on fire! The still-burning ship was towed to the shallow waters of Point Salines where the ship came to its resting place. It's still there now, and is an impressive shipwreck.

KICK 'EM JENNY

Between the island of Carriacou and Grenada lies a growing underwater volcano known as Kick 'em Jenny. Currently lying just 328 ft. (100 m) below the surface, the volcano will one day rise out of the ocean. The volcano's first known eruption was in 1939, creating a 6.5-ft. (2-m) high tsunami that covered Grenada.

UNDERWATER SCULPTURES

Grenada's Underwater Sculpture Park is the world's first underwater art gallery. Located 16 ft. (5 m) underwater, scuba divers can interact with many sculptures that reflect Grenada's culture and history, including lifesize figures, a bicycle, and a statue of Jesus Christ.

TRINIDAD AND TOBAGO

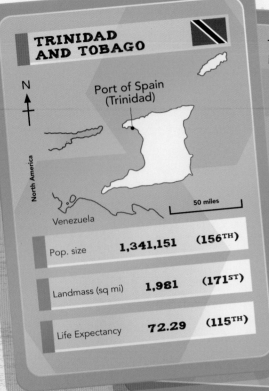

Port of Spain (Trinidad)

N

North America

Venezuela

50 miles

Pop. size	1,341,151	(156TH)
Landmass (sq mi)	1,981	(171ST)
Life Expectancy	72.29	(115TH)

Trinidad and Tobago is a country made up of two small islands floating between the Caribbean Sea and the Atlantic Ocean.

It has given the world so many amazing things it's hard to keep count. Prepare to be surprised . . .

SOMETHING TO REMEMBER

The people of Tobago are called Tobagonians. The people from Trinidad are called Trinidadians, or Trinis. But what is the official name for people from both islands?

A) Trinboggers

B) Trinbagonians

C) Tobagginianans

Answer: B

Moruga scorpion chilli

HOT! HOT! HOT!

One of Trinidad's most famous exports is the moruga scorpion—one of the hottest chillis on the planet. It measures two million on the Scoville Heat Unit (SHU) scale. The heat from one of these tiny-but-mighty peppers can cause blisters to form on your tongue and the back of your throat. Ouch!

PITCH PERFECT

Pitch Lake, in Trinidad, is the world's largest natural deposit of asphalt, and is 246 ft. (75 m) deep. The asphalt in this very black and very sticky lake is used to pave roads all over the world. There are only a few asphalt lakes in existence, three in California and one in Venezuela.

THE BEST PARTY IN THE WORLD

Trinidad and Tobago's annual Carnival now has copycat carnivals all over the world. This is one of the biggest, best, and loudest street party in the world. Preparations begin a month in advance and feature local music and outrageous costumes.

THE LIMBO

How low can you go? This famous dance was invented in Trinidad. It is performed by everyone at the annual Carnival street party!

BEAT OF THE DRUM

Another local invention is the steel drum, one of the few instruments to be invented in the twentieth century. This beat-machine became popular when the U.S. military brought oil drums to the island in an attempt to improve the country's infrastructure.

DISNEYLAND OF DIVING

Tobago has the largest single brain coral in the world, measuring 10 ft. (3 m) high and 16 ft. (5.3 m) wide! Brain coral is very rare. The presence of this coral in Trinidad and Tobago's waters, as well other stunning reefs, has lead many scuba divers to claim that the country is the "Disneyland of diving!"

Leatherback turtle

LEATHERBACK TURTLES

Leatherbacks are the largest turtles on Earth, growing up to 6.5 ft. (2 m) long. They have swum the Earth's oceans for over 100 million years. These amazing creatures live in the waters around Trinidad and Tobago, and come ashore at night to dig holes and lay their eggs—a rare and beautiful sight to behold.

94%
of Suriname is covered by the Amazon rainforest.

THE CENTRAL SURINAME NATURE RESERVE

1.6 million hectares of Suriname—around the size of Northern Ireland—is home to the most diverse ecosystem on planet Earth, including otters, anteaters, and jaguars. There are many insects too, as well as hundreds of species of fish and bats.

Suriname is the smallest sovereign state in South America, both in terms of geography and population size.

Separated from neighboring nation Guyana by the Courantyne River, Suriname is a big jumble of cultures all fused together rather peacefully . . .

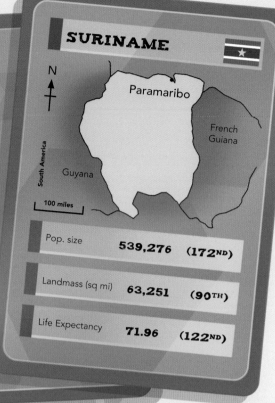

SURINAME

Paramaribo

French Guiana

South America

Guyana

100 miles

Pop. size	539,276	(172ND)
Landmass (sq mi)	63,251	(90TH)
Life Expectancy	71.96	(122ND)

SRANAN TONGO

Dutch may be the official language, but many people in Suriname speak Sranan Tongo. This is a mix of African, Portuguese, and Dutch and was once spoken between slaves and slave owners in the 17th century. Want to count to ten? Try this:

wan, tu, dri, fo, feifi, siksi, seybi, ayti, neygi, tin

THE DUTCH

Despite being nearly 5,000 mi. (8,000 km) away, Suriname has many ties with The Netherlands. It was the Dutch Empire that took control of the land in 1667.

TOAD-ALLY GROSS!

The female Surinam toad grows her baby tadpoles in the spongy skin of her back until they are mini toad-sized! Once they are ready, they simply pop out of her skin!

PARAMARIBO

Over half of the Surinamese people live in the capital city of Paramaribo—"the wooden city." It is full of beautiful old Dutch buildings.

KETI KOTI

To celebrate the end of slavery in Suriname in 1863, the country takes part in Keti Koti, a colorful national festival that, in the unofficial language of the country, means "the chains are cut."

Surinam toad

GUYANA

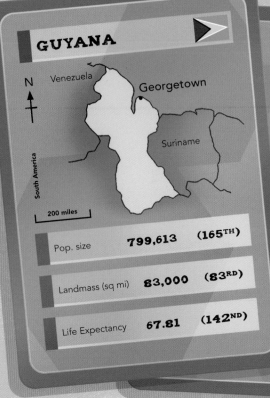

N

Venezuela

Georgetown

Suriname

South America

200 miles

Pop. size	799,613	(165TH)
Landmass (sq mi)	83,000	(83RD)
Life Expectancy	67.81	(142ND)

The only English speaking country in South America, Guyana is known as the "Land of Many Waters" and is a sight to behold.

Full of pristine rainforests yet to be touched by mankind, the country is a fusion of South American and Indian cultures.

FALLING AROUND

Located on the Potaro River in Guyana's rainforest is Kaieteur Falls. This mega waterfall has a drop of 741 ft. (226 m). That's five times larger than Niagara Falls in Canada!

GOING FOR GOLD

In 1879, Guyana struck gold! One of the largest gold mines in the Americas (and the world)—the Omai gold mine in the northwest of the country—is believed to contain 3.7 million ounces of gold. That's over 14 million solid-gold wedding rings!

Where else is Holi a widely celebrated festival? GO TO PAGE 169

HOLI LAND

The famous Hindu festival, Holi, is celebrated here every March. Phagwah, as it is known in Guyana honors good triumphing over evil. People celebrate it by spraying bright powders and colored water, and everyone gets covered in a rainbow of colors!

GIANT ANTEATER!

Guyana's Iwokrama rainforest is one of the last four remaining tropical forests in the world that have yet to be touched by man. The rainforest is home to the magnificent giant anteater, a vulnerable mammal with a 2-ft (60-cm) long tongue that can lap up 35,000 ants a day!

Giant anteater

BRAZIL

NEXT STOP BRAZIL!

The famous Takutu River Bridge transports you not only over a mighty river, but into another country: from Lethem, Guyana to Bonfim, Brazil! Opened in 2009, the bridge is a rare example of a land border where drivers going over the bridge must change from driving on the left (in Guyana) to driving on the right (in Brazil), or vice versa!

GUYANA

MOUNT RORAIMA

Tepuis are types of mountains that look like table-tops. Venezuela's most striking natural landmark, Mount Roraima, is one of the world's most recognized tepuis. This mega mountain is also believed to be the inspiration for Sir Arthur Conan Doyle's famous novel *The Lost World*.

GO TO PAGE 137 Where would you find another tepui mountain?

Venezuela, on the north coast of South America, is stuffed to the gills with lots of exciting things to do.

One of the continent's richest countries financially, thanks to its natural resources, it's also lush and beautiful.

VENEZUELA

Caracas

South America

Colombia

Brazil

200 miles

Pop. size	30,405,207	(41ST)
Landmass (sq mi)	353,841	(33RD)
Life Expectancy	74.39	(90TH)

RAINBOW HEAVEN

Cue drum roll! Ladies and gentlemen, may we introduce to you Angel Falls—the highest waterfall in the world! Clocking in at 3,212 ft. (979 m), 19 times higher than the famous Niagara Falls, Angel Falls is also one of the very few locations on Earth where you can count dozens of rainbows at once, due to the intense moisture and water spray.

THE EVERLASTING STORM

Lasting for up to ten hours a night, around 150 nights a year, gigantic storm clouds gather in the same spot 5 mi. (8 km) above Lake Maracaibo and pummel the planet with electricity. There are over 1.2 million lightning strikes there every year!

NEVER ARRIVE ON TIME

It is a traditional custom in Venezuela never to arrive on time! If you're meeting a local, always arrive 15 minutes late. If you arrive on time, Venezuelans will think you are greedy!

CURRUCHETE
SAMBA PA MI
SOL Y SOMBRA
SAMBA COCO
Mantecado
HALLACA
CALENTAO
COCA-COLA
Lechosa
POR ESTAS CALLES
MEXICO
PERDONAME AMO
FRESA COCO
MELON
WISH YOU WERE HERE
RADIO MERIDA
CAPUCHINO
BRANDY
MANGO
PIMM'S

20 times larger than a rat!

Capybara

BIG FAT RAT

In big cities, so it is said, you are never more than 6 ft. (2 m) from a rat. In Venezuela, it's especially true! Capybaras—the largest rodents on Earth —grow up to 4 ft. (1.3 m) long (the same size as you!) and weigh 100 lb (45 kg). These whoppers are 20-times larger than a normal rat!

NICE CREAM

Tucked away in small town called Merida is an ice cream parlor that sells the largest number of ice cream flavors in the world. Why not order one of the 860 flavors from a menu that includes chilli, tomato, macaroni and cheese, and garlic! Which flavor would you choose?

COLOMBIA

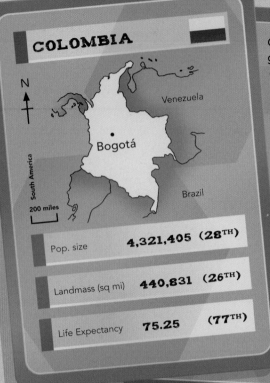

N

South America

200 miles

Venezuela

Bogotá

Brazil

Pop. size	4,321,405	(28TH)
Landmass (sq mi)	440,831	(26TH)
Life Expectancy	75.25	(77TH)

Quibo! ("How's it going!") This exotic country may have a history twice as troubled as its neighbors, but when it comes to staggering beauty, Colombia has it in abundance!

Close to 14 percent of all the world's biodiversity—as well as many lost tribes—can be found deep in the Colombian rainforest.

THE NUKAKS

One of Colombia's lost tribes is the Nukak community. The modern world has only been in contact with this nomadic group of hunter-gatherers since 1988, as they live deep in the Amazon rainforest. In order to survive, the Nukak are skilled at using the medicinal qualities of the rainforest. They dunk types of vine roots in rivers, which release a drug that stuns fish, making them easy to catch!

MAGICAL MUD VOLCANO

Fancy taking a dip in a volcano? Don't worry it's not hot! Colombia's magical mud volcano, El Totumo, is a 50-ft. (15-m) high crater that is full of gooey mud.

KINGDOM OF GOLD

While the legend of El Dorado ("the golden one") is used around the world, its origins lie in Colombia. King of the native Muisca people, El Dorado supposedly honored Guatavita, a goddess, by covering himself in gold dust and throwing precious gems into the middle of the sacred lake where she lived!

El Dorado

EMERALD COUNTRY

While Ireland is considered to be the Emerald Isle, it is Colombia that is the Emerald City! Colombia produces up to 90 percent of the world's greenest gemstone.

FLOWER POWER

450 million flowers are exported from Colombia to the U.S.A. for Valentine's Day every year.

HERE COMES THE BOOM!

Colombia's popular traditional sport, *Tejo*, is a blast to play. Literally! Players throw a metal puck at a target (a metal rod) in a throwing field, and the closest to hitting the rod wins. The metal rod is rigged with small explosives known as *mechas*. When a player hits the rod, the devices explode loudly. Boom!

THE LIQUID RAINBOW

Caño Cristales, or "The Liquid Rainbow" is the most beautiful river in the world. The unique rock formations and diversity of flora and fauna make the water seem a kaleidoscope of colors—red, green, bright blue, yellow, and orange.

CHEESY HOT CHOCOLATE

Colombia is famous for its chocolate. And even more famous for its tradition of adding a huge chunk of cheese to hot chocolate, a popular lunchtime treat for locals. Try one for yourself tonight!

BLUE BOOBIES

Blue-footed boobies are one of nature's oddest birds . . . they love to dance! By lifting their brightly colored feet in a strange ritual, they attract a mate.

Blue-footed boobie

What Ecuador lacks in size it makes up for in natural and cultural wonders.

Its geography is as diverse as its wildlife, from Amazonian rainforest to sky-scraping mountain tops and giant tortoises to boobies with blue feet... it's all here!

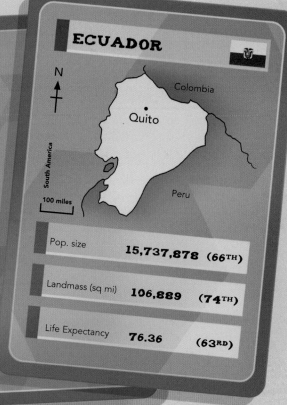

ECUADOR

N

Colombia

Quito

South America

Peru

100 miles

Pop. size	15,737,878	(66TH)
Landmass (sq mi)	106,889	(74TH)
Life Expectancy	76.36	(63RD)

SPLIT IN TWO

Many countries straddle the equator—the imaginary line that goes around the planet, dividing the world's northern and southern hemispheres. But Ecuador has the line to prove it! It also has the "Middle of the World" monument, a place where you can have one foot in the northern hemisphere and one foot in the southern hemisphere.

ECUADOR 0°- 0'- 0" LAT.

HANDY ANDES

The Andes mountain range is the longest in the world. Stretching for more than 4,350 mi. (7,000 km), this collection of snow-capped mega mountains extends through seven South American countries. Can you guess which ones?

Answer: Venezuela, Colombia, Ecuador, Peru, Bolivia, Chile, and Argentina.

EL NIÑO

El Niño is a type of weird weather that sees a surge of warm water rise from the depths of the Pacific Ocean and spread along the equator, jumbling up the Earth's climate and bringing with it drought, hotter temperatures, and flooding. The term *El Niño* (Spanish for "the Christ child") was originally used by fishermen along the coasts of Ecuador to describe this puzzling event.

 Ecuador

GENTLE GIANTS

Ecuador's spectacular Galápagos Islands are home to the world's largest tortoises. Lonesome George was the most famous— a giant Pinta Tortoise, George was known as the rarest creature in the world, the last of his kind. He died in 2012 at 102 years old!

GOING BANANAS

Ecuador is a banana-mad nation and one of the world's biggest banana exporters. A favored dish is *patacones*, fried green bananas, eaten like crisps! There are more than 1,000 varieties of banana, but the one we all know and love (and eat!) is called the Cavendish.

SMELLS LIKE A MAYOR

In 1967, the small town of Picoaza hit the national headlines—it is the only town in the world to elect Pulvapies—a brand of foot powder—as its mayor!

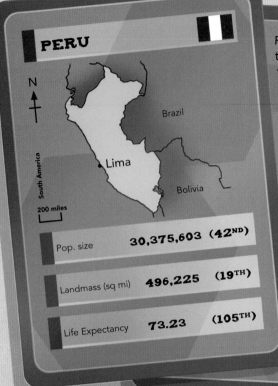

PERU

N

Brazil

Lima

Bolivia

South America

200 miles

Pop. size	30,375,603	(42ND)
Landmass (sq mi)	496,225	(19TH)
Life Expectancy	73.23	(105TH)

Peru is one of the world's most fascinating countries. Contained within its borders are so many natural and man-made wonders that it has become the most popular South American destination for backpackers.

If you want to see coast, mountains, rainforests, and deserts in one go—Peru is the place.

PADDINGTON

The world-famous teddy bear, Paddington, may be a resident of London now, but author Michael Bond's furry creation is actually from "darkest Peru."

THE GRANDEST CANYON

Cotahuasi Canyon, near the city of Arequipa, is the deepest canyon in the world. It is 11,000 ft. (3,354 m) deep. That means you could stack 11 Eiffel Towers on top of each other, and they still wouldn't reach the top!

MASHCO-PIRO

It is said that there are more than 70 uncontacted tribes in the Amazon jungle. The Mashco-Piro are one of Peru's, and to this day they still thrive in the far west of the Peruvian Amazon, remaining separate from the modern world. It is thought it is thought that only 250 people of their kind survive.

POTATOES

When Spanish conquistadors conquered the Inca Empire, the first thing they brought back to Europe was the potato. Peru's Inca Indians first grew the potato thousands of years ago. The ancient Inca Indians valued the potato not only as a food, but as a measure of time. Units of time were related to how long it took a potato to boil.

PIGGIES

To many, guinea pigs are adorable pets. To Peruvians they are a tasty treat! More than 60 million guinea pigs are eaten each year in Peru. Could you eat one?

NAZCA LINES

One of the world's greatest mysteries, the Nazca Lines are a collection of giant pictures scratched on the floor of the Nazca desert. Created around 2,000 years ago, there are over 70 animals and plants drawn into the red desert landscape, including sharks, hummingbirds, spiders, lizards, and whales.

BRIDGE OF EGGS

Puente de Piedra, or the "Bridge of Stone," is, unsurprisingly, made of stone. But rather more surprisingly, it's also made of eggs! Over 10,000 eggs were used to stick the bricks together. It's still standing 400 years later!

WONDER OF THE WORLD

Machu Picchu is an unbelievable ruin of a forgotten Inca city. Perched in the cloud forests of Peru, the city's ruins, containing a palace and other sacred sites, were rediscovered in 1911.

PEOPLE OF THE MOON

The Zo'é tribe, or "People of the Moon," live in the rainforests of northern Brazil. They pierce the bottom of their lips with a large wooden plug called a *poturu*.

South America's biggest country, Brazil has more people in it than the rest of the continent combined.

Brazil is so big it would take 70 hours to drive from Rio Grande to the Northern border with Guyana. But don't rush! There is so much to do while you're in Brazil.

BRAZIL

Brasilia

South America

500 miles

Argentina

Pop. size	200,361,925	(5TH)
Landmass (sq mi)	3,287,956	(5TH)
Life Expectancy	73.28	(104TH)

← HOLY MOLY!

Rio de Janeiro's gigantic statue of Christ the Redeemer, an iconic symbol of Brazil, stands atop Corcovado Mountain, and measures 98 ft. (30 m) tall, 17 times bigger than the average human!

WORLD CUP

The Brazilian national soccer team have won the FIFA World Cup five times, more than any other international squad. They are also the only team to have played at every tournament.

FAVELA FLAVOR

Brazil's slum towns, or *favelas*, are known around the world. Rocinha is the largest *favela* in Brazil, located on a very steep hill, with a population of 70,000 people. Santa Marta *favela*, in Rio de Janeiro, is famous for its colorfully painted residences.

WORLD'S GREATEST PARTY

The Rio Carnival attracts two million partygoers every February. The carnival highlight is the samba float parade, a competition between Rio's 100 samba schools! The carnival begins when Rio's mayor hands over a giant silver and gold key to Rei Momo, the "Fat King."

FIFA World Cup

Santa Marta favela

← Christ the Redeemer statue stands at

98 FT. (30 M)

That's

17

times bigger than the average human

THE REAL AMAZON.COM

Brazil is home to the largest percentage of the Amazon rainforest—a dense jungle with millions of species of insects and animals and more than 16,000 species of trees. Between 2000 and 2006, Brazil lost 57,900 sq. mi. (150,000 km²) of rainforest, an area larger than Greece.

BOLIVIA

N

Brazil

Peru

La Paz
(administrative)

Sucre (judicial)

South America

200 miles

Argentina

Pop. size	10,671,200	(81ST)
Landmass (sq mi)	424,164	(28TH)
Life Expectancy	68.55	(138TH)

Sandwiched in the center of Brazil, Peru, Paraguay, Argentina, and Chile is Bolivia. With a landscape full of salt as well as fertile valleys that produce much of the world's staple food crops, including potatoes and corn, Bolivia is worth exploring.

With the world's highest capital city, this is a country with its head in the clouds.

MR BOLIVIA

Simón José Antonio de la Santísima Trinidad Bolívar y Palacios Ponte y Blanco (or Simón Bolívar as he is more commonly known) liberated several Latin American countries from the hands of their Spanish conquerors, including Venezuela, Ecuador, Peru, and Bolivia. Bolivia is named in his honor.

DEVIL DANCE

Bolivia's most famous festival, *Carnaval de Oruro*, dates back 2,000 years. It begins every March with the Devil Dance. Hundreds of dancers take to the streets dressed as the devil with carved masks and horns.

ISLA DEL SOL

This mysterious island in the centre of Lake Titicaca holds the ruins of the Temple of the Sun, an Inca temple. Inca legend suggests that Viracocha, the bearded god who created the universe, emerged from the waters of Lake Titicaca and created the Sun on this island.

La Paz

CAPITAL CAPITAL

It's official: La Paz is the world's highest capital city. Perched around 11,910 ft. (3,630 m) above sea level, it is not uncommon to see planes fly past at eye level. Clouds have even been seen going through people's living rooms!

AN OCEAN OF SALT ON LAND

Salar de Uyuni, or the Uyuni Salt Flats, seems at first glance to be a white desert. In fact, this is the world's largest inland deposit of salt. The desert becomes a giant mirror of the sky during the rainy season.

Salar de Uyuni

HIGHWAY OF DEATH

On your journey to La Paz, you'll have to drive the most dangerous road in the world. Popularly known as "Bolivian Highway of Death," the North Yungas road is responsible for around 300 deaths every year.

THE BOTTLE DANCE

This traditional Paraguayan dance for women involves stacking bottles on your head, then spinning and shaking around energetically. The more experienced the dancer, the more bottles she can balance on her head!

ONOMATOPOEIA

Paraguay's kind-of official language is Guaraní. It is part of the indigenous Tupian family of languages, and is spoken by more than 4.5 million people. Guaraní is an onomatopoeic language. This means many of its words sound like the thing they are describing.

The geographical heart of South America, Paraguay is slap-bang in middle of the continent.

It is considered a country of contrasts but its laid-back residents are always happy to say *hola*— "hello"—to new visitors.

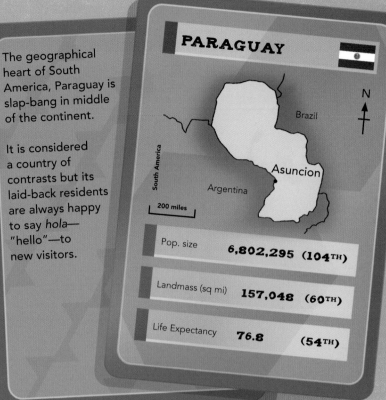

PARAGUAY

Brazil

Asuncion

South America

Argentina

N

200 miles

Pop. size	6,802,295	(104TH)
Landmass (sq mi)	157,048	(60TH)
Life Expectancy	76.8	(54TH)

DAM!

One of the seven wonders of the modern world, the Itaipu Dam is the world's second largest hydroelectric power plant. It produces the same amount of energy as burning 434,000 barrels of oil every day.

TEA DRINKERS

A hot cup of *yerba mate* is Paraguay's national thirst-quencher of choice. This type of herbal tea is packed full of health benefits, and smells like freshly cut grass!

CLAP YOUR HANDS SAY HELLO!

Most Paraguayan homes don't have doorbells. Upon visiting a local residence, simply announce your arrival by clapping your hands!

SMALL BIRD,
BIG VOICE!

The bare-throated bellbird, found in Paraguay, has one of the loudest natural calls in the world. A high pitched blast, it can be heard more than 1 mi. (1.6 km) away!

Bare-throated bellbird

URUGUAY

N

Argentina

Brazil

South America

Montevideo

100 miles

Pop. size	3,407,062	(134TH)
Landmass (sq mi)	69,898	(89TH)
Life Expectancy	76.81	(53RD)

A very peaceful nation, Uruguay is famous for its cowboys, called *gauchos*. It's just as well, as cows outnumber people three to one!

It's also known for its love of soccer and the fact that it's shaped like a real heart. Most of the land is very flat, making it perfect for ranching those 12 million steaks on legs.

ARMADILLO COUNTRY

Uruguay's national animal is the armadillo. This odd little critter is the only mammal on Earth whose body is covered with a hard shell, making it practically invincible!

Armadillo

TWENTY-NINTH

On the 29th of every month it is customary for everyone in Uruguay to eat gnocchi. This tradition relates to the nation's Italian heritage, when only staple foodstuffs such as flour and potatoes remained at the end of a long month.

WORLD CUP WINNERS

The country's national stadium, Estadio Centenario, was built in 1930 to accommodate the world's first ever soccer World Cup. Uruguay won the tournament, beating Argentina 4–2 in front of a crowd of 93,000 people.

COWBOY FESTIVAL

Fiesta de la Patria Gaucha is Uruguay's annual cowboy festival. Riders from Argentina and Uruguay compete in thrilling rodeo events. The winners parade in the streets!

Fiesta de la Patria Gaucha

SAND HAND

Emerging from the Playa Brava beach like a thirsty crab is *Mano de Punta del Este*, the "Hand of Punta del Este." This fascinating sculpture, by Chilean artist Mario Irarrázabal, depicts five human fingers emerging from sand. It was created in 1982 and is now one of Uruguay's defining landmarks.

HAND OF GOD

Argentina is soccer mad. One of the most famous soccer players of all time is Maradona, the player responsible for one of the greatest goals in soccer history. The first Argentinian soccer rulebook stated that a player who had been fouled could accept an apology rather than involve the referee!

Diego Maradona

You would think that the world's largest consumer of cows would also be the, well . . . beefiest nation on Earth.

However, thanks to the tango dance, an Argentinian creation, the locals are able to keep nice and lean, just like their famous steaks!

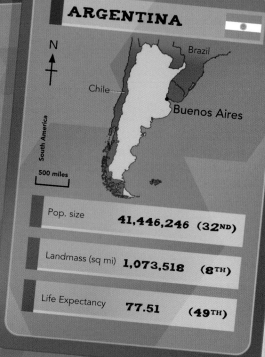

ARGENTINA

N

South America

Brazil

Chile

Buenos Aires

500 miles

Pop. size	41,446,246 (32ND)
Landmass (sq mi)	1,073,518 (8TH)
Life Expectancy	77.51 (49TH)

IGUAZU FALLS

Argentina's "Big Water," sits on the border between Argentina and Brazil and consists of 275 individual waterfalls, with an average height of 220 ft. (67 m). The most impressive of them all is *Garganta del Diablo*, "Devil's Throat," a U-shaped waterfall 269 ft. (82 m) high.

PLAY PATO

Argentina's beloved national sport is called *pato*, a game played on horseback. It combines aspects from polo and basketball. The word *pato* is Spanish for "duck" as early games used a live duck inside a basket instead of a ball!

Whisky!

ARGENTINOSAURUS

The oldest known dinosaur species ever to walk the Earth used to roam the Argentine landscape. Species such as *Eoraptor* is thought to have lived as far back as 230 million years ago. In 2014, palaeontologists announced the discovery of a 77-million-year-old dinosaur in Argentina—the world's largest ever found! Called *Dreadnoughtus schrani*, it was the size of seven Tyrannosaurus rex . . . or roughly the same size as a jumbo jet!

Dreadnoughtus schrani

SAY WHISKEY

When posing for photos in Argentina, they don't say "cheese," they say "whiskey." This helps you widen your smile!

DO THE TANGO

The celebrated music and dance, the tango, originated in Buenos Aires, "the Paris of South America," in the late 19th century. It's a vital part of Argentine popular culture.

CHILE

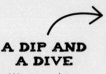

N

Santiago

Argentina

South America

500 miles

Pop. size	17,619,708	(61ST)
Landmass (sq mi)	291,933	(38TH)
Life Expectancy	78.44	(37TH)

The supermodel of countries, Chile is the world's narrowest nation—and one of the longest!

Only 217 mi. (246 km) wide, but approximately 2,700 mi. (4,300 km) long, this gigantic country contains the continent's most bewitching geography.

A DIP AND A DIVE

Want to take a dip in the world's largest pool? Put on your goggles and head to San Alfonso del Mar. This monster swimming pool is 115 ft. (35 m) deep and 3,323 ft. (1,013 m) long—20 times longer than an Olympic-sized pool!

ATACAMA DESERT

The world's driest place! Some unlucky areas of this barren landscape may not have seen a drop of rain in 400 years! This means the skies are amazingly clear, and makes it the perfect place to house the Atacama Large Millimeter Array (ALMA)—a very large telescope that has provided insight into the birth of distant stars during the early universe, as well as detailed knowledge about planet formation in other galaxies.

THE HORNS OF SOUTH AMERICA

Rising out of the Patagonian grassland, are the *Los Cuernos* mountains, known as the "Horns of South America." The distinct geology of these rock formations looks nothing like your average mountain and they are steeped in mysterious history.

HAPPY EASTER!

Easter Island is the world's most isolated destination. Located 2,200 mi. (3,540 km) west of Chile, this elusive isle is renowned for its 887 *moai*—giant heads carved from volcanic stone. The heads have an average weight of 14 tons and height of 13 ft. (4 m). Why were these heads built? No one knows!

TREASURE ISLAND, PART TWO

In 2005, 600 barrels of Spanish gold and Inca jewels were found on Robinson Crusoe Island off Chile's coastline. For centuries, treasure hunters have scoured the island in search of the booty, which was reportedly buried there in 1715 by Spanish sailor Juan Esteban Ubilla y Echeverria. The treasure, worth an estimated $10 billion was found by a mini robot that can scan 164 ft. (50 m) deep into the earth.

THE BLUE LAGOON

The Blue Lagoon is a giant milky bathtub—and the country's most popular hot spot. Literally! Millions of visitors each year come to take a dip in 1.5 million gallons (6 million litres) of geothermal seawater that have travelled from 6,560 ft. (2,000 m) beneath the Earth's surface. By the time it bubbles up to the lagoon, the mineral-rich, aqua-blue water is simmering at 100°F (38°C).

When it comes to Iceland, the name says it all! But don't be fooled, there's more to Iceland than meets the eye.

With its steamy geysers, hot springs, fiery volcanoes, and warm and friendly people (and puffins), it's no surprise that Iceland is known as the land of ice and fire.

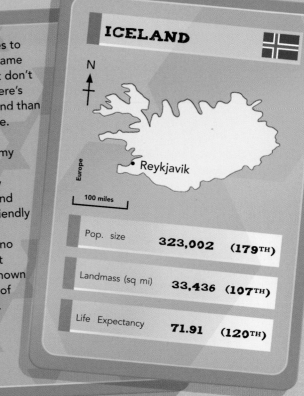

ICELAND

N

• Reykjavik

Europe

100 miles

Pop. size	323,002	(179TH)
Landmass (sq mi)	33,436	(107TH)
Life Expectancy	71.91	(120TH)

Puffin

PUFFIN ISLAND

There are between eight and ten million of these cute little seabirds in Iceland. Visitors can see their feathered friends on the islands off the coast by taking a boat called the *Puffin Express*.

PATRONYMS

In Iceland, it is the law to give children surnames according to the first names of their parents, meaning moms and dads have different surnames to their children. This is known as a "patronym." For example, if your name is John and your father is called Terry, you'd be called John Terryson, and for daughters the word *dóttir* is applied, for example, Rachel Terrydóttir.

SKROKKUR GEYSER

Every four to eight minutes, the Skrokkur Geyser in Selfloss erupts with a jet of hot water that fires up to 131ft. (40m) in the air—the height of four buses stacked on top of each other! Bubbling hot underneath the ground, the water is forced up through cracks in the Earth.

DEEP-BLUE CAVES

To see the land of ice and fire in action, there's no better place than at Skaftafell National Park, where you'll find Svmnafellsjvkull, a crystal ice cave that looks like its ceiling is on fire with deep blue flames. The cave is hidden deep inside a glacier that crackles and pops above.

WHAT A STINK!

A traditional Icelandic food is *hákarl*, which is the definition of an acquired taste! Shark meat is buried in a shallow pit and left to rot, before being cleaned, sliced, and served raw. It has been described as tasting 100 times stronger than blue cheese. Yum!

SCOTLAND

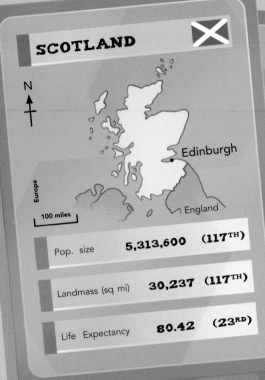

N

Europe

100 miles

Edinburgh

England

Pop. size	**5,313,600**	**(117TH)**
Landmass (sq mi)	**30,237**	**(117TH)**
Life Expectancy	**80.42**	**(23RD)**

Scotland is the head that sits proudly atop the body of Britain.

A nation of outstanding natural beauty, Scotland is world famous for its lochs and mountains, lake monsters, whiskey and so much more!

THE SOUND OF WAR!

They sound like no other instrument on Earth—making a background noise known as a drone—but bagpipes are Scotland's proud national instrument. Centuries ago, Scottish warriors played the bagpipes in battle to intimidate their enemies.

WHERE ELSE IN THE WORLD?

Some of Scotland's most famous icons actually originated elsewhere. Can you take a guess where these Scottish "inventions" actually came from?

1) Bagpipes   **A) Central Asia**
2) Haggis   **B) Greece**
3) Kilts and sporrans   **C) England**
4) Tartan   **D) Ireland**

Answers: 1.B, 2.C, 3.D, 4.A

HIT OR MYTH

Scotland's national animal is the unicorn. In Celtic mythology, the unicorn symbolizes innocence and joy, as well as power!

NATIONAL POET

Scotland's most treasured writer is Robert Burns. He died in 1796 but every year in January there is a national celebration in his honor. A supper of haggis and whiskey is served, and one of Burns' most famous works, *Address to a Haggis*, is traditionally recited to the haggis, before it's cut into and eaten!

LOYAL DOG

The legend of "Greyfriars Bobby" tells of Scotland's most famous dog. This Skye terrier is remembered for his loyalty to his master, Edinburgh policeman, John Gray. The story goes that after his master died, Greyfriars Bobby sat by his grave, protecting it lovingly for 14 years, until his own death.

HAGGIS

So what is this haggis we keep hearing about? Well, it's Scotland's national dish and it consists of the lungs, heart, and liver of a sheep, mixed with onions, stock, and spices, and cooked and served inside a sheep's stomach. Not for the faint-hearted!

FREEDOM!

Scotland fought for independence from England in June, 1314 at the famous Battle of Bannockburn. Led by their warrior king, Robert the Bruce, Scotland defeated the English army.

THE HIGHLAND GAMES

The world's best celebration of Celtic culture, the Highland Games, began in the 11th century. The games include amazing events such as the caber toss—where men throw huge wooden logs as far they can! There's also the stone put, the Scottish hammer throw, and even a haggis-hurling event.

Loch Ness Monster

LOCHS AND LOCHS OF MONSTERS!

Scotland's most famous myth is that of the Loch Ness monster. Many travelers have dredged the loch for the mysterious beastie but have yet to find any concrete evidence of her existence. Local Nessie super-fan, George Edwards, spends sixty hours a week searching for the dino-like creature. He has found nothing so far, except 100,000 golf balls!

THE BIRTH OF THE FUTURE

These days the oceans are full of telegraph cables, helping countries to communicate with each other over enormous distances. But the very first of its kind was laid from western Ireland to eastern Newfoundland—an island off Canada—in 1858. One of the first messages sent was from Queen Victoria to American President James Buchanan. It began: "The Queen desires to congratulate the President upon the successful completion of this great international work." It reduced the communication time between North America and Europe from ten days—the time it took to deliver a message by ship—to just hours!

Located 50 mi. (80 km) west of Great Britain, Ireland is the internationally loved "Emerald Isle," with its rolling hillsides of green.

With national icons aplenty—from shamrocks to fiddles and dancing jigs to jugs of Guinness, it's official: Ireland is amazing!

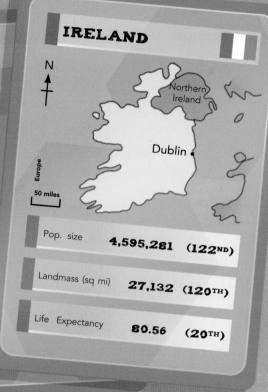

IRELAND

N↑

Northern Ireland

Dublin

Europe

50 miles

Pop. size	4,595,281	(122ND)
Landmass (sq mi)	27,132	(120TH)
Life Expectancy	80.56	(20TH)

THE WHITE HOUSE

America's most famous residence, The White House in Washington, D.C., was designed by an Irishman—James Hoban. The architect entered and won a competition, designing the Presidents' house from top to bottom in 1792.

GO TO PAGE 48

Which other world-famous building was designed by the winner of a contest?

THE DINGLE DOLPHIN

Off the coast near the town of Dingle is an underwater celebrity. Fungie the dolphin has been guiding fishing boats to and from Dingle's harbor for years. He's a well loved member of the community, and tourists often take boat trips out to see him and say hello!

LUCKY CHARM

The shamrock is recognized as the symbol that encapsulates the "luck of the Irish." However, there is a more significant backstory to Ireland's lucky charm. Saint Patrick, the patron saint of the nation, used the shamrock to teach people about the Christian Holy Trinity—the three leaves represent the Father, the Son, and the Holy Spirit.

Lucky shamrock

With eleven consonants and eleven vowels, Muckanaghederdauhaulia is Ireland's longest place name. Try and say it five times fast!

10,000,000

. . . pints of Guinness, Ireland's most famous alcoholic drink, are sold every single day in 150 countries around the world. It's so popular that it's known as "black gold!"

MUCKANAGHEDERDAUHAULIA

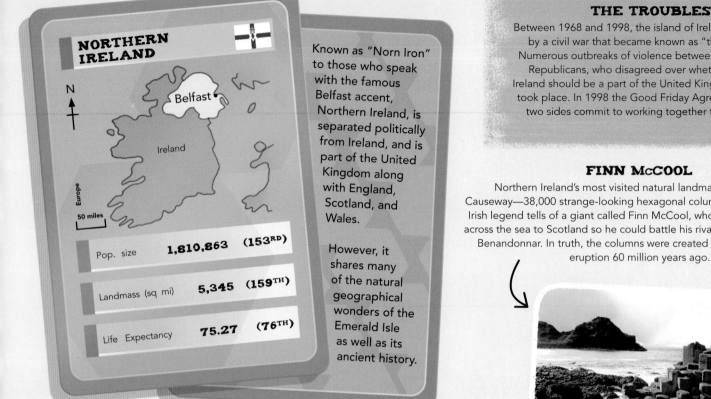

NORTHERN IRELAND

N

Belfast

Ireland

Europe

50 miles

Pop. size	1,810,863	(153RD)
Landmass (sq mi)	5,345	(159TH)
Life Expectancy	75.27	(76TH)

Known as "Norn Iron" to those who speak with the famous Belfast accent, Northern Ireland, is separated politically from Ireland, and is part of the United Kingdom along with England, Scotland, and Wales.

However, it shares many of the natural geographical wonders of the Emerald Isle as well as its ancient history.

THE TROUBLES
Between 1968 and 1998, the island of Ireland was divided by a civil war that became known as "the Troubles." Numerous outbreaks of violence between Unionists and Republicans, who disagreed over whether Northern Ireland should be a part of the United Kingdom or Ireland, took place. In 1998 the Good Friday Agreement saw the two sides commit to working together to find peace.

FINN McCOOL
Northern Ireland's most visited natural landmark is the Giant's Causeway—38,000 strange-looking hexagonal columns of basalt. Popular Irish legend tells of a giant called Finn McCool, who built a path of rocks across the sea to Scotland so he could battle his rival, another giant called Benandonnar. In truth, the columns were created by a super-volcanic eruption 60 million years ago.

THINKING UP THE UNSINKABLE
The world's most famous ship, RMS *Titanic*, was designed by Northern Irishman Thomas Andrews and built at Belfast's iconic shipping port. On April 15, 1912, RMS *Titanic* sank in the North Atlantic Ocean after colliding with a gigantic iceberg. More than 1,500 people died.

RMS *Titanic*

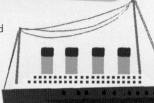

A-SCARY-ROPE-BRIDGE
Connecting the mainland to Carrick-a-Rede Island, the Carrick-a-Rede Rope Bridge originally consisted of just two ropes: one to walk on and one for a hand guide. Today, the rope bridge is a bit sturdier, and it's a fun way to explore the tiny island and get the heart pumping!

THE DARK LEGEND OF THE GRAY LADY
The Dark Hedges, an avenue of intertwined, 300-year-old beech trees in Ballymoney, is one of Northern Ireland's most striking natural landmarks. The road of trees is supposedly haunted by the "Gray Lady"— a ghost who appears at dusk, silently gliding and hiding among the trees. Spooky!

HAUNTED CASTLE
Ballygally Castle in County Antrim (now run as a hotel) is said to be the most haunted place in Northern Ireland. The ghost of Lady Isobel Shaw, who fell to her death from the turret of the castle, supposedly knocks on guests' doors at night!

PRINCE OF WALES

Llywelyn the Last, or Llywelyn Ein Llyw Olaf (say that five times fast!) was the last prince of an independent Wales before the country's conquest by Edward Longshanks (Edward I of England). Llywelyn died in 1282 at the Battle of Orewin Bridge at Builth Wells. His head was cut off and sent to Edward, who stuck it on a lance outside the Tower of London, where legend says it remained for 15 years.

Llywelyn Ein Llyw Olaf

Stuffed with enough geographical wonders and strange place names to keep you entertained for centuries, Wales is full of castles and legends, sheep and leeks, and a proud obsession with rugby, its national sport.

Cymru am byth— "Wales Forever!"

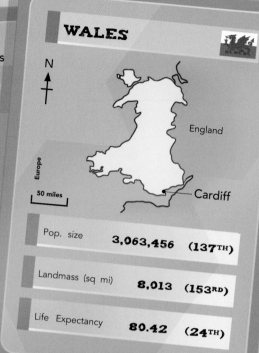

WALES

N

Europe

50 miles

England

Cardiff

Pop. size	3,063,456	(137TH)
Landmass (sq mi)	8,013	(153RD)
Life Expectancy	80.42	(24TH)

A MOUTHFUL OF LETTERS

Meaning "Saint Mary's Church in the hallow of the white hazel near a rapid whirlpool and the Church of Saint Tysilio of the red cave," *Llanfairpwllgwyngyllgogerychwyrndrobwllllantysiliogogogoch* is more of a mouthful than a tasty Welsh rarebit! With 58 letters to its name, the town has Europe's longest place name.

CHEESE ON TOAST

Everybody loves grilled cheese, but in Wales it's a true delicacy! Welsh rarebit, a popular lunchtime treat, is beer-soaked cheese and mustard mixed together, then melted on toast!

In which country would you find Mount Everest?

GO TO PAGE 172

MABINOGION

This collection of magical Welsh tales is over 1,000 years old. Full of giants, dragons, enchanted trees, beautiful, cunning women, and brave men, these stories have stood the test of time.

EVEREST

Colonel Sir George Everest never visited the world's tallest mountain, nor even saw a picture of it, but he will forever be associated with Mount Everest. The rocky skyscraper was named after the famed mountain surveyor, by the Royal Geographical Society. Weirdly, the mountain is not pronounced like Everest's own name, which was pronounced *Eve-rest.*

Everest

Mabinogion

ENGLAND

Pop. size — 53,493,700 (23RD)

Landmass (sq mi) — 50,346 (96TH)

Life Expectancy — 80.42 (22ND)

The British Empire sent English culture all over the world, and the English language was the most spoken language on Earth for centuries.

With its rolling hills of green, skies of gray, buses of red and cliffs of white, not to mention the world's first mega-city—England has given the world over 4,000 years of fascinating history.

KING HENRY VIII

England's most controversial king, reigning 1509–47, is probably most famous for having six wives. Can you name them all?

The Beatles

BIG BEN

In Chinese, Big Ben—the bell in London's historic timepiece—is known as *Dà běn zhōng,* or "big stupid clock." The clock tower itself was officially named Elizabeth Tower to celebrate Queen Elizabeth II's diamond jubilee.

BAND OF BEATLES

The Beatles are the most successful and influential group in the history of recorded music. Forming in 1960, in Liverpool, John Lennon, Paul McCartney, George Harrison, and Ringo Starr had 17 number one singles in under ten years—and sold more than 1.5 billion records.

THE BARD

William Shakespeare is celebrated as the greatest writer of all time. His comedies, tragedies, histories, and sonnets are still performed all over the world, and he is credited with the invention of 1,700 words, including "dawn," "bump," and "ladybird!"

William Shakespeare

FULL ENGLISH

Baked beans Bacon Sausage
Eggs Toast / fried bread

FANCY A FRY-UP?

A full English breakfast is the only way to start the day! There are many variations on this classic meal, but you'll always find sausages, eggs, bacon, baked beans, toast or fried bread, and lots of tea to wash it down. Yum!

IT'S A MYSTERY

Stonehenge is one of the most valuable prehistoric sites in the world. The construction and pattern of the peculiar standing stones began around 2500 B.C. Evidence suggests some of the iconic stones traveled all the way from the Preseli Hills, Wales — 155 mi. (250 km) away. Some of the stones weigh a whopping 27 tons. How did they get there?

GARDEN OF EDEN

The Eden Project in Cornwall is a space-age collection of bubbles or "biomes" rising out of an old clay pit. These are the largest greenhouses on Earth, housing a fantastic array of plants and flowers from all over the world.

AN IMPORTANT DIARY

Anne Frank was just an ordinary German Jewish teenager. Her family moved to Amsterdam before the outbreak of World War II. As things got worse for the Jews, her family hid in their house in a small loft. From this cramped space, Anne wrote her diary, detailing her life in hiding from Adolf Hitler's Nazis. Her diary was published after her death in 1945, and has since been translated into many languages.

ON YOUR BIKE!

The Dutch love their bicycles. The country is known as the bicycle capital of the world—more than 18 million are seen on the streets every day.

Along with Belgium and Luxembourg, the Netherlands makes up the Low Countries—an area of Europe that is extremely flat and lies completely below sea level.

From the windmills in Zaanes Schans to the famous tulip gardens of Keukenhof and Amsterdam's historic canals, the Netherlands is packed with amazing things to see.

NETHERLANDS

Amsterdam

Europe

50 miles

Germany

Belgium

Pop. size	16,804,224	(64TH)
Landmass (sq mi)	16,158	(133RD)
Life Expectancy	81.12	(18TH)

VINCENT VAN GOGH

This master of art produced more than 2,100 paintings, drawings, and sketches. Tragically though, he only sold one of them during his lifetime. His true success came after his death.

AMSTERDAM

The Netherlands' treasured capital city has more than 165 canals and 1,281 bridges. Because Amsterdam was originally a swamp, all of the city's buildings are built on long wooden poles, pushed deep into the sandy river floor below. The Royal Palace is perched on 13,659 poles!

WIND POWER

The windmill is a historic icon of the Netherlands, with over 1,000 mills still in working condition. Windmills pump excess water from the land back into the river, so that the land can be farmed. There were once 10,000 windmills dotted around the landscape.

CITY OF FLOWERS

More than seven million tulips, daffodils, and hyacinths take over the world's most beloved Flower Garden at Keukenhof, in the city of Lisse. Tulips are a Dutch national symbol, however tulip bulbs aren't native to the country—they were once imported from Turkey.

FIERLJEPPEN

Fierljeppen, the Netherlands' traditional sport, originated as a way for Dutch people to get around (and over!) the canals easily. The game consists of running towards the river or canal with a long pole in your hand, and then leaping over the water as far as possible—while climbing to the top of the pole, too!

DENMARK

N

Europe

Sweden

Copenhagen

50 miles

Pop. size	5,613,706	(113TH)
Landmass (sq mi)	16,639	(132ND)
Life Expectancy	79.09	(34TH)

It's impossible to get bored in Denmark. It is the birthplace of Lego and amusement parks, fairy tales, Danish pastries, Vikings, and 300 uninhabited islands.

You are never more than an hour's drive from the sea, and never more than one minute away from a happy Danish person! Denmark has it all.

ONCE UPON A TIME

Known as *eventyrs* in Denmark, Hans Christian Andersen's fairy tales have captivated the world for over 175 years. The Danish author's *The Snow Queen* was the inspiration for Disney's smash hit movie *Frozen*. He also wrote *The Emperor's New Clothes* and *The Little Mermaid*, among many others. As Albert Einstein once said: "If you want your children to be intelligent, read them fairy tales. If you want them to be more intelligent, read them more fairy tales."

A LAND OF LEGO

Lego is the world-famous brick toy. It was created in Denmark by carpenter Ole Kirk Kristiansen in 1932. Lego, from the Danish phrase *leg godt*, means "play well." 20 million Lego bricks are made every year at the factory!

HAPPY

It's official. Danes are the happiest people in the world. According to the UN's 2013 World Happiness Report, with a score of 7.6 out of 10, Denmark triumphed over every other country.

SYDNEY OPERA HOUSE

The man who designed the Sydney Opera House—Australia's most famous building—was Danish architect Jørn Utzon. He won a competition to design the building in 1957, beating over 230 other entries.

DANISH FOOD

The Danes love their food. From *wienerbrød* (Danish pastries) to *frikadeller* (Danish meatballs) to *Gravad laks* (salt-cured salmon) there is quite literally a *smorgasbord* (a Swedish word) of choice!

Wienerbrød

Gravad laks

THE COMFORT IN HYGGE

The Danish have a special word —*hygge*. Pronounced "hooga," the word translates as "tranquility," or a warm feeling that comes from that cozy comfort you feel in a warm, soft bed, or by a blazing fire, when everything surrounding you is cold and dark.

THE BIRTH OF FUN

Dyrehavsbakken, opened in 1583, is the world's first amusement park! The second oldest, Tivoli Gardens, is just down the road and has the oldest operating wooden rollercoaster on the planet, dating back to 1914.

ERIC THE BLOODAXE

Once upon a time, more than 1,000 years ago, Eric Fairhair was the son of the Viking king of Norway. His father, Harald Fairhair, had many sons who could inherit the throne. Eric solved that problem by murdering all his brothers, a fact that earned him his nickname "Bloodaxe."

Polar bears, skiing, ice driving, glaciers, fjords—Norway has all these and so much more!

Wrap up warm, because there are so many amazing outdoor events to do in Norway—the land of the north —that you won't want to miss out.

NORWAY

N

Europe

200 miles

Sweden

Finland

Oslo

Pop. size	5,084,190	(119TH)
Landmass (sq mi)	125,021	(68TH)
Life Expectancy	81.6	(14TH)

JOSTEDALSBREEN

The world's glaciers—massive chunks of slow moving ice—are disappearing by the second. So, before it vanishes forever, take a walk over Jostedalsbreen, the largest glacier in Europe.

FAMOUS FJORD

Fjords are formed when glaciers retreat, leaving sea waters to rise and flood the valleys created by the glaciers. Norway has the highest concentration of fjords in the world. The mighty Geirangerfjord is the country's most visited natural landmark and is in the shape of a "U."

LONDON'S POLAR BEAR

In 1252, Henry III of England received a present from King Haakon of Norway. It was a polar bear. The bear lived in the Tower of London but had a very long leash, which meant it could swim and catch fish in the River Thames!

MUSH! MUSH!

Head north to Finnmark for the nation's best dog sledding. When a driver calls "mush," a pack of strong huskies will dash off at speed, pulling a sled behind them. Each year, Norway hosts two world-famous dog sled races. It's the only way to travel!

GLOBAL SEED VAULT

On the remote Norwegian island of Svalbard is a vault where scientists are keeping 2.25 billion of the world's flower, vegetable, and grain seeds. Stored at a very low temperature, the seeds can last for thousands of years. If there were ever a global disaster that wiped out the world's crops then Norway would come to our rescue!

BETWEEN A ROCK AND A HARD PLACE

A rock, called the Kjeragbolten boulder, lodged 3,280 ft. (1,000 m) above the ground, is one of Norway's greatest places to get your adrenalin pumping. Climbers and daredevils (and some sheep!) psyche themselves up to walk out on the rock for a photo opportunity. However, if the wind picks up, it's a long way down!

WOW!

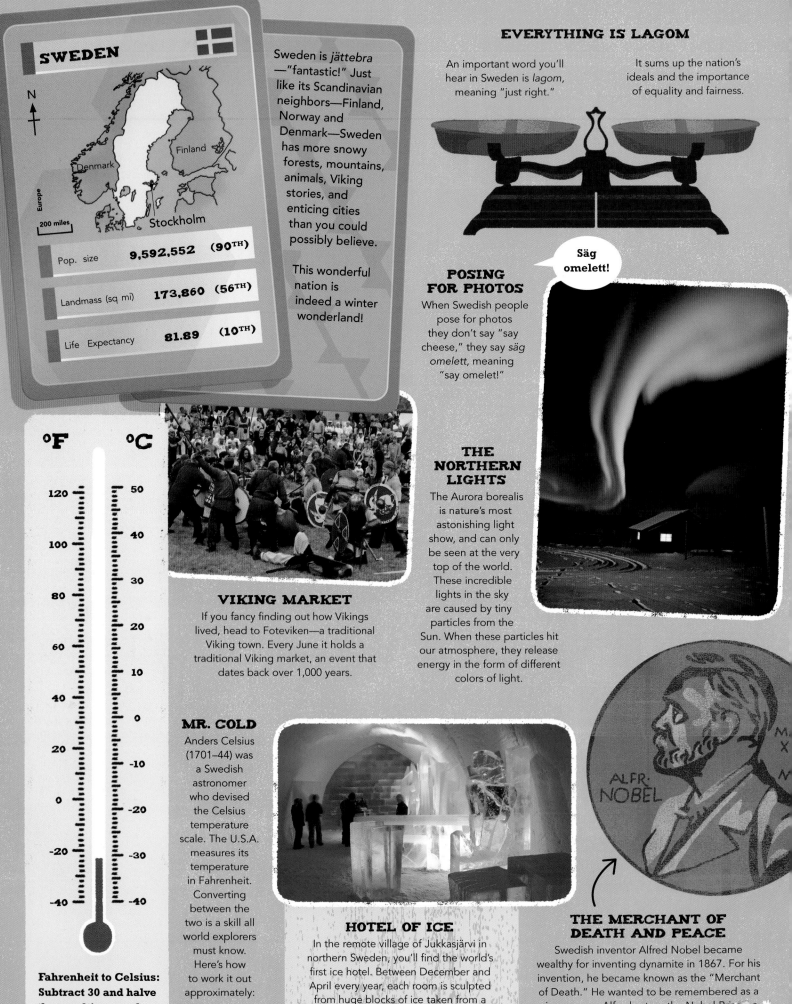

SWEDEN

N

Denmark
Finland
Stockholm

Europe

200 miles

Pop. size	9,592,552	(90TH)
Landmass (sq mi)	173,860	(56TH)
Life Expectancy	81.89	(10TH)

Sweden is *jättebra* —"fantastic!" Just like its Scandinavian neighbors—Finland, Norway and Denmark—Sweden has more snowy forests, mountains, animals, Viking stories, and enticing cities than you could possibly believe.

This wonderful nation is indeed a winter wonderland!

EVERYTHING IS LAGOM

An important word you'll hear in Sweden is *lagom*, meaning "just right."

It sums up the nation's ideals and the importance of equality and fairness.

POSING FOR PHOTOS

When Swedish people pose for photos they don't say "say cheese," they say *säg omelett*, meaning "say omelet!"

Säg omelett!

THE NORTHERN LIGHTS

The Aurora borealis is nature's most astonishing light show, and can only be seen at the very top of the world. These incredible lights in the sky are caused by tiny particles from the Sun. When these particles hit our atmosphere, they release energy in the form of different colors of light.

°F   °C

120 — 50
— 40
100 —
80 — 30
— 20
60 —
— 10
40 —
— 0
20 —
— -10
0 —
— -20
-20 —
— -30
-40 — -40

Fahrenheit to Celsius: Subtract 30 and halve the resulting number.

Celsius to Fahrenheit: Double the number and add 30.

VIKING MARKET

If you fancy finding out how Vikings lived, head to Foteviken—a traditional Viking town. Every June it holds a traditional Viking market, an event that dates back over 1,000 years.

MR. COLD

Anders Celsius (1701–44) was a Swedish astronomer who devised the Celsius temperature scale. The U.S.A. measures its temperature in Fahrenheit. Converting between the two is a skill all world explorers must know. Here's how to work it out approximately:

HOTEL OF ICE

In the remote village of Jukkasjärvi in northern Sweden, you'll find the world's first ice hotel. Between December and April every year, each room is sculpted from huge blocks of ice taken from a nearby river. The temperature remains at 23°F (-5°C), and guests are given warm coats and hot drinks to keep them cosy.

ALFR. NOBEL

THE MERCHANT OF DEATH AND PEACE

Swedish inventor Alfred Nobel became wealthy for inventing dynamite in 1867. For his invention, he became known as the "Merchant of Death." He wanted to be remembered as a nice man, so Alfred set up the Nobel Prize, a series of annual honors to those who [...] science and the arts. The Nobel P[...] the most prestigious award you ca[...]

OLD GUM

The world's oldest piece of chewing gum was found in Finland. The 5,000-year-old gum, a lump of birch bark tar, was used by Finland's Neolithic people to treat gum infections . . . as well as for glue!

With more than 180,000 lakes and with 70 percent of the country covered by forest, it's no wonder Finland is an elusive land where great mythologies hide, and completely crazy local traditions are proudly upheld.

It may often be cold and dark but as one of the top ten happiest countries, no one seems to mind!

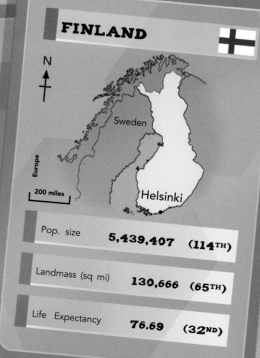

FINLAND

N

Europe

200 miles

Sweden

Helsinki

Pop. size	5,439,407	(114TH)
Landmass (sq mi)	130,666	(65TH)
Life Expectancy	76.69	(32ND)

SÁMI PEOPLE

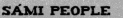

The Sámi people of Finland are a major indigenous tribe that have existed for more than 5,000 years. There are roughly 9,000 Sámi living in Finland today, surviving on reindeer herding, hunting, and fishing. The Sámi used to use a measurement of distance called *Poronkusema*—the distance a reindeer can walk before needing to pee!

Air guitar world champion

FUNKY FINNISH FESTIVALS

?

The Finnish love to celebrate the bizarre. Throughout the year there are lots of crazy festivals that are now internationally envied. Swamp Soccer, Air Guitar World Championships, and the Cell Phone Throwing Championship are just a few examples!

DEAR SANTA . . .

You might know him as Father Christmas or Santa Claus but in Finland he is known as *joulupukki* or the "Christmas Goat". Finland's *joulupukki*, officially resides in the northern province of Lapland with *joulutonttu*, his dwarf-like assistants. Santa's post office receives over 550,000 letters every year from children all over the world!

WIFE-CARRYING CHAMPIONSHIP

Wife carrying is a traditional sport in Finland, with competitors from all over the world congregating in Sonkajarvi each year. The sport dates back to the 19th century, when it is thought a local villain called Ronkainen used to steal local women, put them on his shoulders and run away! The length you have to carry your wife is 831 ft. (253.3 m), over a track made of quicksand, grass, and 3 ft. (1m) deep water.

To: Father Christmas, Santa Claus Post Office, FI-96930 Arctic Circle, FINLAND

KAKSLAUTTANEN

There is a remote part of the northern Finnish Lapland, called Kakslauttanen where you can sleep in igloos with glass roofs. These are built for one sole purpose—to view the Aurora borealis—nature's light show.

ESTONIA

N

Tallinn

Europe

Latvia

50 miles

Pop. size	1,324,612	(158TH)
Landmass (sq mi)	17,462	(131ST)
Life Expectancy	74.07	(97TH)

Named after the Ests people who inhabited the region two thousand years ago, Estonia is effectively 50 percent forest.

Welcome to a flat and snowy, forward-thinking country that's roughly the same size as Switzerland but a little more mysterious.

TAKE A TRIP TO TALLINN

The 406-ft (124-m) tower of St Olaf's church in the Old Town of Tallinn has been struck by lightning and burned to the ground three times in its 700-year history, but has always been rebuilt.

LEAN ON ME

Similar to Italy's world-renowned Leaning Tower of Pisa, the Leaning House of Tartu is just as curious! Slowly sinking due to one side of its foundations being built on wooden blocks, the building has become a crazy cultural landmark. Don't stare at it too long—you'll get neckache!

St. Olaf's church

ALIVE AND KIIKING

Imagine being on a swing and pushing yourself so hard that you go all the way round! Well, that's *kiiking*! Estonia proudly invented *kiiking*, and it's often considered a national sport. Competitors fasten themselves to a large swing, and then skillfully push and pump until they gain enough momentum to rotate a full 360 degrees.

Wheeeeeeeeeeeeeeeeeeeee!

NIAGARA FALLS OF THE BALTIC

Estonia's Jägala Falls is the country's largest waterfall and in winter it freezes over!

TOELL THE GREAT

Estonian folklore tells of tales of Toell the Great—a giant hero who helped the people of Tõlluste. It is said that when an enemy decapitated him during a battle, Toell put his head on his sword and walked to his grave.

METEOR COUNTRY

Estonia has the highest number of meteorite craters of any country in the world. Scientists believe that the meteor site at Kaali was the only meteor impact ever to be witnessed by early humans, up to 7,500 years ago. The impact was equivalent to that of the Hiroshima bomb, a nuclear weapon unleashed by the U.S. Air Force on Japan during World War Two.

LATVIAN DELICACY

River lampreys, long eel-like fish with no jaws that suck the blood of other fish for food, are a national delicacy in Latvia. In fact, Latvia is the only country to eat these 15-in-(40-cm-) long slippery creatures, usually after marinating them in coffee!

A BIG SONG AND DANCE

Held every five years since 1873, the Latvia Song and Dance Festival is one of Latvia's most important cultural events, and the largest amateur choral tradition in the world. In 2018, at the next event, more than 30,000 people will sing Latvian folk songs together, usually a cappella (without musical accompaniment).

WOW!

Located on the banks of the blustery Baltic Sea, Latvia is a beautiful country with enough weird and wonderful features to keep you enthralled for hours.

A nation of record breakers and crocodile hunters; singers and dancers; ice-hockey players and eel-eaters, Latvia is a place to have a *Riga*-rous look around!

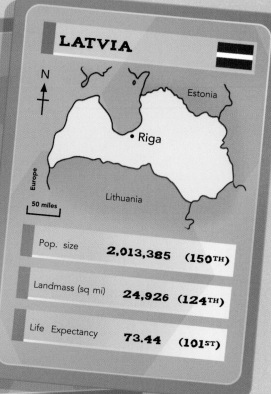

LATVIA

N

Estonia

• Riga

Europe

50 miles

Lithuania

Pop. size	2,013,385	(150TH)
Landmass (sq mi)	24,926	(124TH)
Life Expectancy	73.44	(101ST)

FREEDOM MONUMENT

Latvia's most famous landmark is the Freedom Monument, in Riga. Honoring the 3,000 soldiers killed during the 1918–20 Latvian War of Independence from Russia, the needle-shaped structure is 137 ft. (42 m) high and a symbol of the nation's struggle for freedom.

FACE IN THE WALLS

Latvia's capital city, Riga, is famous for its Art Nouveau architecture. This style of architecture is inspired by nature and defined by its use of curved lines, floral motifs, and decorative gargoyles, like this one . . .

CROCODILE DUNDEE

The real-life inspiration for Crocodile Dundee—a famous movie character from the 1980s —was Latvian Arvids Blumentāls, from Dundaga. He moved to Australia after World War Two and became a crocodile hunter (known as Crocodile Harry), reportedly killing more than 40,000 crocodiles!

A BELT TO KEEP

Given to children at a young age, *Lielvārde* belts play an important part in traditional Latvian culture. Worn to all special occasions and festivals, the symbolic belts, with unique, brightly woven patterns are individually made for each person, and are kept by Latvians for the whole of their lives.

TĒVZEMEI UN BRĪVĪBAI

LITHUANIA

N

Latvia

Vilnius

Belarus

Europe

Poland

50 miles

Pop. size	2,956,121	(139TH)
Landmass (sq mi)	25,212	(123RD)
Life Expectancy	75.98	(68TH)

Hello, or *Labas* as the Lithuanians might say.

Lithuania is the largest and most southerly of the three Baltic states, and is also the absolute center of Europe. Take a look on the map if you don't believe us!

EASTER GRANNY

In Lithuania, according to ancient tradition, the Easter Bunny doesn't bring you Easter eggs. Instead Velykų Senelė (the Easter Granny) does! On Easter Sunday, Easter Granny distributes eggs—brightly painted and full of treats —around the villages to all the good children. Naughty children receive only a single, plain white egg. Those are the rules!

The Easter Granny's basket of decorated eggs

HILL OF CROSSES

When Lithuania was under the control of the Soviet Union, its people put up crosses on Kryzių Kalnas, (the Hill Of Crosses) as a sign of resistance. In the 14th century, the Hill of Crosses was a burial site where Lithuanians mourned the dead lost at war. It is now one of the country's most distinctive landmarks!

SCENT OF LITHUANIA

Think of Switzerland and you smell chocolate. Think of England and you smell tea. But think of Lithuania and what smell comes to mind? Exactly. In 2011, Lithuania became the only country in the world to create its own official fragrance, called the Scent of Lithuania. The goal when creating the smell was to "tell a story about its cities and villages, its nature, ancient traditions and cultural heritage, the character and the achievements of its people." So what does Lithuania smell like? The scent is a mix of bergamot, wildflowers, ginger, raspberry, and grapefruit. The perfume is available to buy in all supermarkets!

DEVILISHLY INTERESTING

One of the world's most unusual museums is found in Kaunas and features a collection of devil statues from all over the world. With over 3,000 pieces in the Devils' Museum collection, there are wooden devils, red devils, porcelain devils, paper devils, carved devils, household devils, and lots more. Phew!

Raspberry

Ginger

Bergamot

Grapefruit

Wildflowers

Kūčios

KŪČIOS CHRISTMAS

Christmas Eve dinner in Lithuania is a traditional event. Known as *Kūčios*, the Christmas feast includes 12 dishes, with no meat and no dairy allowed. The most traditional of these dishes are small sweet biscuits soaked in poppy seed milk. The food can only be eaten when stars appear in the sky, and any leftover food must remain on the table for ghostly spirits of deceased relatives to come and enjoy during the night.

SPUTNIK

The world's first satellite, Sputnik, was launched by the Soviet Union in 1957. It spent three months in orbit around the globe and traveled more than 40 million mi. (64 million km)! Its successful launch triggered the race to the Moon in the 1960s.

WORLD'S OLDEST LAKE

Lake Baikal is 25 million years old, a thousand times older than any other lake on Earth! It is the deepest lake too, accounting for 20 percent of the entire world's fresh water.

Stretching across 11 time zones above Europe, Asia, and the Pacific Ocean, Russia is the world's largest country, almost twice the size of the United States and one-eighth of the entire planet's land mass!

As you might expect, a country this big has lots of things to explore. Let's get started . . .

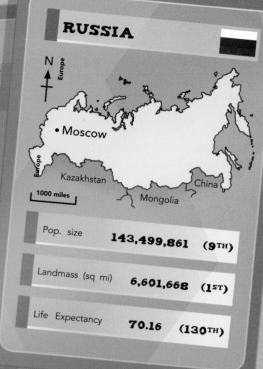

RUSSIA

• Moscow

Kazakhstan

Mongolia

China

Europe

Europe

N

1000 miles

Pop. size	143,499,861	(9TH)
Landmass (sq mi)	6,601,668	(1ST)
Life Expectancy	70.16	(130TH)

A DOLL WITHIN A DOLL

Russian dolls, or *matryoshkas*, are symbols of Russia. These wooden dolls separate across the middle, revealing a smaller doll inside, and another doll inside of that. The first *matryoshka* dates back to 1890.

TRAVEL IN TECHNICOLOR

The Aquarelle Train, known as the "watercolor train," was launched in 2007 to remind commuters in Moscow to look up from their daily newspapers and enjoy their surroundings more. The train is a movable art museum with framed paintings on every carriage wall!

The Aquarelle Train

St. Basil's Cathedral

IVAN THE TERRIBLE

Russia's first tsar—a word meaning "leader"—was Ivan the Terrible. Ivan ruled 16th-century Russia, turning it from a medieval state into a world empire, and making it the size that it is today. He was notorious as a cruel and insane dictator.

BEARD IDEAS

For centuries, everyone in Russia had beards (except the girls). But after 1698, any Russian who wanted to grow a beard had to pay 100 roubles to Peter the Great, the country's revolutionary tsar! Peter wanted to westernize his nation's fashion, and encourage men to adopt a clean-shaven look. After payment, men were given a beard license, a copper token that stated: "The beard is a useless burden."

ДЕНГИ ВЗАТЫ

FLAMES IN THE SKY

Russia's most visited landmark is St. Basil's Cathedral, located in Red Square, Moscow. Ordered to be built by Ivan the Terrible in 1555, the building is shaped like giant flames rising into the sky! The church's iconic colors were not painted on until 200 years after it was completed.

BELARUS

N

Lithuania

Russia

Minsk

Europe

100 miles

Pop. size	9,466,000	(91ST)
Landmass (sq mi)	80,155	(84TH)
Life Expectancy	72.15	(117TH)

Vitayu! 40 percent of Belarus is covered in thick forests (reflected in the green stripe on the flag).

With another 13 percent made up of swamp, plus 21,000 rivers and 11,000 lakes, Belarus—or White Russia, as it is known—is one big wet place. Grab your rain slicker and see what it has to offer!

BANYAS FOR THE BRAVE

Traditional Belarusian bathhouses, called *banyas*, are definitely not for the fainthearted. First take a steam in a sauna, then douse yourself in ice-cold water, and hit yourself with bunches of birch twigs. Then go back and do it all again.

OUCH!

HOCKEY WORLD CHAMPIONSHIPS

One of Belarus's national sports is ice hockey. In 2014, the nation hosted the World Hockey Championships. The home team to support are HC Dinamo Minsk!

SAY HI TO BISON →

Belarus's national animal is the bison. One of the few places you can see this majestic creature in the wild is at Belovezhskaya National Park. These massive beasts are the biggest native mammals in all of Europe.

BEST CAT OF BELARUS

Every year the International Cat Show, an exhibition held in the Belarusian capital, Minsk, shows off the world's best cats! Furry friends are dressed in elaborate outfits and paraded before the judges.

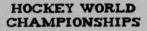
It is illegal to drive a dirty car in Belarus!

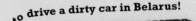

CLEAN ME!

DEEP, DEEP DOWN

The deepest cave found anywhere on Earth is the Krubera Cave in Ukraine. Once thought to be bottomless, the depth has now been measured at 7,208 ft. (2,197m)—almost seven Eiffel Towers stacked on top of each other!

Ukraine is the second largest country in Europe. It is huge—second only to its neighbor, Russia.

This enormous land is sometimes known as "the breadbasket of Europe" because of all the wheat it grows.

UKRAINE

N

Belarus

Russia

Kiev

Europe

200 miles

Pop. size	45,489,600	(30TH)
Landmass (sq mi)	233,013	(46TH)
Life Expectancy	69.14	(135TH)

7

6

5

4

3

2

1

Depth of Krubera Cave
7,208 FT.
(2,197 M)

Eiffel Tower →
1,062 FT.
(324 M)

Chornobyl

CASTLE ON THE CLIFF

The Swallows Nest is a flamboyant castle balanced precariously on the edge of a 131 ft. (40 m) cliff. It overlooks the infamous Crimean Peninsula—the bit of land that divided the Classical World of "civilized" Ancient Greek and Roman empires from the nomadic tribes of Huns, Cimmerians, Mongols, Goths, and Hazars.

CHORNOBYL

On April 26, 1986, one of the biggest catastrophes in history occurred: the Chornobyl Nuclear Power Plant disaster. After the devastating explosion, it was reported that radioactive rain fell as far away as Ireland. Large areas surrounding the plant are known as the "zone of alienation." These won't be safe to live in for at least 20,000 years.

TUNNEL OF LOVE

This romantic destination has to be seen to be be-*leafed*! Located in the town of Klevan, the Tunnel of Love is a working railway line engulfed in a tunnel of leaves! Couples come here to make a wish and if their love is true, then their wish will be granted!

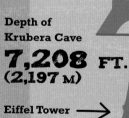

Trembita

TREMBITA

The longest musical instrument in the world, at a whopping 10 ft. (3 m), the *trembita* is a horn that, when blown, makes a high-pitched sound. It's used to signal the start of a celebration, or a funeral.

MOLDOVA

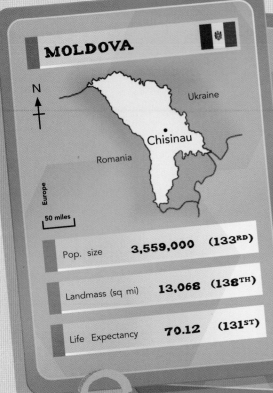

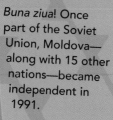

N

Europe

50 miles

Pop. size	**3,559,000**	**(133RD)**
Landmass (sq mi)	**13,068**	**(138TH)**
Life Expectancy	**70.12**	**(131ST)**

Chisinau

Ukraine

Romania

Buna ziua! Once part of the Soviet Union, Moldova—along with 15 other nations—became independent in 1991.

This picturesque nation is passionate about making and drinking wine and is the only country named after a dog . . .

DOG TAG

According to legend, Moldova inherited its name from Prince Dragoș' dog, Molda. Prince Dragoș was the first ruler of the historical territory of Moldavia, and his poor dog drowned in the local river while out hunting. The prince named the river "Molda," and the country's name quickly followed suit!

ORHEIUL VECHI

Hidden in a wild and remote part of the country lies Moldova's most fantastic cultural delight. Orheiul Vechi is a cave monastery carved into the limestone cliffs by monks in the 13th century. The complex was inhabited until the 18th century. Since 1996, the incredible site is being slowly restored by a small group of dedicated monks.

WINE TIME!

The world's largest wine cellar, located in Mileștii Mici, contains two million wine bottles!

CANDLE OF THANKS

Moldova's Thanksgiving Candle monument is a different kind of memorial. Rather than honoring fallen soldiers, this striking site remembers all the cultural monuments that have been destroyed in Moldova.

HOT COALS

Nestinarstvo, a fire ritual of dancing on hot coals, is a unique Bulgarian tradition, preserved from ancient times. The temperature of the fiery embers danced upon is 500–700°F (300–400°C). The dancers enter a sort of spiritual trance as they step on the embers, and seem to feel no pain.

Bulgaria is one of Europe's oldest countries and is sandwiched between Romania and Greece.

This eastern European country is often overlooked, but from folk music to flowers, Bulgaria is a land of hidden treasures.

BULGARIA

N

Romania

• Sofia

Europe

50 miles

Greece

Turkey

Pop. size	7,265,115	(100TH)
Landmass (sq mi)	42,811	(104TH)
Life Expectancy	74.33	(91ST)

A ROSE BY ANY OTHER NAME

It is believed that 80 percent of all rose oil—a vital ingredient for making some of the world's most popular and expensive perfumes—comes from the Bulgarian roses farmed at the Rose Valley. One million rose flowers are needed to make 2.1 pints (one liter) of essential rose oil—making it more valuable than gold.

OLDEST AND GOLDEST

The world's oldest gold treasure was located at Bulgaria's Varna Necropolis and dates back 6,000 years! The burial site contains almost 300 tombs, including the skeletons of famous warriors buried with scores of gold jewelry items. Since the site's discovery in 1972, more than 3,000 pieces of ancient gold have been found.

POPULATION DECLINE

The world's population is getting bigger by the day, except in Bulgaria. It's the only country in the world to have a smaller population today than in 1950. The nation is currently experiencing negative population growth, "losing" two million people since 1988.

MARTENITSI

On the first day of March each year, Bulgarians exchange red-and-white woven bracelets, called *Martenitsi*. They wear them throughout the month, until they see a tree in bloom. They then tie their bracelet to the tree, symbolizing the beginning of spring and the end of winter.

RIDING HIGH

In northeast Bulgaria is a curious carving. A man riding a horse has been chiseled into a sheer cliff 75 ft. (23m) above the ground. He stabs a lion with a spear while an eagle rides out ahead of him. This carving dates back to the 8th century, and no one is quite sure who it depicts.

A martenitsa

SERBIA

Romania

Belgrade

Bosnia & Hercegovina

Kosovo

N

Europe

100 miles

Pop. size	7,163,976	(102ND)
Landmass (sq mi)	34,116	(112TH)
Life Expectancy	75.02	(81ST)

Like the variation between the fertile land in the north and the mountainous areas in the south, Serbian people can switch between the Cyrillic and Latin alphabets without flinching.

This is a difficult feat that perfectly highlights the multicultural diversity and history of this landlocked nation.

GENEX TOWER

The Genex Tower is designed to look like a huge gate, greeting visitors as they arrive in Serbia's capital, Belgrade. The building has been declared an "ugly" example of Brutalist architecture and is often regarded as one of the world's strangest skyscrapers!

Novak Djokovic

WORLD'S NUMBER ONE

Novak Djokovic is one of tennis's all-time great players. Ranked number one in the world, he has won eight Grand Slam singles titles putting him in the top ten of the greatest champions ever.

RASPBERRIES

Serbia is the world's largest raspberry exporter. Producing 95 percent of the global supply, Serbia is the world's largest exporter of raspberries, known locally as "red gold." The area of Arilje, is known as the world's raspberry capital.

DOUGH IN THE DOUGH

To celebrate a traditional Christmas lunch, a *česnica*— a special kind of bread containing a gold coin is baked. During the feasting, members of the family tear up the bread. The person who finds the coin will receive good luck in the New Year.

SOUND THE TRUMPETS!

Serbia's Guča festival is one loud party. Every year hundreds of brass bands and trumpet players compete for a chance to perform at the festival, and the tunes they play are sure to get people dancing!

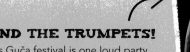

ZEUS!

The most important god in Greek mythology was god of the sky and ruler of other Olympian gods, Zeus. His most famous power was the ability to throw lightning bolts while flying on his winged horse, Pegasus. Zeus's oldest brother, Hades, ruled the Underworld, while his other brother, Poseidon, was god of the sea.

Zeus

Pegasus

GREECE

Bulgaria

N

Turkey

Europe

100 miles

Athens

Pop. size	11,032,328	(79TH)
Landmass (sq mi)	50,962	(95TH)
Life Expectancy	80.3	(25TH)

From ancient mythology to ancient philosophy, Greek culture has influenced and inspired the whole world.

These days, Greece is a popular tourist hot spot due to its landmarks of outstanding beauty and history, sandy beaches, and *saganaki*—fried cheese.

PARTHENON

Built in honor of the goddess Athena, the Parthenon still stands after 2,600 years. With its famous Doric columns, it expertly shows off the intelligence and sophistication of the ancient Greek architects and builders.

WINNERS OF THE OLYMPICS

Held in honor of Zeus, The Greek Olympics are thought to have begun in the city of Olympia in 776 B.C. They were the inspiration for the modern Olympic Games, which began in 1896 at the mighty Panathenaic Stadium, Athens.

LABYRINTH

First developed in Crete as a puzzle to contain the legendary bull creature called the Minotaur, a labyrinth is a complex structure that has only one path to the centre. Ancient Greek hero Theseus was able to find his way through the labyrinth using a ball of twine to mark his path, and he slayed the Minotaur.

A SANTORINI SUNSET

More than 6,000 sun-drenched islands belong to Greece, and one of the most popular with visitors is stunning Santorini. The village of Oia on this island is famous for the incredible sunsets you can see from its clifftop hotels and houses.

SWEET LIKE HONEY

More than 12,000 tons of honey are made in Greece every year. With flavors from herbs and wildflowers, it's thought to be the finest in the world.

MACEDONIA

N

Kosovo

Bulgaria

Skopje

Europe

Greece

50 miles

Pop. size	2,107,158	(146TH)
Landmass (sq mi)	9,928	(148TH)
Life Expectancy	75.8	(70TH)

With 80 percent of the nation made up of massive mountains, and a history that belies its geographical size, Macedonia may be small . . . but it packs a punch.

Are you ready? *Haydemo*— "let's go!"

ANCIENT STARGAZING

A fascinating place most people have never heard of, Kokino megalithic observatory in northeast Macedonia is a Bronze Age archaeological site discovered in 2001. The seemingly random pile of rocks is a window to an ancient civilization. The sacred site was used thousands of years ago to look at the stars and other celestial bodies.

GALICHKA SVADBA

Every year, on July 12, the village of Galičnik celebrates Galichka Svadba —Macedonia's ancient wedding festival. Couples enter a competition to be selected as the bride and groom. On the wedding day, all of the townspeople walk through the streets in traditional clothing to the chosen groom's house where his face is shaved. His facial hair is collected in a cloth and is believed to bring good health. The bride rides a white horse through the village to the church.

SHAKE IT OFF!

Tresenica, (Shaking Dance) is a traditional Macedonian dance, which starts off slow and speeds up, with dancers shaking energetically while joined in a circle. Dancers wear a traditional costume.

HOW OHRID!

Lake Ohrid is 18 mi. (30 km) long and one of the deepest lakes in Europe at 945 ft. (288 m) deep—that's almost three soccer pitches! It contains 200 species that haven't been found anywhere else in the world, including eels with scales that pearls can be made from!

KUKLICA

Kuklica is a geological curiosity —a stone town that was formed as a result of rock erosion over the past 100,000 years. The rocks that remain are now 30 million years old. A local legend surrounding the formation of these strange stone pillars tells of a man who could not decide which of two women he wanted to marry. So, he planned to marry both of them on the same day at different times! When the second bride saw her future husband marry another woman, she turned everyone at the wedding into stone!

TREE DAY

In March 2008, Macedonia celebrated its first Tree Day. More than 200,000 residents took the day off work and planted six million trees in one day. In 2009, even more trees were planted. Macedonian Tree Day is now an established annual tradition that hopes to offset the country's deforestation of local woodlands.

FAMOUS ALBANIAN

She may have been born in Skopje (now Macedonia) but Agnes Gonxha Bojaxhiu—or Mother Teresa as she became known—is celebrated as the only Albanian (so far!) to win a Nobel Prize. Mother Teresa was made a saint in 2003, for dedicating her life to helping the poor, the sick and the helpless.

Mother Teresa

The Albanians call Albania Shqiperia, which means "land of the eagles," the bird of prey that sits proudly on their national flag.

With famous missionaries and ancient ruins, plus a language that is as fun to say as it is to listen to, Albania is back from lunch and open for business . . .

ALBANIA

N

Kosovo

Tirana

Macedonia

Europe

50 miles

Greece

Pop. size	2,773,620	(141ST)
Landmass (sq mi)	11,100	(143RD)
Life Expectancy	77.96	(45TH)

TWO FINGERS

You may only need two fingers to play it, but the *çifteli* string instrument is an incredibly difficult instrument to master. It is played predominantly by the Gheg people of northern and central Albania.

SAY YES WITH NO!

Albanians nod their head up and down to mean "no," and shake it from side to side for "yes." You have been warned!

APOLLONIA

Bang in the middle of the country you can find the ruins of an ancient town, named after the Greek god, Apollo. Once upon a time, Apollonia was the most important city in the ancient world, said by Roman philosopher Cicero to be a *magna urbs et gravis*, "a great and important city." Today, there are many ruins that show how thriving and civilized it used to be.

KING ZOG

He may sound like a villain Superman might do battle with, but Zog, King of the Albanians was, in real-life, indestructible. During his ten-year reign (1928–39), he survived more than 50 assassination attempts and is the only national leader known to have shot someone in return for being shot at!

THE XHIRO HOUR

One of the most popular pastimes in Albania is *xhiro*, the word that means "evening walk." Some of the towns even close roads at certain times of the evening so that residents can enjoy their *xhiro* uninterrupted.

Çifteli

King Zog

SAY IT ISN'T SO

The Albanian language is unrelated to any other in Europe and derives from ancient Illyrian. Albanian has 27 words for types of moustache and 30 to describe different eyebrows, one being *vetullushe*, which means "a goat with brown eyebrows!"

KOSOVO

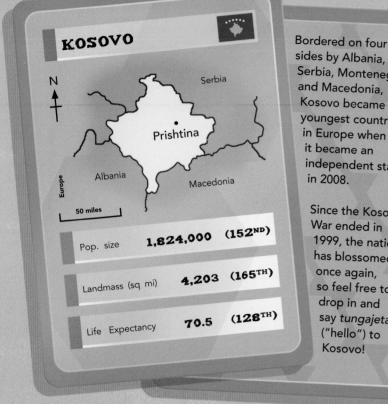

N

Serbia

Prishtina

Europe

Albania

Macedonia

50 miles

Pop. size	1,824,000	(152ND)
Landmass (sq mi)	4,203	(165TH)
Life Expectancy	70.5	(128TH)

Bordered on four sides by Albania, Serbia, Montenegro, and Macedonia, Kosovo became the youngest country in Europe when it became an independent state in 2008.

Since the Kosovo War ended in 1999, the nation has blossomed once again, so feel free to drop in and say *tungajeta* ("hello") to Kosovo!

THE VOICE

The most famous Kosovar of recent years is pop star and *The Voice U.K.* judge Rita Ora, who was born in Kosovo's capital Prishtina, to Kosovar-Albanian parents. Rita's father changed her birth name of "Sahatçiu" to "Ora" when she was younger, as it was easier to pronounce. *Sahatçiu* is Albanian for "watchmaker," *Ora* means "hour". Rita moved to London when she was one.

Rita Ora

HERE COMES THE BRIDE

The bride-painting traditional wedding ceremony of Kosovo is more than a thousand years old! In remote villages such as Lubinje, a bride's face is painted in many layers by the village's respected grandmothers. Three golden circles symbolize the cycles of life, and red and blue dots mean babies.

RESTAURANT BEARS

For decades, Kosovo's wild brown bears were kept chained up in some traditional restaurants and were used to attract customers and entertain them as they ate. These days, the practice is illegal and the bears are more likely to be found foraging happily in Prishtina's Bear Sanctuary national park, a rescue home for restaurant bears.

NEWBORN

On the day Kosovo proclaimed its independence from Serbia, the symbolic Newborn Monument was revealed in Prishtina's main square. Every year, on February 17, the letters are painted differently and unveiled. The monument has achieved worldwide acclaim.

Mimosa

FLOWER FESTIVAL

The seaside town of Herceg Novi is transformed in February every year for the Mimosa Festival. Parades, feasts, and masked balls are held, all in honor of the yellow mimosa flower, to herald the start of spring.

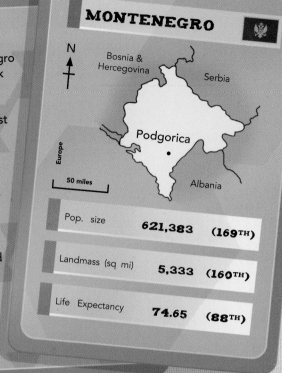

MONTENEGRO

N

Bosnia & Hercegovina

Serbia

Europe

Podgorica

Albania

50 miles

Pop. size	621,383	(169TH)
Landmass (sq mi)	5,333	(160TH)
Life Expectancy	74.65	(88TH)

Tara River Canyon

THE BIG DEEP

The Tara River Canyon is the continent's deepest river canyon. In places it is 4,265 ft. (1,300 m) deep, and it runs for more than 50 mi. (80 km). Hidden within the canyon's cliffs are 80 large caves—some as big as houses!

WITH THIS OLIVE I THEE WED

A Montenegran tradition that was made into law by King Nikola in the late 19th century, means that newlyweds must plant an olive tree on their wedding day as a symbol of a fruitful and long-lasting marriage. Indeed, the oldest olive tree in the country, an estimated 2,000 years old, resides in the grounds of King Nikola's palace.

OUR LADY OF THE ROCKS

An artificial island created from sunken ships and rocks, Our Lady of the Rocks began to form out of a legend that started in 1452. Two sailors saw a mysterious picture of the Virgin Mary on a rock in the sea. After this, each successful voyage out to sea would lead sailors to place rocks and sunken ships in the bay until eventually a small island was created. The sailors laid these rocks in the hope that one day a church could be built on the site to honor the Virgin Mary.

OSTROG! OSTROG!

Built into the steep cliffs of Ostroška Greda is the gleaming white Monastery of Ostrog. Founded in the 17th century, the monastery is dedicated to Saint Basil of Ostrog, and it attracts more than a million visitors every year.

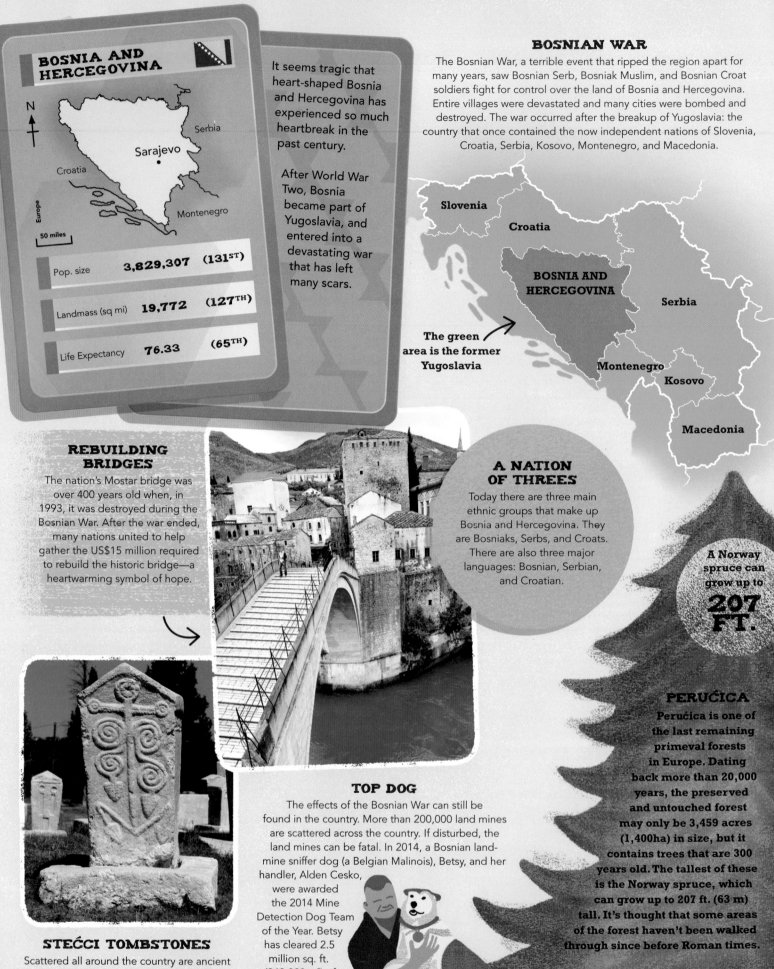

BOSNIA AND HERCEGOVINA

N

Serbia

Sarajevo

Croatia

Montenegro

Europe

50 miles

Pop. size	3,829,307	(131ST)
Landmass (sq mi)	19,772	(127TH)
Life Expectancy	76.33	(65TH)

It seems tragic that heart-shaped Bosnia and Hercegovina has experienced so much heartbreak in the past century.

After World War Two, Bosnia became part of Yugoslavia, and entered into a devastating war that has left many scars.

BOSNIAN WAR

The Bosnian War, a terrible event that ripped the region apart for many years, saw Bosnian Serb, Bosniak Muslim, and Bosnian Croat soldiers fight for control over the land of Bosnia and Hercegovina. Entire villages were devastated and many cities were bombed and destroyed. The war occurred after the breakup of Yugoslavia: the country that once contained the now independent nations of Slovenia, Croatia, Serbia, Kosovo, Montenegro, and Macedonia.

Slovenia

Croatia

BOSNIA AND HERCEGOVINA

Serbia

The green area is the former Yugoslavia

Montenegro

Kosovo

Macedonia

REBUILDING BRIDGES

The nation's Mostar bridge was over 400 years old when, in 1993, it was destroyed during the Bosnian War. After the war ended, many nations united to help gather the US$15 million required to rebuild the historic bridge—a heartwarming symbol of hope.

A NATION OF THREES

Today there are three main ethnic groups that make up Bosnia and Hercegovina. They are Bosniaks, Serbs, and Croats. There are also three major languages: Bosnian, Serbian, and Croatian.

A Norway spruce can grow up to

207 FT.

PERUĆICA

Perućica is one of the last remaining primeval forests in Europe. Dating back more than 20,000 years, the preserved and untouched forest may only be 3,459 acres (1,400ha) in size, but it contains trees that are 300 years old. The tallest of these is the Norway spruce, which can grow up to 207 ft. (63 m) tall. It's thought that some areas of the forest haven't been walked through since before Roman times.

STEĆCI TOMBSTONES

Scattered all around the country are ancient medieval tombstones, known as *Stećci*. It is believed more than 60,000 of them can be found across the land. Engraved with epitaphs written in the Bosnian Cyrillic alphabet, they also contain many patterns and pictures whose meaning has yet to be discovered!

TOP DOG

The effects of the Bosnian War can still be found in the country. More than 200,000 land mines are scattered across the country. If disturbed, the land mines can be fatal. In 2014, a Bosnian land-mine sniffer dog (a Belgian Malinois), Betsy, and her handler, Alden Cesko, were awarded the 2014 Mine Detection Dog Team of the Year. Betsy has cleared 2.5 million sq. ft. (240,000 m²) of land since 2009.

Betsy the land-mine sniffer dog

SINJSKA ALKA

Since 1715, Croatians have competed in the traditional *Sinjska Alka* contest. Contestant —called Alkars and dressed in traditional clothes—gallop on horseback and score by piercing their lances through a hanging metal ring.

Croissant-shaped Croatia, with its clear blue seas and thousands of islands, has become the "pearl of the Adriatic."

The Adriatic is a thin sliver of sea that separates Italy from the Balkan countries (Croatia, Bosnia, Montenegro, and Albania).

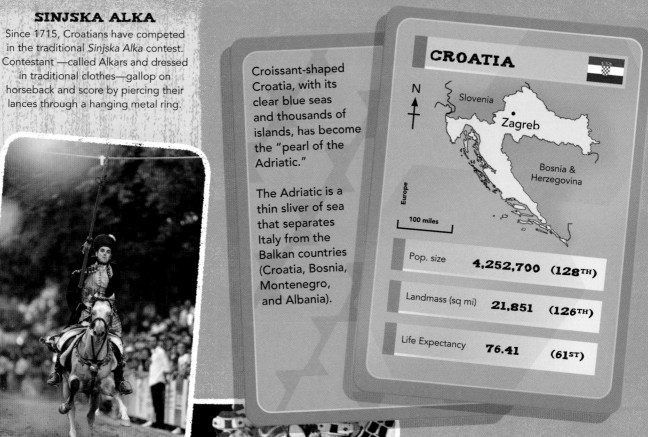

CROATIA

N

Slovenia

Zagreb

Bosnia & Herzegovina

Europe

100 miles

Pop. size	4,252,700	(128TH)
Landmass (sq mi)	21,851	(126TH)
Life Expectancy	76.41	(61ST)

DRAW! DANCE!

On the island of Korcula, a unique dance called the *Moreška* is performed. It tells the story of two kings who fight for the love of a maiden. What makes this dance so special is that the performers spin and clash swords as they dance!

I GIVE YOU MY HEART

Little gingerbread hearts, known as *licitars*, are a famous symbol of Zagreb, Croatia's capital. They're decorated with colorful icing and sometimes little mirrors. Meant as an ornament rather than a sweet snack (even though they are edible), these little hearts are so popular that they've made it into the logo of the Zagreb tourist board!

LOOSEN UP!

In the 17th century, Croatia invented the world's best fashion accessory: the tie. Worn by the Croatian military when fighting for the French, the neckties caught the eye of French king Louis XIV and they quickly became a fashion trend that has survived to this day.

DUBROVNIK

As Irish writer George Bernard Shaw once exclaimed about Croatia's esteemed city: "Those who seek paradise on earth should come to Dubrovnik." Perched next to the clear blue sea, Dubrovnik is one of the world's greatest walled cities.

LAND OF DALMATIANS

Dalmatia is one of Croatia's historical regions. It's famed as the birthplace of the Dalmatian breed of dog, loved for its spotted black-and-white fur, and it gives its name to the Dalmatian Coast, which stretches from Istria in the north of Croatia down to the top of Albania.

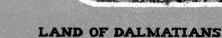

SLOVENIA

Austria

Ljubljana

Croatia

Europe

N

50 miles

Pop. size	2,060,484	(148TH)
Landmass (sq mi)	7,827	(154TH)
Life Expectancy	77.83	(46TH)

Dober dan! Or "good day," as a Slovenian may say. This tiny green country is a picture-perfect place of cobblestone streets, epic mountains, castles, and ancient natural landmarks.

Slovenia is bordered by Italy, Austria, Hungary, and Croatia.

WRONG ADDRESS

In Washington, D.C., the capital of the United States, the Slovakian and Slovenian embassies meet once a month to exchange mail that has been mistakenly sent to each other's country!

~~SLOVAKIA~~
~~SLOVENIA~~

IDRIJA ŽLIKROFI

Stuffed with potato, bacon, and onions, these delicious little dumplings are a traditional Slovenian delicacy.

KURENTOVANJE

Slovenia's largest traditional folk festival is Kurentovanje. Townspeople of the city of Ptuj dress up in large sheepskin costumes, known as *kurents*, and ring loud bells to scare off winter and evil spirits.

DEEPER UNDERGROUND

Slovenia's Postojna Cave has a train that takes visitors deep into the subterranean world of stalagmites and stalactites. The cave is famous for a stalagmite (a pin-shaped rock rising up from the floor) named Brilliant. Brilliant!

BEAR BONES

A Neanderthal flute made of cave-bear bone and thought to date back 45,000 years was discovered at Slovenia's Divje Babe archaeological site in 1995. It is the oldest example of a musical instrument in the world!

DING, DONG!

Lake Bled looks like something out of the pages of a fairytale. On an island in the center of the lake is a tiny white church. If you row out to the island, make sure you ring the church bell—legend says it will grant you a wish.

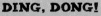

NAUGHTY OR NICE?

In Austria, you might come across the legend of Krampus. He's Santa Claus's evil twin brother—a terrifying figure that's half man, half goat—and he punishes children who have been naughty during the year. Eek!

Krampus

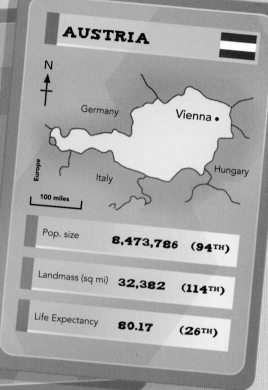

Mountains, Mozart, *The Sound of Music*, markets, and salt mines . . .

Austria may be bordered by seven much bigger countries and share its language with Germany, but its people, and its history are one of a kind.

AUSTRIA

N

Germany

Vienna •

Europe

Italy

Hungary

100 miles

Pop. size	8,473,786	(94TH)
Landmass (sq mi)	32,382	(114TH)
Life Expectancy	80.17	(26TH)

TRACHT UND DIRNDL

Austria's traditional national costume, known as *tracht*, is an iconic symbol of Austrian and Bavarian culture. *Tracht* consists of *lederhosen* for men and *dirndl* for women. *Dirndls* originated from the uniform of Austrian servants in the 19th century—*dirndlgewand* means "maid's dress."

WOLFGANG AMADEUS MOZART

Born in Salzburg in 1756, Mozart—who had a genius IQ of 165—is regarded as the world's most famous composer. He began to play and compose music from the age of four. He also had a rather unusual sense of humor and often mentioned . . . poo in his letters and diaries!

CRYSTAL KALEIDOSCOPE

Take a trip to Innsbruck to see the Chambers of Wonder at Swarovski Crystal Worlds. Discover a giant in the hillside and 14 underground lairs of illuminated crystals that change color and sparkle!

SUBTERRANEAN

Austria is treasured for its salt mines and crystals deep underground, but it is also the location of the World of the Ice Giants, the largest ice caves in the world.

FINGERHAKELN

Austria's traditional game of competitive finger-pulling—or *Fingerhakeln*—is a serious sport, with very strict rules! In order to win, competitors must drag their opponent across a table . . . by just the finger!

HUNGARY

N

Slovakia

Budapest

Romania

Serbia

Europe

100 miles

Pop. size	9,897,247	(89TH)
Landmass (sq mi)	35,918	(109TH)
Life Expectancy	70.46	(73RD)

Tucked in between Croatia, Serbia, Romania, Slovakia, and Slovenia, Hungary is one of Europe's oldest countries, founded in 897.

With thermal springs, inspiring inventors, world-famous food, and one of the most notorious leaders in history, Hungary will whet your appetite for more!

A MAGYAR NATION

People from Hungary call themselves Magyars, not Hungarians. Magyars were the earliest tribe to settle on the land and the term is also the name of the Hungarian language. Magyar has no words for "son" or "daughter" but has nine specific words for different kinds of cousins. The Magyar alphabet consists of 44 letters! They look like this:

A	Á	B	C	Cs	D	Dz	Dzs	E	É	F	G	Gy	H	I
Í	J	K	L	Ly	M	N	Ny	O	Ó	Ö	Ő	P	Q	R
S	Sz	T	Ty	U	Ú	Ü	Ű	V	W	X	Y	Z	Zs	

RUBIK'S TRICK

Created by Hungarian inventor Ernő Rubik, the Rubik's Cube remains a worldwide phenomenon. If you want to solve one, here's a clue: the color of a side is always determined by the color of the center cube of that side. Shh . . . don't tell anyone!

BOTTOMS DOWN!

If celebrating with a Magyar, do not clink glasses when toasting. During the 1849 war with Austria, Austrian leaders executed Hungary's rebel generals and were later seen celebrating smugly by clinking their beer glasses. For the next 150 years, Hungarians vowed to never clink glasses and the custom is considered bad manners to this day!

THERMAL LAKE

Hungary has more than 1,000 thermal springs, making it one of the best places to take a fizzy swim! Lake Hévíz is the largest natural thermal lake in Europe and is home to bacteria believed to have special healing powers.

Rubik's Cube

ATTILA THE HUN

Known as the "Scourge of God" by the Roman Empire, Attila the Hun was the ruthless and barbaric leader of the Huns and one of the world's most infamous warriors. He killed his own brother and invaded much of Europe. Legend tells that he died of a nosebleed on his wedding night.

GOULASH

Goulash is world famous and is the national dish of Hungary. It's a red stew with meat, potatoes, and other vegetables, all seasoned with loads of paprika. The recipe dates back 1,200 years!

LABYRINTH OF HORROR

Six miles (10 km) of complex labyrinth lies buried under Buda Castle in Hungary's capital city, Budapest. The creepy cave system was a prison and torture chamber in the 16th century. A ghost known as the Black Count apparently haunts the labyrinth.

MUSIC NATION

The Sziget Music Festival is often voted Europe's greatest. Held every August in Budapest, the week-long event attracts almost 400,000 music fans! Over 1,000 performances take place incorporating every genre of music.

BIGĂR AND BETTER

It may not be big or clever, but Bigăr Waterfall in southwestern Romania (the halfway point between the equator and the North Pole) is often voted the most unusual waterfall in the world. When the water falls it spreads into tiny streams running over moss.

The mighty Danube River separates the nation from its neighbor, Bulgaria, but it is also surrounded by Hungary, Ukraine, Serbia, and Moldova.

It was the birthplace of Dracula, the iconic Transylvanian vampire, but there's more to Romania than that. Lots more.

ROMANIA

Pop. size	19,963,581	(59TH)
Landmass (sq mi)	92,043	(81ST)
Life Expectancy	74.69	(87TH)

PALACE OF PARLIAMENT

The Palace of Parliament in Bucharest is the largest building in Europe as well as the world's heaviest. This monster structure, with 3,100 rooms and an underground car park that can hold 20,000 cars, was ordered to be built by Romanian dictator Nicolae Ceaușescu.

POTTY TREES

In the Maramures region of Romania, it's not unusual to pass people's gardens and see colorful pots and pans strung from the branches of the trees. This isn't to scare away birds, but rather is a traditional sign that a girl of marrying age lives in the house!

FACE IN THE ROCK

Rising out of the Danube River in Orsova is the stony face of King Decebalus, who was ruler of what is now Romania almost 2,000 years ago. Taking ten years to complete, it is the tallest rock sculpture in Europe.

Which other country sees famous faces carved into rock on a giant scale?

GO TO PAGE **7**

TASTE FOR BLOOD

Created by Irish writer Bram Stoker in 1897, Count Dracula was inspired by the Romanian Prince Vlad III (1431–77), infamously known for his fondness of impaling enemies through their heads. Bran Castle is supposedly the home of this terrifying vampire.

SLOVAKIA

Poland

Bratislava

Europe

Hungary

50 miles

Pop. size	5,414,095	(115TH)
Landmass (sq mi)	18,933	(129TH)
Life Expectancy	76.69	(57TH)

Slovakia is a nation with as much going on underground as there is above ground.

With a whole world of subterranean cave systems full of 6,000-year-old bat bones, to some of the world's tallest stalagmites and stalactites, Slovakia will knock your socks off!

QUEEN NAPKIN
Possibly the most famous Slovakian of the modern age is Antonia Kozakova. She has collected a record-breaking 62,757 unique napkins from all over the world. Her prized collection is said to be worth almost US$500,000.

SPIŠ CASTLE
The magnificent Spiš Castle is one of the oldest and biggest castles in Europe. Built more than 900 years ago, the magical fortress has been used as a location in many blockbuster movies. Inside the castle, the ruins of torture chambers and devices remain!

BEER BATH
In Bratislava there is a peculiar type of spa. Visitors can take a relaxing bath in barrel-shaped tubs full of warm, frothy beer! The brew is supposed to be very good for the skin, but it's certainly a strange-smelling bubble bath!

DRAGON'S CAVE
The Demänovská Ice Cave is home to the bones of various animals, including those of a huge cave bear, which was once thought to be a dragon's bones. These bones gave the caves their scary name: the Dragon's Cave.

Elizabeth Báthory de Ecsed

BLOOD BATH
Known to locals as Countess Dracula, Elizabeth Báthory de Ecsed (1560–1614) was the world's first female serial killer, murdering over 650 people, many of them young girls. Elizabeth lived in Castle Cachtice and, according to legend, bathed in the blood of young women she had murdered, believing it had a youthful effect on her skin.

On the Revolutions of the Celestial Spheres

WORLD CHANGING

Polish-born astronomer Nicolaus Copernicus is thought to be the first person to propose that Earth was not the center of the universe. In the 16th century, Copernicus suggested the sun was the center of the universe in his *De revolutionibus orbium coelestium* (On the Revolutions of the Celestial Spheres). His theory rocked the world—and changed it too!

Surrounded by seven other nations, Poland stands at the center of Europe. It's a nation that has survived being at the center of two world wars, as well as having been completely wiped off the map.

However, it bounced back, and with a unique culture and national identity, Poland is here to stay.

POLAND

N

Europe

100 miles

Warsaw

Belarus

Czech Republic

Ukraine

Pop. size	**38,530,725**	**(34TH)**
Landmass (sq mi)	**120,726**	**(70TH)**
Life Expectancy	**76.65**	**(58TH)**

Auschwitz

PIEROGI

Poland's national dish is pierogi—dumplings filled with cheese and potatoes and topped with fried onions. Yum!

UGLY HISTORY

During World War Two Poland was occupied by the Nazis, Adolf Hitler's German soldiers. At the time, Poland had 3.3 million Jewish residents. Over the course of the war Hitler's concentration camps were designed to exterminate the Jewish people from the world. These "death camps" executed more than six million Jewish people, and the most notorious of them all—Auschwitz—was in Poland.

Corporal Wotjek

MARIE CURIE

The only recipient to win Nobel prizes in two sciences, one in chemistry and the other in physics, and the first woman to win one at all, Marie Curie pioneered research in radioactivity and discovered two elements on the periodic table: radium and polonium.

TRUMPET TIME

Kraków, one of Poland's major cities, is home to a historic tradition. At the top of St. Mary's Basilica, a trumpeter plays a series of notes on a golden trumpet every hour on the hour. This custom has continued for 600 years!

WAR BEAR

During World War Two, the Polish army became the first and only army to recruit a bear as a soldier. Wotjek (a name meaning "he who enjoys war") would help transport ammunition and kept the troops' morale up. He saluted whenever a high-ranking officer walked by and drank beer with his fellow soldiers!

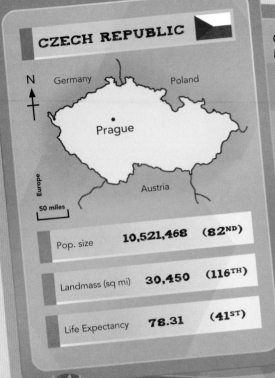

CZECH REPUBLIC

N

Germany   Poland

Prague

Austria

Europe

50 miles

Pop. size	10,521,468	(82ND)
Landmass (sq mi)	30,450	(116TH)
Life Expectancy	78.31	(41ST)

Once known as the Kingdom of Bohemia, the Czech Republic is now dubbed the "Castle Capital of the World" with more than 2,000 historic castles!

With Prague at its center—once the capital of Europe—the Czech Republic is very much the Central European culture of the future to keep an eye on!

POLKA, POLKA, POLKA

Created in the Czech Republic more than a century ago, this beloved dance and form of folk music started a worldwide phenomenon called "Polkamania" when it was introduced to the ballrooms of Prague in 1835.

WORLD'S LARGEST CASTLE!

Prague Castle is the largest ancient castle in the world, 426 ft. (130 m) wide and over 1,870 ft. (570 m) long—more than five football fields! Dating back to the 9th century, Prague Castle is the most visited landmark in the Czech Republic.

GOOD KING WENCESLAS

Did you know that "Good" King Wenceslas once ruled the Czech kingdom? He is remembered today as the inspiration for the famous English Christmas carol—but 1,000 years ago he was the Duke of Bohemia, who risked his life to feed the poor . . . and was eventually murdered by his brother.

ASTRONOMICAL CLOCK

Every hour on the hour, Prague's astronomical clock strikes and the procession of the 12 apostles begins. A small trapdoor opens and figures march around ringing bells. The clock is 600 years old!

DANCING HOUSE

Designed by the famous architect Frank Gehry and built in 1996, Prague's Dancing House is unusually shaped. Part of the deconstructivist style of architecture, it looks a bit unsteady!

Czech Republic

VELVET REVOLUTION

Until 1993 the Czech Republic and the Slovak Republic were one country: Czechoslovakia. The two countries became independent of one another after peaceful demonstrations. They were influenced by the dismantling of the Berlin Wall—the political line that divided Eastern and Western Germany.

Slovakia

The Velvet Revolution, as it is known, is considered the most peaceful division of two nations in history.

BIRTH OF ROBOTS!

In 1920, the word "robot" was introduced to the world in a play by Czech writer Karel Capek. The story was called *R.U.R.* (Rossum's Universal Robots).

WORLD WARS

In the twentieth century, Germany was at the center of two world wars: the first, known as the Great War (1914–18), and World War Two (1939–45). World War Two was the most widespread and the deadliest war in history, with over 85 million people from 30 countries losing their lives.

Germany boasts awe-inspiring castles, landmarks, festivals, and natural wonders—not to mention 1,200 types of sausage!

It's one of the most bewitching and forward-thinking countries in Europe and has a history—both modern and ancient—as dramatic and dynamic as its language.

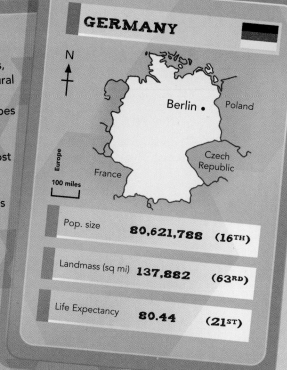

GERMANY

N

Berlin •
Poland

Europe
France
Czech Republic

100 miles

Pop. size	80,621,788	(16TH)
Landmass (sq mi)	137,882	(63RD)
Life Expectancy	80.44	(21ST)

THE DEVIL'S IN THE DETAILS

Germany is known as *das Land der Dichters und Denkers*, a land of writers and thinkers. One of the country's greatest *dichter-denkers* is Johann Wolfgang von Goethe (1749–1832). His drama *Faust I* is considered the greatest work of German literature. It tells the now legendary story of a scholar who makes a deal with the devil: his soul in exchange for unlimited power on Earth while he lives.

Germany is famous for having over 1,200 types of sausage, including the sausage dog!

HOT OFF THE PRESS!

Germany is a nation of famous inventors. However, without Johann Gutenberg you would not have heard of any of them! In the early 1450s, Gutenberg invented the printing press and published the first ever book in Europe—the *Gutenberg Bible*. This machine changed the world. The invention of the movable-type printing press meant that books could now finally be produced in large quantities and distributed in a short period of time, helping to improve and spread education and study. Without Gutenberg, you probably wouldn't be reading this book right now!

NEUSCHWANSTEIN CASTLE

"Mad" King Ludwig (1845–86), a former monarch of Germany's Bavarian state, is famous for the construction of his Neuschwanstein Castle. Completed around 1892, the castle is an icon of Bavaria and one of the main inspirations for Cinderella's Castle at Disneyland.

OKTOBERFEST

Every autumn, millions of visitors flock to the German city of Munich to experience its world-famous beer festival. Sitting at long tables inside enormous tents, revelers drink beer from huge tankards, and enjoy traditional German food. More than 500,000 chickens and 50,000 pork knuckle servings are dished up during the festival.

BELGIUM

Netherlands

N

Brussels

France

Europe

50 miles

Pop. size	11,195,138	(78TH)
Landmass (sq mi)	11,787	(139TH)
Life Expectancy	79.92	(29TH)

Belgium is located slap-bang in the middle of Western Europe, bordered by the Netherlands, Germany, Luxembourg, and France.

This friendly nation is treasured for its waffles, chocolate, sprouts, mussels, beers, and fries as well as its castles, cathedrals, and quirky traditions.

THE COSMIC EGG

In 1927, a Belgian priest and physicist George Lemaître, published his theory about the beginning of the universe, or as he put it, "the Cosmic Egg exploding at the moment of the creation." The Big Bang, as we know it now, was actually first used as an insult to describe Lemaître's theory by another astronomer, Fred Hoyle . . . and the name famously stuck!

FRITKOT

While the dispute rages over who invented french fries—was it the French or the Belgians?—one thing is for sure: the Belgians have perfected them, always double frying them for extra crunch. *Fritkots* (mobile fry shops) are national institutions. In 2010, the Belgian Chris Verschueren set a world record for continuous frying by spending 83 hours making 3,300 lb. (1,500 kg) of french fries!

ATOMIUM

An architectural marvel, the Atomium is Brussels' oddest-looking landmark. Originally constructed for the 1958 World Fair, the building is now considered a symbol of peace among all the world's nations. With nine interconnected spheres rising 335 ft. (102 m) in the air, the Atomium is the shape of an iron crystal enlarged 165 billion times!

SINTERKLAAS

Every year on December 6, a holy figure called Saint Nicholas (*Sinterklaas*), with his red coat and white beard, rides into town on a white horse and descends the chimneys of Belgium's houses leaving presents and sweets for children. You might know him as Santa Claus!

BATTLE OF WATERLOO

One of history's most notorious conflicts, the Battle of Waterloo was fought in the Walloon region of Belgium. The 1815 clash saw the British Duke of Wellington defeat of France's famous emperor, Napoleon Bonaparte, as part of the Napoleonic Wars. 50,000 soldiers died. The actual battle took place 2.5 mi. (4 km) from Waterloo, but the duke liked to name battles after the place he stayed the previous night!

THE FIRST SPA

The Belgium town of Spa is where the word "spa" comes from. The town has been visited as far back as the 14th century, when people came to the town to bathe in the cold, natural mineral springs for health and healing purposes.

GRAND OLD DUKE

Becoming an independent nation in 963, Luxembourg is the world's only grand duchy (country ruled by a grand duke). In 1919, Grand Duchess Charlotte put the royal family up for a public vote—should they remain as the head of state or not? The people voted to keep the grand duchy in place and that was that. The present grand duke is named Henri.

Crest of the grand duchy

Europe's seventh smallest nation, Luxembourg is a fairytale kingdom for the modern age.

This is a country where old fortresses, forests, and picturesque castles meet contemporary architecture, big business, and banking. History and rolling hills clash with the high tech here.

LUXEMBOURG

N

Germany

Europe

Belgium

Luxembourg City

20 miles

Pop. size	543,202	(171ST)
Landmass (sq. mi.)	998	(175TH)
Life Expectancy	80.01	(28TH)

SMALL BUT WEALTHY

Luxembourg may be a small nation but, incredibly, it's the second richest in the world—according to size. The tiny country is one of the world's leading financial centers, with more than 150 banks.

THE ECHTERNACH DANCE

Once every year the people of Echternach dance through the town's streets to honor and celebrate the life of St. Willibrord, the monk who founded the town's abbey in 698. In the lively procession, 9,000 performers hop from left to right while holding a white handkerchief.

KING OF THE CASTLE

Luxembourg's impressive Vianden Castle was built between the 11th and 14th centuries, but fell into ruin after 1820, when the king of the Netherlands sold off parts of it. Today it has been restored and is now one of Luxembourg's best landmarks.

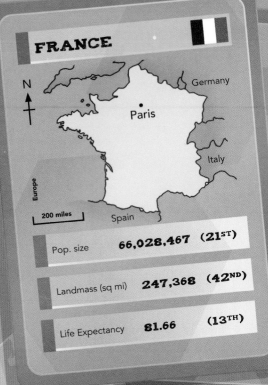

FRANCE

N

Germany

Paris

Italy

Europe

200 miles

Spain

Pop. size	66,028,467	(21ST)
Landmass (sq mi)	247,368	(42ND)
Life Expectancy	81.66	(13TH)

Bonjour! Baguettes, croissants, crêpes, croque-monsieur, pain au chocolat. One thing's for sure—in France you won't go hungry!

When it comes to spoiling the world with treats—both cultural and culinary—nobody does it better. The world's most popular tourist destination has a lot to celebrate.

THE HUMBLE CROISSANT

Ever wondered why a croissant is shaped the way it is? According to legend, the first croissant ever made was in Vienna, Austria, in 1683, when the nation was under attack by the Turkish Empire. On the outskirts of Vienna, Turkish soldiers decided to dig a tunnel to enter the city more easily. Viennese bakers, who worked underground at that time, heard noises and called in the Austrian army. The solders were caught! In remembrance of their actions, the bakers decided to make a treat in the shape of a crescent moon—the symbol on the Turkish flag. A century later, Marie Antoinette, the famous Austrian princess who married Louis XVI, served the croissant to French aristocrats, helping it become the icon it is today!

Mona Lisa

AROUND THE WORLD

The brilliant French writer Jules Verne was one of science fiction's earliest literary masters. In 1873 Verne wrote *Around the World in Eighty Days*, in which the esteemed Phileas Fogg takes on a bet to travel around the entire world in 80 days.

GOING TO THE LOUVRE

Paris is one of the world's most visited cities, thanks in part to the Louvre. Nine million people visit this famous museum each year to see Leonardo da Vinci's *Mona Lisa*, but the average time spent looking at it is just 15 seconds. The Louvre is one of the largest museums in the world and houses over 35,000 works of art!

BREAD END

France is famous for its food, and in particular its baked goods. More than 10 billion baguettes are sold in France every year. That works out to be 156 baguettes per person per year!

FRENCH TONGUE TWISTER!

Un chasseur sachant chasser sait chasser sans son chien de chasse.

A hunter who knows how to hunt knows how to hunt without his hunting dog.

LOUIS' HOME

With over 700 rooms, the Palace of Versailles—just outside Paris—was King Louis XIV's grand home. It has a room called the Hall of Mirrors, originally lit with 3,000 candles! It was in this room that the Treaty of Versailles was signed in 1919, officially ending World War One.

TOUR DE FRANCE

The world's most astonishing race of endurance and human spirit, the Tour de France has been around for more than a century! Every July, brave cyclists race approximately 2,200 mi. (3,500 km) around France in a series of stages over 23 days. The fastest cyclist at each stage gets to wear the iconic yellow jersey. In 2016, Andorra will host a stage of the race!

MONACO GRAND PRIX

Formula One boasts 20 races every year, but the Monaco Grand Prix is the most prestigious. The Monte Carlo circuit is one of the most demanding tracks in Formula One racing, as it twists and bends through the city streets. It contains both the slowest corner (the Fairmont Hairpin) and the fastest, where speeds can reach 160 mph. (260 km/h)!

Monaco may be smaller than one square mile and tinier than New York's Central Park, but don't underestimate it.

Despite its diminutive size, Monaco means business when it comes to billionaires, boats, and betting big!

MONACO

N
France
Europe
Monaco

1 mile

Pop. size	**37,831**	**(197TH)**
Landmass (sq mi)	**0.78**	**(202ND)**
Life Expectancy	**89.57**	**(1ST)**

DYNASTY

The wealthy and powerful Grimaldi family has ruled Monaco for centuries. In 2002, a treaty between Monaco and France was signed stating that if the reigning prince of Monaco failed to have any offspring, the power of the country would revert to France. It is law that all leaders of Monaco must bear the surname Grimaldi.

Fairmont Hairpin

PALAIS DU PRINCE

The official residence of Albert II, the prince of Monaco, is one of the most decadent palaces in the world, with 235 rooms! At 11:55 A.M. every day, the changing of the guard outside the palace's entrance is observed by thousands of tourists.

Grimaldi coat of arms

DEO JUVANTE

BET BIG!

The Casino de Monte-Carlo is the national symbol of Monaco and main source of its income! Built in 1863, it is forbidden to this day for citizens of Monaco to even enter the casino, let alone place a bet. In 1913, during a game of roulette, a ball fell on black 26 times in a row: a very rare occurrence.

FISH AND CLIFFS

Perched on top of the historic Rock of Monaco and overlooking the famed French Riviera, Monaco's Oceanographic Museum and Aquarium has kept an eye on the ocean for centuries. Featuring a shark lagoon, the aquarium houses an incredible 6,000 species of undersea creatures.

SWITZERLAND

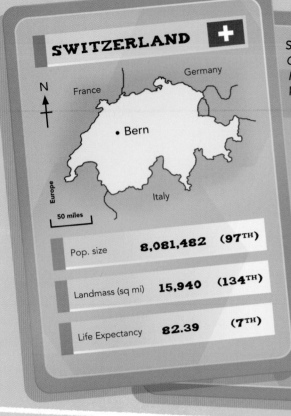

France
Germany

N

Europe

• Bern

Italy

50 miles

Pop. size	8,081,482	(97TH)
Landmass (sq mi)	15,940	(134TH)
Life Expectancy	82.39	(7TH)

Switzerland, or *Confoederatio Helvetica*, as it is known in Latin, is a nation built on meandering alpine roads, mountain tunnels, muesli, cheese fondue, and glistening ski slopes.

With breathtaking landscapes and clean mountain air, it's as picture perfect as it gets.

THE ORIGINS OF THE UNIVERSE

Located deep underground in Switzerland is a 17-mile-long tunnel and super machine called the Large Hadron Collider. It has been designed to reveal, and recreate, the conditions that existed immediately after the Big Bang that created the universe, 13.7 billion years ago. Beams of protons are sent around the tunnel at 99.9 percent of the speed of light before colliding into one another, generating temperatures 100,000 times hotter than the Sun.

Large Hadron Collider

MATTERHORN

The iconic Matterhorn is one of the highest summits in the Alps mountain range and is noted for its distinctive mountain peak. A treacherous beast to climb, the Matterhorn is one of the most dangerous mountains in the world for climbers, with over 500 fatalities to date.

GO TO PAGE 76

A physicist from which country came up with the Big Bang theory?

BROKEN CHAIR

This wooden sculpture was created by Swiss artist Daniel Berset in 1997. It is made out of wood and is 39 ft. (12 m) high. A symbol for peace that represents the campaign against land mines, this is a simple but incredibly powerful work of art.

CAN YOU HEAR IT?

Farmers in Swiss mountain pastures often have to communicate over large distances to call their animals back to the farm. They developed two ways of doing this, which have both become symbolic of Switzerland. Some choose yodeling—a way of singing that quickly changes between a low and high pitch during a single note. Try it out:

Sing the phrase "*yodel-A-E-D*" in an ascending pitch. Say the word "yodel" as deep as possible, then "A" in a higher pitch, then "E" higher still, then "D" in your highest pitch! Then repeat: that's yodeling!

If that's not your thing, then how about the alphorn? This is a long, thin instrument that produces a rich note, which can be heard several miles away.

COOL CRESTA RUN

Situated in St. Moritz, the Cresta Run is the oldest natural ice toboggan run on the planet. On this treacherous speed track, the rider zooms straight down the 0.75 mi. (1.2 km) track headfirst while lying on a toboggan. Rakes on the end of special boots are used to brake and steer, and racers can reach speeds of 80 mph. (130 km/h)!

HOW TO BUY A COUNTRY

Austrian Prince Johann Adam Andreas I von Liechtenstein bought the nearby counties of Schellenberg and Vaduz in 1699 and 1712. He merged them into one and gave the country his name: Liechtenstein. But he never lived there or even visited! In fact, no ruler of the nation actually lived in the country until 1938!

A country roughly the same size as Washington, D.C., Liechtenstein is a snow-filled treat sandwiched between Switzerland and Austria.

It's the only country named after its ruling family, where the money spent on the streets is the Swiss franc and the language spoken is German!

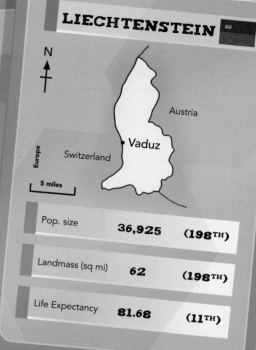

LIECHTENSTEIN

N

Austria

Vaduz

Europe

Switzerland

5 miles

Pop. size	36,925	(198TH)
Landmass (sq mi)	62	(198TH)
Life Expectancy	81.68	(11TH)

A KING'S CASTLE

Vaduz Castle is the home of Prince Alois. It can be found 400 ft. (120 m) up on a hillside, overlooking the country's capital city, Vaduz. For centuries the castle has remained closed to visitors. Every year on August 15, the country celebrates its national day with a huge firework display from the castle lighting up the skies.

ABSOLUTE POWER

Prince Hans Adam II and his son, Crown Prince Alois, rule Liechtenstein with absolute power. In 2003, as voted by the 37,000 locals, Prince Hans was given powers that allow him to dismiss the government and reject new laws!

Barbara Erni

THE GOLDEN BOOS

According to the 18th-century legend the Golden Boos, Barbara Erni was a Liechtenstein woman with striking red hair who travelled throughout Europe with a large treasure chest strapped to her back. Wherever she rested for the night, she would demand that the chest be locked in the best room available. Once it was locked away and night fell, a small man would emerge from it and steal any valuables he could find. Erni and the man would then flee during the night! Barbara Erni was the last person to be executed in Liechtenstein in 1785.

LOVERS NOT FIGHTERS

Liechtenstein is one of the few countries in the world that maintains no military and follows a policy of neutrality during wars. In 1868, during Liechtenstein's last military engagement, legend reports that 80 soldiers were sent to fight in Italy. The next day, 81 soldiers returned—an Italian soldier who wanted to live in Liechtenstein had returned with them! The army was promptly disbanded.

ITALY

Europe

Austria
Croatia
France

N

Rome

Pop. size	59,831,093	(22ND)
Landmass (sq mi)	116,347	(72ND)
Life Expectancy	82.03	(9TH)

Italy was the country that kickstarted modern civilization. Being shaped like a boot probably helped!

It's home to the ancient ruins of Rome and has brought us some of the greatest thinkers, artists, and explorers that have ever lived. Hey Italy, *grazie mille!*

THE COLOSSEUM

Rome has many ancient ruins from its powerful empire, founded over 2,000 years ago, but it's the Colosseum that's the mightiest. As many as 80,000 ancient Romans could fit inside, often to watch gladiators do battle. The Colosseum was designed so that it could be emptied in less than ten minutes. Called a *vomitorium*, this exit passage is located under the seats. Big crowds can exit through it, and this is what makes modern stadiums usable today.

BATTLE OF THE ORANGES

Every February the town of Ivrea throws Italy's largest food fight, a re-enactment of a medieval battle. The town imports 57,000 crates of oranges. Then thousands of people, divided into nine teams, dress up in medieval costumes and throw oranges at each other for three days!

SUPERCARS

Nobody makes super-fast cars look as cool as the Italians: think Ferrari, Lancia, Maserati. Many consider the best of the bunch to be the Lamborghini Aventador, with a top speed of 217 mph (350 km/h).

Lamborghini Aventador

A SLICE OF HISTORY

Legend says that a man named Raffaele Esposito created the Pizza Margherita in 1889, to honor the Italian queen Margherita of Savoy. A Margherita is a pizza garnished with tomatoes, mozzarella and basil, the colors of the Italian flag.

Da Vinci's design for a flying machine

TREVI FOUNTAIN

Rome's famous wishing well, Fontana di Trevi, receives €3,000 worth of coins every day. Legend has it that if you throw a coin into its waters, you will return to Rome one day.

Gondola

RENAISSANCE MAN

Italy's greatest overachiever, Leonardo da Vinci (1452–1519) was a man ahead of his time. As well as painting masterpieces like the *Mona Lisa* and *The Last Supper*, da Vinci also invented the parachute, the diving suit, and the helicopter, among many other things, long before the technology was available to make them!

VIBRANT VENICE

Known as the floating city—even though it's sinking!—Venice is made up of 118 islands and connected by more than 150 canals and 400 bridges. Long, black boats called gondolas have become the symbol of Venice. Each one is made of eight different types of wood; they're often seen with ornate chairs and decorations inside.

SERENE SAN MARINO

The country's official name is the Republic of San Marino, but by most residents it is referred to as the "Most Serene Republic of San Marino." How soothing!

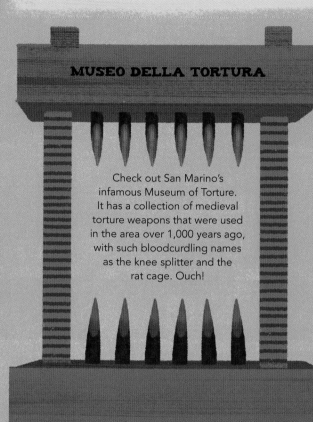

MUSEO DELLA TORTURA

Check out San Marino's infamous Museum of Torture. It has a collection of medieval torture weapons that were used in the area over 1,000 years ago, with such bloodcurdling names as the knee splitter and the rat cage. Ouch!

Surrounded by Italy on all sides, San Marino is situated near the back of the knee on the "boot"—you'll never forget that now!

It is a super microstate, less than half the size of Liechtenstein. It's also completely mountainous, so get your hiking boots ready.

SAN MARINO

N

San Marino

Europe

Italy

5 miles

Pop. size	31,448	(199TH)
Landmass (sq mi)	24	(199TH)
Life Expectancy	83.18	(4TH)

OLDEST COUNTRY IN THE WORLD

San Marino is the oldest surviving country in the world. Its borders date back to September 3, A.D. 301, when it was founded by Saint Marinus, a stonecutter, who set up shop in San Marino. His dying words were "*Relinquo vos liberos ab utroque homine*" (I leave you free from both men). No one knows what he meant!

THE THREE TOWERS

San Marino's citizens are fiercely proud of their independence, which has been defended over the centuries from the republic's three stone towers, built into the rocks of Mount Titano. Two of these are now open to the public, and there are incredible views to be had.

The Guaita Tower

MR. PRESIDENT

One of San Marino's most famous dead citizens is President Abraham Lincoln! In 1861, the government of San Marino wrote a letter to the U.S. commander-in-chief hoping for an alliance between the two nations, and offered Lincoln an honorary citizenship. He warmly accepted!

The Montale Tower

The Cesta Tower

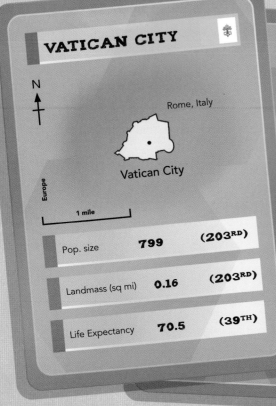

VATICAN CITY

N

Rome, Italy

Vatican City

Europe

1 mile

Pop. size	**799**	**(203RD)**
Landmass (sq mi)	**0.16**	**(203RD)**
Life Expectancy	**70.5**	**(39TH)**

Ladies and gentlemen, welcome to the world's smallest country: Vatican City.

Sitting within a walled enclave, slap-bang in the middle of Rome, Vatican City is home to the leader of the Catholic Church— the Pope.

THE POPE

The Pope is the worldwide leader of the Catholic Church, a religion that has over 1.2 billion members. Every Wednesday morning the Pope holds a papal audience, during which he addresses thousands of people in St. Peter's Square in multiple languages, and blesses his Catholic followers.

POPE ARMY!

Dressed in its colorful uniform, the world's smallest army—known as the Swiss Guard—only has one job: to protect the Pope. The army, made up of Swiss citizens, only has 110 soldiers and has been keeping the Pope safe since 1506. They are extremely well trained and skilled marksmen.

THE HOLY DOOR

The Holy Door is the northernmost entrance to St. Peter's Basilica. It is cemented shut and only opened by the Pope for Jubilee years, once every 25 years or so, when pilgrims who are allowed to walk through the door are forgiven of all sins. The Pope opens the door with a silver hammer.

UNDERGROUND SECRETS

The Vatican's Secret Archives is an underground vault in the Apostolic Palace that contains a vast collection of important historical documents—all sealed in climate-controlled rooms—that date back 1,200 years. Letters from Michaelangelo, Abraham Lincoln, and writings by astronomer Galileo Galilei are all kept under guarded lock and key.

PUTTING THEIR STAMP ON IT

Vatican City has its own postal service and has been producing its own series of decorative stamps since 1929. These are hugely sought after by stamp collectors (known as philatelists) all over the world. The postal service is famous for its efficiency and there are more letters sent per inhabitant from Vatican City than anywhere else on Earth!

SEDE VACANTE SETT. 1978

ST PETE'S PLACE

St Peter's Basilica is the holy resting place of previous popes. The church was built on its current location because it was the burial site of Saint Peter—a disciple of Jesus Christ. Visitors rub or kiss the foot of the bronze statue of Saint Peter inside the basilica to bring them good luck and blessings for the future.

THE FIRST PET CAT

In 2004, archaeologists discovered the 9,500-year-old remains of a person buried with a cat, from the Neolithic village of Shillourokambos, Cyprus. The find has been hailed as the oldest-known pet cat. The poor kitty was buried alive with its owner.

HELLO HALLOUMI!

It may be a land packed with ancient myths and legends, but one of the more modern Cypriot phenomena that has taken the world by storm is halloumi: the famous mixture of goat's and sheep's milk cheese. If you eat it raw, halloumi should squeak in your teeth; if you it grill or fry it, it becomes crispy and gooey. Many Cypriot families make it themselves. The EU has recognized halloumi as a traditional Cypriot product, so officially halloumi is only halloumi if it's made in Cyprus.

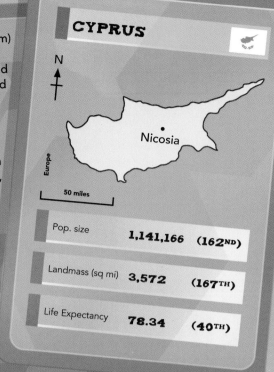

CYPRUS

Almost 50 mi. (80 km) away from Turkey sits Cyprus, an island nation that emerged from the sea 30 million years ago.

Its ancient birth is linked to the origin myth of Aphrodite, the famed goddess of love, and was the gift Roman Emperor Mark Anthony gave to his Egyptian queen and the last of the pharaohs, Cleopatra.

N

Nicosia

Europe

50 miles

Pop. size	1,141,166	(162ND)
Landmass (sq mi)	3,572	(167TH)
Life Expectancy	78.34	(40TH)

HOLY COAST!

Cyprus's coast is chock full of holes. Made out of limestone, the island's cliffs are the perfect place to hide.

APHRODITE AND PAPHOS

When Aphrodite (the Romans knew her as Venus), the beautiful goddess of love, appeared in the water near Paphos, she grew from foam in the sea (aphros means "sea foam") and traveled to shore on a scallop shell. Visitors to Paphos can gaze in awe at Aphrodite's Rock, the exact craggy spot at which, legend tells us, the goddess was born.

MOUFLON AND ON

Cyprus is famous for its sheep. But the mighty mouflon—with its distinct spiraling horns—is thought to be the ancestor of all modern sheep. The mouflon is very shy in real life, but in Cyprus you can spot them—they're the symbol of the national rugby team!

MT. OLYMPUS

Despite being an island nation in the middle of the Eastern Mediterranean, Cyprus is still renowned as a great place for winter sports! Pack your skis and pick a slope on Cyprus's highest peak: Mt. Olympus. The Aphrodite run is perfect for beginners

MALTA

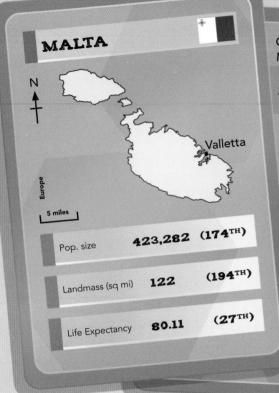

N

Europe

Valletta

5 miles

Pop. size	423,282	(174TH)
Landmass (sq mi)	122	(194TH)
Life Expectancy	80.11	(27TH)

On a map, you'll find Malta dangling in the Mediterranean Sea, just off the bottom of the Italian island of Sicily.

An archipelago made up of three sun-bleached islands—Malta, Gozo, and Comino—Malta is renowned for its crusading knights, blue lagoons, and ancient temples.

KNIGHTS OF MALTA

The Knights of the Order of Saint John arrived in Malta in 1530, having established themselves 500 years earlier as a group of monks who looked after the sick and dying in Jerusalem. The knights later fought in the Crusades. In 1565, Malta was the location of an epic battle, during which the nation was under siege from the Ottoman Empire. The knights had 700 men; the Turkish soldiers had 30,000. And yet the knights won the battle! The emblem of the knights—the Maltese Cross—is now the symbol of the country of Malta.

ARCH WITH A VIEW

One of Gozo's most famous tourist attractions is a natural limestone arch. It's nicknamed "The Azure Window" because of its framed blue view of the Mediterranean Sea.

NOT A DROP TO DRINK?

Malta has no rivers and very little rainfall. Over the centuries, the people have learned to extract fresh water from the salty sea in order to survive.

ANCIENT EARTH

Some of the oldest religious sites on Earth are the huge stone temples of Ħaġar Qim and Mnajdra, a Unesco World Heritage Site that dates back over 5,000 years!

MDINA

Situated on a hill in the center of Malta, Mdina is a 4,000-year-old walled city. Only residents of Mdina are allowed to drive their cars on the roads inside the city.

LOVELY LUZZUS

Traditional Maltese fishing boats are called *luzzus*. They're painted in bright colors and often decorated with eyes on the front, to protect the fishermen from harm when they're at sea.

F185

TWO PRINCES

Andorra is the world's only co-principality. This means it is a country traditionally governed by two princes. Today though, the job is split between Spain's Bishop of Urgell and the president of France.

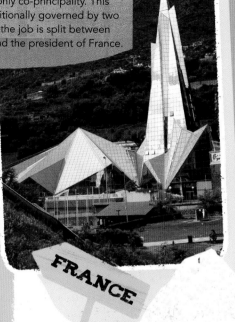

SPACE-AGE SPA

Heated by natural hot springs, which bubble bountifully underneath the ground at a pleasant 89.6°F (32°C), and featuring a massive lagoon in the center, Andorra's Caldea Spa Complex is a modern marvel. The huge glass building may stick out from the natural landscape like a sore thumb, but it is Europe's largest spa destination.

FRANCE

ANDORRA

N

Europe

France

Andorra la Vella

Spain

5 miles

Pop. size	**79,218**	**(193RD)**
Landmass (sq mi)	**181**	**(187TH)**
Life Expectancy	**82.65**	**(6TH)**

Located in the Pyrenees mountains, and squished between Spain and France, the country of Andorra is a mini-nation with as many valleys as you can shake a ski pole at.

Andorra's Grandvalira is the largest ski area in the Pyrenees.

SKY HIGH
Sitting 3,356 ft. (1,023m) above sea level, Andorra la Vella is the highest capital city in Europe!

MOUNTAIN WALL

Stretching 270 mi. (430 km) in length, the Pyrenees divide southern France and northeast Spain. Throughout history, the Pyrenees have separated Spain and Portugal from the rest of Europe. The mountains made it difficult to travel between the two areas by land and hard to make maps. It was for this reason that the Spanish became brilliant sailors!

SPAIN

SHOPAHOLIC!
Andorra contains more than 2,000 shops. That's more than one shop for every 40 people who live there!

THE COUNTER STEP

Known as the *Contrapás*, or "counter step," this local chain dance is performed at Easter after Mass in the town squares. Wearing traditional Andorran dress, dancers form a big circle and move their feet in a peculiar fashion known as the grapevine.

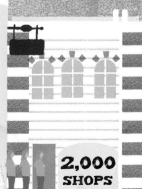

2,000 SHOPS

One shop per **40** PEOPLE

SPAIN

France
Portugal
Europe
Madrid

N

200 miles

Pop. size	46,647,421	(29TH)
Landmass (sq mi)	195,365	(52ND)
Life Expectancy	81.47	(15TH)

Spain is internationally known for its *fiestas* (parties) as much as it is envied for its *siestas* (nap times).

When not sleeping, eating, or dancing, Spaniards are dedicated to making the world more colorful with their art, architecture, fiery language, and fascinating local traditions.

A COUNTRY DIVIDED

Spain is divided into 17 communities, which effectively govern themselves. These regions are: Madrid, Galacia, Asturias, Cantabria, Basque Country, Navarra, La Rioja, Castilla y León, Aragorn, Catalonia, Castilla-La Mancha, Valencia, Murcia, Andalucía, Extremadura, the Canary Islands, and the Balearic Islands.

SIESTA TIME

¿Qué hora es? (What time is it?) Enjoyed as soon after lunch as possible, Spaniards love their *siestas*, a short nap taken in the early afternoon, often for a period of two to three hours. Businesses and shops close, the streets turn quiet, and nobody likes to be disturbed. If you can't beat them, join them!

PICASSO

Pablo Picasso was one of Spain's most famous artists. In his lifetime, he produced an incredible 147,800 works of art—many of them masterpieces.

FLAMENCO

The fiery and passionate flamenco is a Spanish music and dance style that expresses deep emotions between the *bailaor* (male) and *bailaora* (female) dancers. There are three different components of flamenco: *torque* (played on guitar), *cante* (the song), and *baile* (the dance).

FOOD FIGHT!

La Tomatina, held in the small town of Buñol, Valencia, is not a festival for those who don't like to get messy! Every August, more than 50,000 revelers descend on the town to throw the world's biggest food fight—and one hundred tons of overripe tomatoes—at each other!

HUMAN PYRAMIDS

Built and enjoyed at traditional Spanish festivals, a *castell* is a human tower that is comprised of scores of people climbing on top of each other. In 2010, Unesco added *castells* to the List of Intangible Cultural Heritage of Humanity.

La Sagrada Família

THE NEVER-ENDING BUILDING

The most visited landmark in Spain is architect Antoni Gaudí's La Sagrada Família cathedral. Located in Barcelona, the architectural wonder is still being built, 130 years after work first began. It is expected to be completed in 2026 and will have 18 towers. How old will you be then?

RUNNING OF THE BULLS

The Running of the Bulls, held in the small city of Pamplona every July, is one of the world's longest standing (and most dangerous) traditions, dating back to 1385. The idea is simple: six bulls chase *mozos*, a group of young men who traditionally wear white with a red sash, while they dart around the city streets, trying very hard not to be run over and trampled.

TREATY OF TORDESILLAS

In 1494, the Treaty of Tordesillas was signed between the Spanish and Portuguese empires, effectively dividing the "New World" in two: Portugal ruled the eastern half (such as Brazil and Africa), while the Spanish occupied the West (such as the Caribbean Islands). The Portuguese Empire was the first global empire in history.

Bom dia! Situated on what is known as the Iberian Peninsula, sandwiched between Spain and the Atlantic Ocean, Portugal used to own half the world.

These days, it's known as the home of the beautiful Algarve coastline and is one of the most peaceful nations on the planet.

PORTUGAL

Europe

N

100 miles

Spain

Lisbon

Pop. size	10,459,806	(84TH)
Landmass (sq mi)	35,560	(110TH)
Life Expectancy	79.01	(35TH)

PUT A CORK IN IT

Portugal produces 50 percent of the world's cork exports and is home to the oldest cork tree on the planet. The bark of a cork oak tree is stripped from its trunk—without harming the tree—and then shaped into corks for wine bottles. Cork oak trees can live for more than 250 years, growing new cork "skin" every nine years.

A NATION OF NINE

Because of the spread of the Portuguese Empire in the 15th century, Portuguese is the official language of nine countries. Can you guess which?

Portugal, Brazil, Cape Verde, Angola, Guinea-Bissau, Mozambique, Timor-Leste, Sao Tome and Principe, and Equatorial Guinea.

TONGUE TWISTER!

O rato roeu a roupa do rei de Roma

The rat gnawed the king of Rome's clothes

TEA TIME

As the wife of King Charles II, Portuguese princess Catherine of Braganza was Queen of England, Scotland, and Ireland from 1662 to 1685.

It was Catherine who introduced the habit of drinking tea to Britain, now a national pastime and an icon of Britishness.

WOW! 100 FT. WAVE

10
9
8
7
6
5
4
3
2
1

SURF'S UP!

With a coastline that spans 497 mi. (800 km), Portugal is a surfer's paradise. In 2013, Brazilian surfer Carlos Burle took on a 100-foot monster wave off the coast at Praia do Norte in Nazare, Portugal. It is believed to be the biggest wave ever surfed—the same size as a ten-story building! It's no surprise that Portugal is also home to the first commercial wave farm, started in 2008, which creates and sells electricity harnessed from the ocean's waves.

THE LAND OF SAND

The world's most amazing sandcastles are built at Pera, on the Algarve, at the FIESA festival—a mega sand-sculpture exhibition. It displays 40,000 tons of sand, transformed into unbelievable sculptures by sand artists from all over the world. Some sand structures reach 39 ft. (12m) in height!

FERDINAND MAGELLAN

Ferdinand Magellan (1480–1521) was a famed Portuguese explorer, the first European to cross the Pacific Ocean, and, in 1522, the first person to captain a ship that sailed all around the world—(although he died along the way). He also gave the Pacific Ocean its name: *Mar Pacifico*, which means "peaceful sea" in Portuguese.

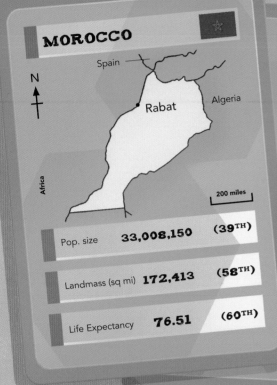

MOROCCO

Spain

N

Rabat

Algeria

Africa

200 miles

Pop. size	33,008,150	(39ᵀᴴ)
Landmass (sq mi)	172,413	(58ᵀᴴ)
Life Expectancy	76.51	(60ᵀᴴ)

In the northwestern corner of Africa sits the magical and mysterious land of Morocco.

Only 8 mi. (13 km) from the tip of southern Spain, this mystical country is full of spicy smells such as ginger and cinnamon, iconic cities such as Casablanca and Tangier, and ancient traditions such as snake charming!

FEZ
Often called "the most complete medieval city in the Arab World," Fez is a magical place, full of locals wearing fezzes: the nation's iconic red felt hat with a black tassel. The fez was introduced to the population by Sultan Mahmud II of the Ottoman Empire in 1826.

COUSCOUS
The national dish of Morocco is *seksou*, or couscous. This tasty dish consists of grains of steamed semolina and is often served with a meat and vegetable stew cooked in a clay pot known as a tagine.

HAGGLE, HAGGLE, HAGGLE!
Known as bazaars throughout Asia, in Morocco markets are called souks. These open-air marketplaces, such as the one near Djemaa el-Fna in the "red city" of Marrakesh, are internationally famous for their fragrant food carts, colorful produce, and haggling—a process where you negotiate the cost of what you want to buy with the owner until you reach a price you're both happy with!

ERG CHEBBI
At sunset, Morocco's Erg Chebbi sand dunes look like no other place on earth. These Saharan sand dunes can reach a height of 492 ft. (150 m), the equivalent of 15 houses stacked on top of each other!

SNAKE CHARMERS
The city of Tangier is well known for its snake charmers—people who sit on the street and pretend to hypnotize snakes in baskets with a musical instrument called a *pungi*, in exchange for money.

PAINT THE TOWN BLUE
In northeast Morocco lies Chefchaouen, where all the buildings and streets are painted blue! This symbolic gesture by Jewish refugees in the 1930s was to show that they could live peacefully alongside their native Muslim neighbors.

THE SAHARA

Eighty percent of Algeria is covered by the world's second-largest desert: the mighty Sahara. It is second only in size to the ice deserts of Antarctica. The Sahara Desert is so big that you could fit the U.K. in it 35 times! In Arabic, the word *sahara* means "desert," so it's technically called the "Desert Desert."

CAMEL RACING

Every year in Hassi Messaoud, the native Touareg people from neighboring villages race their camels to mark the changing of the seasons. Camels may look slow and doddery, but they can reach speeds of 40 mph. (65 km/h)!

Algeria is Africa's largest country. And wow, it's a whopper!

After many years of brutal civil wars, Algeria is now a peaceful place to visit, a land where the phrase *salaam alaikum* ("peace be with you") is the common way to say hello and goodbye. Algeria is also where you can discover the Sahara.

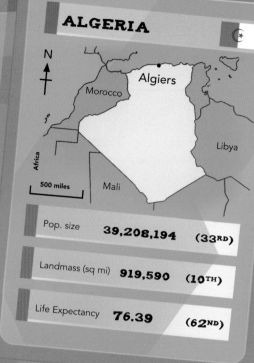

ALGERIA

Pop. size	39,208,194	(33RD)
Landmass (sq mi)	919,590	(10TH)
Life Expectancy	76.39	(62ND)

EARLY GRAFFITI

Between 8,000 and 1,000 years ago, Algeria's native Phoenician cave dwellers painted more than 15,000 pictures on the walls at Tassili N'Ajjer. The paintings depict men, women, and children, as well as animals such as giraffes, crocodiles, and cows, dancing and hunting (not at the same time!).

WAR FOR INDEPENDENCE

The Maqam Echahid memorial is an iconic monument that commemorates Algeria's war for independence from France, its colonial ruler from 1954 to 1962. The monument shelters a flame that is never extinguished, to symbolize the Algerian people's struggle for freedom.

LIVING ON THE EDGE

Algeria's best-known city, Constantine, sits on the edge of a cliff. It's also split in half by the Rhumel River. If you want to see the city, you must crisscross the valley over many suspension bridges.

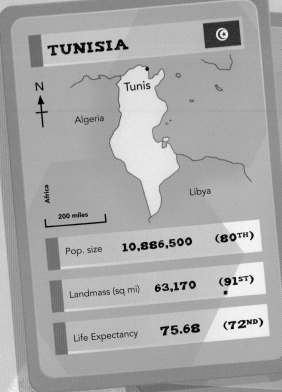

TUNISIA

N

Tunis

Algeria

Africa

Libya

200 miles

Pop. size	10,886,500	(80TH)
Landmass (sq mi)	63,170	(91ST)
Life Expectancy	75.68	(72ND)

Sandwiched in the middle of its big brothers, Algeria and Libya, on its eastern and western sides respectively, Tunisia is the northernmost point of the African continent.

Star Wars may have put it on the global map in 1977, but the local Berber people have existed in the region for more than 3,000 years.

FEEL THE FORCE

Once up a time in a galaxy far, far away, storyteller and filmmaker George Lucas picked the deserts of Tunisia for many famous scenes in his *Star Wars* movie trilogy. Almost 40 years later, director J.J. Abrams returned to Tunisia and Ksar Hadada to film sequences for the eagerly anticipated sequel.

FATA MORGANA

Chott el Djerid is the largest salt lake within the Sahara Desert and a place where the mysterious optical phenomenon of fata morgana occurs. Named after the sorceress Morgan le Fay in the King Arthur legend, this superior type of mirage occurs when a layer of cooler air lies beneath a layer of warmer air. Observers might see weird shapes in the distance floating and transforming in front of their eyes!

FESTIVAL OF THE SAHARA

The International Festival of the Sahara is held in Douz every December and is the country's oldest and most popular festival, which celebrates the customs and traditions of the nomadic way of life. Every year thousands of people travel to Tunisia to watch events such as camel marathons, a Bedouin marriage, and traditional music and dancing.

EL JEM

After the battle of Carthage ended in A.D. 238, the Roman conquerors built El Jem—Africa's largest Roman colosseum. More than 35,000 people attended the amphitheater to watch gladiators fight!

HANNIBAL

Near the city of Tunis lie the ruins of the once-great city of Carthage, a place treasured and envied by the Romans. Almost 2,000 years ago, the legendary general of Carthage, Hannibal, invaded Italy using an army of elephants to up the element of surprise! After wars that lasted 118 years, the Romans claimed Tunisia for Italy, recreating Carthage as a Roman city in Africa.

Hannibal

GLORY TO ZEUS!

Located in the ancient city of Cyrene—the "Athens of Africa"—and built by the Greeks 2,500 years ago, the ruined Temple of Zeus was once a bigger necropolis than the Parthenon in Athens.

Libya is 95 percent desert. For every sand dune, however, there is an ancient Roman ruin or bustling city that adds a flash of African color.

From tranquil Mediterranean coastlines to lakes in the middle of deserts, Libya is a land of contrasts.

LIBYA

N

Tripoli

Egypt

Africa

200 miles

Niger

Chad

Pop. size	6,201,521	(109TH)
Landmass (sq mi)	679,358	(16TH)
Life Expectancy	76.04	(67TH)

SALTY SAHARA

In the middle of the Sahara at the Ubari Sand Sea you can a swim in an oasis where the water is five times saltier than regular seawater!

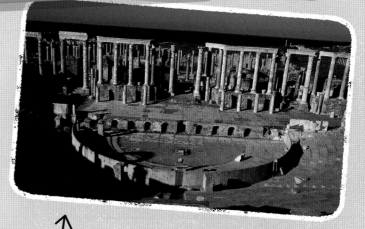

LEPTIS MAGNA

Among the world's best-preserved archaeological ruins, the once-powerful Roman city of Leptis Magna still stands near Khoms. Over 2,000 years later, the Arch of Septimius Severus, the marketplace, and the amphitheater are still standing intact!

SHAKE UP YOUR BREAKFAST

A popular breakfast dish in Libya is *shakshuka*. This colorful meal consists of baked eggs with tomatoes, onions, chilies, and spices. It's usually served with bread to mop up all that delicious sauce. Yum!

WAW AL-NAMUS

Translated as the "Oasis of Mosquitoes" and located in the center of the Sahara Desert, Waw-an-namus is an extinct volcano with a crater 2.5 mi. (4 km) wide! One of the most remote places in the world, Waw Al-namus consists of three salt lakes that form a watery oasis in the center, which are surrounded by 12 mi. (20 km) of jet-black ash. From space, it looks like a big black hole in the desert!

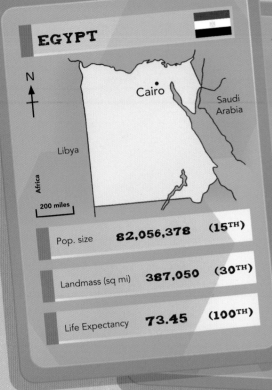

EGYPT

N
200 miles

Cairo
Libya
Africa
Saudi Arabia

Pop. size	82,056,378	(15TH)
Landmass (sq mi)	387,050	(30TH)
Life Expectancy	73.45	(100TH)

As the driest nation in Africa, Egypt can get as hot as its history.

With the magnificent life-giving Nile River that splits the country in two, the beautiful Red Sea coast, and the ancient culture of pharaohs and their pyramids, Egypt is seriously epic.

LUXOR

Located on the east and west banks of the Nile River in southern Egypt, the modern city of Luxor is the world's greatest open air museum. Within, you will find tombs and monuments dedicated to the pharaohs (kings) of ancient Egypt, including the Temples of Karnak and Luxor, the Valley of the Kings and the Valley of the Queens, and the ancient ruins of the city of Thebes. Egyptians built underground tombs for their kings so that when they died they could be buried with food and possessions ready for the afterlife.

THE SUEZ CANAL

Egypt's Suez Canal, a 101-mi. (163-km) long waterway, links the Mediterranean to the Red Sea. Eight percent of all the world's ocean-going ships pass through it. Like the Panama Canal, it can save ships thousands of miles in the journey between east and west.

ABU SIMBEL

The Abu Simbel temples were carved to celebrate the reign of Pharaoh Ramesses II and his queen Nefertari. These gigantic rock temples show Ramesses II sitting on his throne guarding the entrance. The location of the temple is amazing too: twice a year the sun's rays pinpoint the statues of other great pharaohs buried deep within the temple and illuminate them.

CLEOPATRA

The most famous of all the Queen Cleopatras (there were six in total) was the last one, the Cleopatra who became the last pharaoh of Egypt in 51 B.C. Following her death, the Egyptian Empire crumbled and the Romans took control. Legend tells that Cleopatra once entered a bet with the Romans to see who could throw the most expensive party. Cleopatra simply dissolved her pearl earring in a glass of wine and then drank it. She won!

THE CAT'S PYJAMAS

Ancient Egyptians thought of cats as mythical and sacred creatures. The ancient Egyptian word for cat was pronounced "miaow!"

THE PYRAMIDS

When the Pyramids in Egypt were built, woolly mammoths still roamed the earth. Think about that! Many thousands of years ago, the sun was considered the one and only god: that is why Ancient Egyptians were fascinated with pyramids—the shape of the sun's rays is like a pyramid! The three pyramids of Giza were built for the Egyptian rulers Khufu, Khafre, and Menkaure. After these kings had died, their bodies were placed inside tombs deep inside the pyramids. The most famous is the Great Pyramid, built for Pharaoh Khufu; it is the largest and oldest pyramid and was built around 2560 B.C. For 3,800 years it was the tallest structure in the world!

NUBA PEOPLE

The native peoples who inhabit the remote and inaccessible Nuba Mountains are called Nuba. Though often grouped as one, the Nuba are many distinct peoples and speak different languages. They often live in houses called *shal*, except for the unmarried men – they live in separate houses called *holua*. Nuba people are primarily farmers and herders and the women and young girls spend many hours of each day carrying clean water to the family home just to survive.

It's got more ancient pyramids than Egypt, a large percentage of the Nile River, and was the home of the ancient kingdom of Nubia: the oldest known monarchy in the world.

Sudan has a lot more going on than just being the point where Africa meets Arabia!

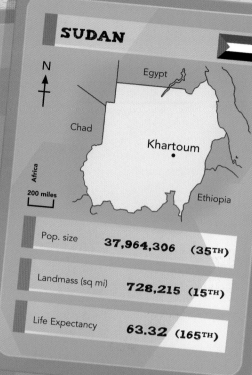

SUDAN

N

Egypt

Chad

Khartoum

Africa

200 miles

Ethiopia

Pop. size	37,964,306	(35TH)
Landmass (sq mi)	728,215	(15TH)
Life Expectancy	63.32	(165TH)

DERVISH DANCERS

In Sudan's capital, Khartoum, crowds gather to watch the Dervish ceremonies near the largest mosques of the city. The Dervishes dance in circles to the beat of drummers and rhythmic chanting, whirling faster and faster until they spin themselves into a mystic trance.

HAMMERHEAD!

Port Sudan is not an incredibly exciting city above ground, but under the water it's a different story. It's famous for its wet and wild scuba-diving sites, and if you're lucky, you might see the unique silhouette of a hammerhead shark gliding through the water.

NUBIAN PYRAMIDS

Egypt's pyramids might be the most famous in the world, but Sudan has some incredible examples too. Once the capital of the Kingdom of Kush, the ancient city of Meroë is the location of a royal cemetery where more than 200 pyramids contain the tombs of hundreds of kings and queens from Nubian royalty.

NEVER SMILE AT A CROCODILE

Growing up to 16 ft. (5 m) in length and living for as long as 100 years, the Nile's most famous resident is the Nile crocodile. These scaly beasts are the second-largest reptile species in the world and can catch prey as large as buffalo and wildebeest in their huge, powerful jaws.

SOUTH SUDAN

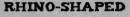

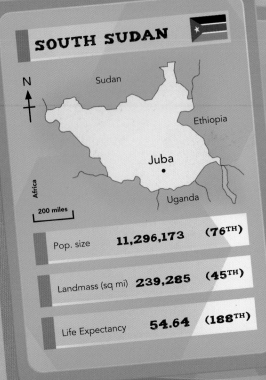

N

Sudan

Ethiopia

Juba

Uganda

Africa

200 miles

Pop. size	11,296,173	(76TH)
Landmass (sq mi)	239,285	(45TH)
Life Expectancy	54.64	(188TH)

Welcome to South Sudan—the world's newest country!

Born in 2011, after a destructive civil war with Sudan, landlocked South Sudan, with its grasslands, swamps and tropical rainforests (as well as the life-giving White Nile River), gained independence from its northern neighbor.

RHINO-SHAPED

Imagine if a nearby town or city was shaped like your favorite animal—how cool would that be? Well, it's possible this crazy idea might become a future reality in animal-mad South Sudan. In 2010, architectural design "blueprints" were drawn up to rebuild the country's capital city Juba in the shape of a rhinoceros—with a huge park located in the shape of the rhino's horn and a 5-star hotel where its eye would be. If it goes ahead, the US$11 billion redevelopment could take up to 20 years to complete. It is hoped that it will breathe life into one of the world's poorest regions.

A BRAINY SNACK

A staple food in South Sudan is a floury pancake called *kisra*. While these can be made using oil, if you want to fry them the authentic South Sudanese way then you'll need to grease your pan with a healthy dollop of cow brains. Yummy!

THE MUNDARI

Covering themselves in a light brown dust known as ochre to stay protected from the sun while herding their precious cattle, the Mundari tribe, one of the smallest tribes in South Sudan, are renowned for being good wrestlers as well as for their distinct facial scars. Every young man in the tribe must complete a rite-of-passage ritual known as scarification. The scars take the form of three lines pointing from the forehead towards the nose.

LONG-HORNED BULL

As with many African nations, the majority of the population relies on their animals for food, breeding, jobs, transport, trade, and social status. Around these parts, the most iconic creature seen wandering the dusty grasslands is the Ankole-Watusi breed of long-horned bull: an emblem of South Sudan and a much-loved beast. The horns on these loveable monsters can grow as wide as 8 ft. (2.5 m) from tip to tip!

BIG OL' SUDD

Home to the black crowned crane, the Sudd is one of the world's largest swamps and is as big as England! Due to the thick vegetation that grows on top of the water in the Sudd, the whole area is difficult to travel through; boats cannot travel through the boggy water and there is no dry land to build roads on. Despite this, many remote swamp villages have sprung up and people have built homes on top of the water!

LAKE CHAD

Once one of the largest freshwater lakes in the world, Lake Chad is rapidly vanishing before our eyes. More and more is becoming part of the Sahara each year. Within decades, the lake will have completely dried up, causing severe drought and problems for the millions of locals, as well as the country's farmers and fishermen.

Lalê ("hello") as they say in this very dry and poor nation.

Chad is a sub-Saharan country where elephants and hippos roam and storks fly. But the water to sustain this beautiful exotic wildlife, as well as more than 200 ethnic groups, is in short supply. The next few years for Chad are vital.

CHAD

N

Niger

Sudan

Africa

200 miles

N'Djamena

Pop. size	12,825,314	(73RD)
Landmass (sq mi)	495,755	(20TH)
Life Expectancy	49.44	(203RD)

CLEAN WATER

Outside the nation's capital, N'Djamena, clean water is scarce. Most people, rely on wells for their fresh water. Once the water is brought up from the ground, it is carried in a large jug perched on the head, often for several miles.

SECRET STONES OF THE SAHARA

The remote Ennedi rock formations emerge from the floor of the Sahara Desert on Chad's Ennedi Plateau. These mammoth monoliths—some over 330 ft. (100 m) tall—come in all shapes and sizes, and rock climbers from all over the world come to conquer them.

FAMOUS OASIS

Chad's Guelta D'Archei is the most famous oasis in the Saharan Desert. Located in one of the most far-flung parts of the world—many days' drive from N'Djamena—Guelta D'Archei is an ancient pool of water, surrounded by high canyon walls on either side, where Nile crocodiles, camels, and hundreds of other animals come for precious water—water that has been turned black by thousands of years of camel poo!

AFRICAN ELEPHANTS

There are two types of elephant in the world, the African and the Asian. At its heaviest, an African elephant can weigh seven tons—by far the largest land animal in the world. Seven tons is the equivalent of seven medium-sized family cars! These species can live up to 70 years, and their ears are shaped just like the African continent!

NIGER

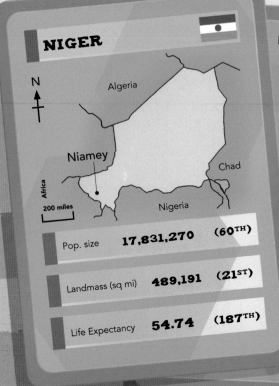

N

Algeria

Niamey

Chad

Africa

200 miles

Nigeria

Pop. size	17,831,270	(60TH)
Landmass (sq mi)	489,191	(21ST)
Life Expectancy	54.74	(187TH)

Life in Niger is hard. But the country thrives and survives despite the toughest conditions.

Surrounded by Mali, Algeria, Libya, Chad, Nigeria, Benin, and Burkina Faso, Niger—named after the mighty Niger River—is two-thirds desert, and has been described as the "frying pan of the world" because it's so hot!

THE LOST TREE

The Tree of Ténéré was a very lonely acacia tree. It was the only surviving tree in the whole of the Sahara Desert: there wasn't another one for over 250 mi. (400 km)! This sacred tree was, tragically, knocked down by a drunk truck driver in 1973. RIP, tree!

NIGER RIVER

Despite the constant heat, the Niger River brings much-needed water to the savanna grassland and farmland. The river is the third longest in Africa after the Congo and Nile and is 2,600 mi. (4,200 km) long: about the same distance as Route 66 in the United States!

GIRAFFES 'R' US

Head to Kouré to see some of Africa's last wild giraffe herds. In the 1980s, wild giraffe numbers reached as low as 50 here, but now there are almost 200. Giraffes are the tallest mammal on earth—their legs alone are as high as a tall human! A giraffe's patterns are much like human fingerprints. No two individual giraffes have exactly the same one!

WODAABE TRIBE

The Wodaabe tribe, a subgroup of Niger's Fulani people, are a tribe of nomadic farmers who do not have a written language. Every year, they celebrate *gerewol*—a ritual courtship competition where young men dance the *yaake* to impress the girls, wearing make-up that emphasizes the whiteness of their eyes and teeth.

NIGERSAURUS

Nigersaurus was a type of long-necked dinosaur called a Sauropod and is one of the strangest creatures ever to walk the earth. Fossils found of this 9-m-(30ft)-long creature, show that it had 500 teeth!

HIP HIPPOS

Hippos are Mali's mascot. In fact, the word *mali* means "hippopotamus" in Bamanakan—the main language of the country. These chubby creatures never have to worry about getting burned in the hot sun, because their skin naturally secretes an oily, reddish type of sunscreen!

Known as the jewel in West Africa's crown, Mali is a landlocked location famous for its music, masks, mosques, and King Mansa Mūsā, as well as the Saharan city of legend, Timbuktu.

With incredible mud-brick buildings, lazy rivers, and friendly people, Mali's got a bit of everything.

MALI

Mauritania

Algeria

Bamako

Burkina Faso

Africa

200 miles

Pop. size	15,301,650	(68TH)
Landmass (sq mi)	478,841	(23RD)
Life Expectancy	54.95	(185TH)

Mansa Mūsā

THE DOGON PEOPLE

Mali's famous ethnic group, the Dogon, are best known for their masked dance, where performers stand on 10-foot-tall stilts and dance a wild and energetic dance to celebrate their beliefs, wearing colorful skirts and big wooden masks. The Dogon people live in the mud-houses built into the cliffs of Bandiagara.

KING OF KINGS

Mansa Mūsā, known as the King of Kings, ruled Mali in the 14th century. He's known as the richest man in all of history, thanks to Mali's huge gold deposits. In 1324, Mūsā made a pilgrimage to Mecca, Saudi Arabia (the holiest place in Islam and birthplace of Muhammad, believed by Muslims to be a prophet of God), with 60,000 people following him. Along his way, he handed out gold dust to the poor.

THE GRANDE MOSQUÉE

The Grande Mosquée in Djenné is the largest mud structure in the world. Made entirely of sun-baked mud bricks, it is a holy place of Islamic worship that is 328 ft. (100 m) long and 131 ft. (40 m) wide. It is one of the most famous buildings in Africa; it also looks like the biggest sandcastle ever built!

Djenné's Grande Mosquée

MAURITANIA

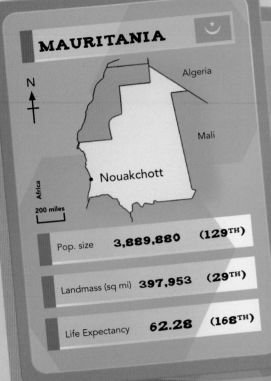

Africa
200 miles

Algeria

Mali

Nouakchott

N

Pop. size	3,889,880	(129TH)
Landmass (sq mi)	397,953	(29TH)
Life Expectancy	62.28	(168TH)

Larger than its nearest neighbors, The Gambia and Senegal, Mauritania is 90 percent desert.

It is considered by many to be the bridge between North and West Africa, as well as being a unique blend of African and Arab cultures.

THE EYE OF THE SAHARA

The Richat Structure, or the "Eye of the Sahara," is found in western Mauritania. It's a large dome of concentric circles that is a prominent landmark for astronauts as they orbit the earth in the International Space Station. Once thought to be an asteroid impact crater, the Richat Structure is now considered to be one of Earth's most symmetrical and mysterious rock structures—no one is sure how it formed.

ANIGUR

One of the country's best-loved traditional games is *anigur*. It's a pretend sword fight, with sticks instead of swords. Two players compete fiercely in a mix of dueling and dancing to entertain spectators, who clap and sing along. There are no winners or losers. Competitors in the game are usually important people in the community and perform *anigur* at official celebrations and ceremonies.

Kediet ej Jill

The ritual game of Anigur

MAGNET MOUNTAIN

The highest peak in Mauritania is Kediet ej Jill, standing at 3,001 ft. (915 m) tall. It's no Everest, but it is one of the few mountains in the world that is made almost entirely out of magnetite, which gives it a blue color. This material also makes it seriously tricky for hapless adventurers who get themselves lost, as the magnetite stops compasses from working!

DELICIOUS DATES

Mauritania produces a whopping 60,000 tons of dates a year. These sweet, dark brown fruits are popular in pastries all over the world. The desert palm trees they grow on provide lots of uses for the dedicated Mauritanian date farmers, who weave baskets and mats from the leaves.

IRON-ORE TRAIN

One of the longest trains in the world is the Mauritania Railways iron-ore train. Over 1.5 mi. (2.4 km) long, the train ferries deposits of iron from the Zouerat mines to Nouadhibou. Passengers can jump on the train and travel with the iron ore, and see a massive swathe of the country in one long 12-hour trip!

PICO DO FOGO

If you head inside the ancient crater of the still-active volcano Pico do Fogo, you won't find a river of bubbling, red-hot, molten lava. No! You'll find a village community who have decided to call the crater their home.

Cut off from the rest of Africa, the nation of Cape Verde emerges from the dark depths of the Atlantic Ocean 310 mi. (500 km) off the West African coast.

Cape Verde consists of ten volcanic islands scattered about the Atlantic Ocean. If you go, say *ola* ("hello") from us!

CAPE VERDE

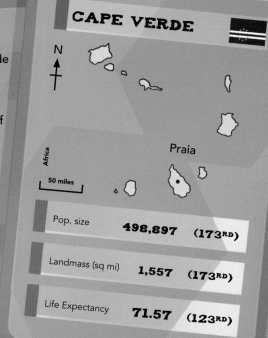

Praia

50 miles

Africa

Pop. size	498,897	(173RD)
Landmass (sq mi)	1,557	(173RD)
Life Expectancy	71.57	(123RD)

MORNA

Cape Verde's most recognized form of music is *morna*—soulful melodies sung in Cape Verdean creole accompanied by musicians on guitar, violin, and clarinet.

AT LOGGERHEADS

Loggerhead turtles drag their gigantic hardback shells up the beach, lay eggs deep in the sand . . . and then make the trip back down.

HIKER'S PARADISE

The island of Santo Antão is made up entirely of volcanic rock. It's not surprising then that this is an island with lots of lumps and bumps! The mountains and lush valleys make this a dream destination for hikers from all over the world.

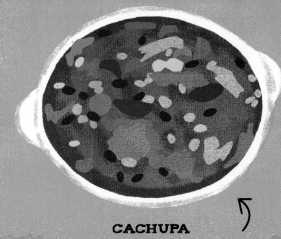

CACHUPA

Cape Verde's national dish, *cachupa*, is sure to put some meat on your bones! This hearty stew is made with beans, mashed corn, onions, sweet potatoes, tomatoes, cabbage, yams, green bananas, and bacon. Phew! Cape Verdeans love this dish so much that they eat it at any time of the day, for breakfast, lunch, or dinner!

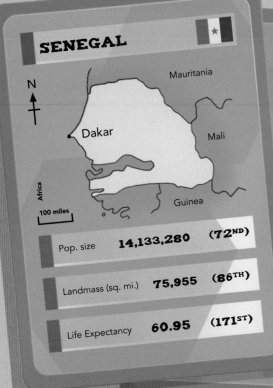

SENEGAL

N

Mauritania

Dakar

Mali

Africa

Guinea

100 miles

Pop. size	**14,133,280**	**(72ND)**
Landmass (sq. mi.)	**75,955**	**(86TH)**
Life Expectancy	**60.95**	**(171ST)**

A fusion of French and African cultures, Senegal is one of West Africa's most bewitching places. It's similar in size to Cambodia.

Keep your eyes on the skies when in Senegal; it's on the flyways of millions of birds as they migrate south for the winter.

MAJOR TRIBES

Accounting for six million people—almost half the Senegal population—the Wolof are the largest ethnic group in Senegal. Originating in the area in 1100 B.C., the Wolof people have a popular saying: "A man with a mouth is never lost."

MBALAX

Senegal's world famous musical style, Mbalax, is a fusion of Western musical styles such as jazz and soul along with the African rhythms of the traditional sabar drum. The Mbalax Dance is very popular, and many movements can be compared to twerking as well as "the dog," where dancers imitate a dog peeing!

DOOR OF NO RETURN

Though historians are unsure of its real place in history, the House of Slaves on Gorée Island was the site where hundreds of thousands of captured Africans were imprisoned in chains, before being sent on slave ships to the Americas, a journey known as the Middle Passage.

ROSY PINK

Lake Retba, or Pink Lake, is named for its pink water! The exotic color is caused by a type of algae called *Dunaliella salina*. The lake also has 40 percent more salt than normal saltwater lakes—so much so that it is impossible to sink!

Where else can you find water that's a crazy color? GO TO PAGE **197**

MMM MBUBB

Known to the Wolof people as *mbubb*, the Senegalese kaftan is an ankle-length robe made of light (and often colorful) fabric that keeps the locals cool in the desert heat. Along with the kufi cap, it is the most common and traditional of clothing.

AFRICA'S LARGEST STATUE

The African Renaissance Monument in Dakar is Africa's largest statue and is even taller than the Statue of Liberty. It caused some controversy when it was erected, as people thought it was too brash and expensive, but it is a lasting symbol of Senegal's independence from France.

SACRED CROCODILES

The Kachikally crocodile pool in Bakau is a sacred spot, renowned for its supernatural healing powers as well as its 80 adult crocodiles (and the occasional albino crocodile)! Couples hoping for children bathe in the pool as a fertility ritual, believing the waters can bring them good luck.

Once a British colony, The Gambia achieved independence in 1965.

This tiny finger of a nation, the filling between two bits of Senegalese bread, might be the smallest country in mainland Africa (it's roughly the same size as Yorkshire, England), but it sure packs a lot in.

THE GAMBIA

N

Senegal

Banjul

Senegal

Africa

50 miles

Pop. size	1,849,285	(151ST)
Landmass (sq mi)	4,361	(163RD)
Life Expectancy	64.36	(156TH)

THE RIVER

Seven hundred miles (1,120 km) long and twice the length of the nation that gives it its name, the Gambia River flows through the center of the country. Oysters are harvested from the river by local tribeswomen and used to make oyster stew, a traditional dish in The Gambia.

KUNTA KINTE

Perhaps the most well-known African to be sold into slavery in the Americas was Gambian Kunta Kinte. Born in 1750 in the village of Juffure, Kinte was part of the Madinka people, the ethnic group that makes up almost half of the Gambian population. According to the stories that have been written about Kinte, one day in 1767, while he was searching for wood to make a *djembe* drum for his younger brother, four men took him captive. When Kinte awoke he was a prisoner due to be shipped to America—a dangerous journey that took four months—to begin life as a slave.

TWENTY-ONE STRINGS

A traditional instrument of the people of The Gambia is the *kora*. It's a 21-string instrument that's a cross between a lute and a harp. Musicians who play are called *griots*— storytellers and singers who relay the history of the Mandinka people through song, poetry, and music.

MONKEYING AROUND

The Western red colobus monkey calls The Gambia home. Living in families of more than 50 members, these ginger-haired Old World monkeys have long fingers but no thumbs, and impressively large stomachs that let them pack in large amounts of leaves, fruit, and seeds. Yum!

GUINEA-BISSAU

N

Senegal

Bissau

Africa

Guinea

50 miles

Pop. size	1,704,255	(154TH)
Landmass (sq mi)	13,948	(137TH)
Life Expectancy	49.87	(201ST)

Sitting below Senegal and in front of Guinea, this tiny nation—around the size of Switzerland—was once colonized by the Portuguese.

Parts of Guinea-Bissau have a matriarchal society, which means that women are the head of families and tribes.

Shake that calabash!

GUMBE
The traditional music of Guinea-Bissau is *gumbe*. This fast-paced style of music, incorporating many styles that are popular, uses the calabash—a shaker that provides percussive rhythm.

BUSHPIGS
Known as red river hogs or bushpigs, or even *Potamochoerus porcus* if you prefer, this wild member of the pig family snuffles around Guinea-Bissau's rainforests, chomping on dead animals. The pigs have bright red fur and a white strip running along their backs.

THE BIJAGÓS
In a bid to impress a potential wife, young Bijago men take part in an acrobatic dance in which they contort themselves together in elaborate shapes. The Bijagós are the most traditional, and mysterious, community in Guinea-Bissau.

CASHEW CARRY!
90 percent of the country's economy comes from the production of cashew nuts.

BIJAGÓS FERRY
The beautiful Bijagós islands are accessible by boat, but the ferry from the mainland only makes the trip once a week. If you miss it, you might have to brave the six-hour journey by cancel.

LITTLE PIGGIES

Guinea pigs don't come from Guinea, but it's said that en route from Peru (where they're seen as a tasty snack) to Europe (where they're popular as a cuddly pet), the little furry creatures stopped off in Guinea—and the name stuck! Guinea pigs have been domesticated by humans for more than 7,000 years.

It may be one of the poorest nations on the planet, but Guinea pulsates with life and heritage.

Here you can dance to the real rhythms of West Africa, accompanied by *balafon* and *kora* players, but don't forget your umbrella, because Guinea is one of Africa's wettest countries!

Guinea pig

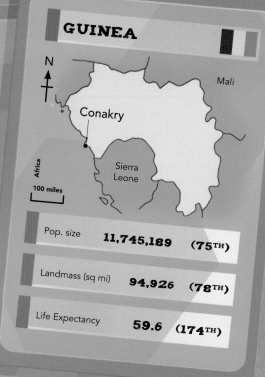

GUINEA

Mali

Conakry

Africa

Sierra Leone

100 miles

Pop. size	**11,745,189**	**(75TH)**
Landmass (sq mi)	**94,926**	**(78TH)**
Life Expectancy	**59.6**	**(174TH)**

DO THE KANKAN

Guinea's largest city, Kankan, is famed for its bustling and colorful markets. It's also well known for its trade of the kola nut—a type of fruit that contains caffeine. You may know it as cola! Kola nuts are chewed in West Africa and are an important part of social gatherings and ceremonies.

BALAFON BONANZA

It looks like a big xylophone, but the *balafon* is much more fun! This definitive Guinean instrument uses dried calabashes to amplify the sound of the keys. It has been played in Africa since the 13th century.

CIRCUS BAOBAB

Guinea's national circus troupe is well known for its incredible acrobatics, juggling, trapeze artistry, and dancing. Performers swing and leap from a stage built to look like a huge baobab tree. The most popular performance from Circus Baobab is based on a traditional Guinean legend, in which a curious hunter steals a mythical drum from a monkey! The group is now so famous that they take their show on tour all over the world.

SIERRA LEONE

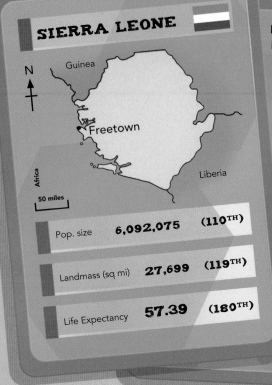

Guinea

N

Freetown

Africa

Liberia

50 miles

Pop. size	6,092,075	(110TH)
Landmass (sq mi)	27,699	(119TH)
Life Expectancy	57.39	(180TH)

Barely larger than Ireland, Sierra Leone is one of West Africa's nearly forgotten gems, a land steeped in more than 30 percent exotic rainforest.

Here you'll find diamonds and gold, hippos and leopards, a brutal history of civil war and slavery, and a future full of freedom. But there is much recovery left to do.

OWDIBODY

In Sierra Leone, the four main languages are English, Krio, Mende, and Temne. If you want to ask how someone is, however, why not ask them *Owdibody*, translated as "How's the body?" Brilliant!

DIAMONDS ARE FOREVER

Most diamonds found in Sierra Leone are more than three billion years old. The country is among the top ten diamond-producing nations in the world, with many diamonds being mined by hand—so grab your sieve and get looking!

CIVIL WAR

Sierra Leone's civil war, from 1991 to 2002, cost the lives of more than 50,000 people. The war was funded by the country's vast natural resources (gold and diamonds) and ended when the United Nations sent in soldiers to negotiate a ceasefire.

DID YOU KNOW

... there are enough diamonds in existence to give everybody on earth a cupful AND that under extreme pressure diamonds can be made from peanut butter?

PEANUT BUTTER

TEMNE PEOPLE

Sierra Leone's largest group of people is the Temne tribe. The culture revolves around paramount chiefs and secret societies. Each society has its own initiation rites and ceremonies, where the initiated are painted white, have their heads shaved, and wear ceremonial masks.

Sparkling rough-cut diamonds

LITTLE HIPPOS

Take a hippo and shrink it down to pocket size—that's a pygmy hippo. Growing no bigger than 3 ft. (1 m) high, these cuties take baths in the waters of Tiwai Island.

FREETOWN

In the 16th century, the area now known as Freetown was to become the place from which thousands of African people left their homeland for a treacherous journey across the Atlantic Ocean to become slaves in the Americas. In 1787, some Africans returned home and Freetown was declared a safe home for freed slaves. Look out for the colorful stilt houses and the bustling Saturday market.

GENERAL BUTT NAKED

Now a Christian Priest, Liberian warlord Joshua Milton Blahyi was once better known as General Butt Naked. During battle in the First Liberian Civil War, Blahyi would lead his soldiers into battle naked, except for shoes and a gun, believing his nudity would protect him from the bullets. Years later, the warlord would inspire a character in the hit Broadway musical *The Book of Mormon*.

In 1821, Liberia become the only country ever to be founded by the freed slaves who had returned to Africa from the United States.

However, over the past half-century, the nation has been occupied by warlords, child soldiers, and secret societies. Only now is it stable enough to welcome travelers.

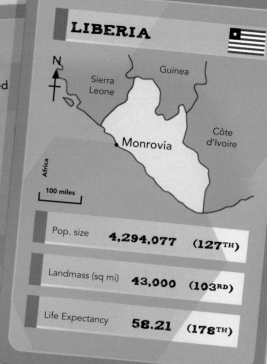

LIBERIA

Guinea
Sierra Leone
Côte d'Ivoire
Monrovia
Africa
100 miles

Pop. size	4,294,077	(127TH)
Landmass (sq mi)	43,000	(103RD)
Life Expectancy	58.21	(178TH)

WHAT A PALAVER

Palaver sauce is a popular stew in Liberia and other West African countries. It's made with spices, palm oil, onions, beef or shrimp, and thick green leaves a bit like spinach. "Palaver" means a long and fuss-filled conversation, and some people believe the stew is so named because the spices mix together in the pot like raised voices mix in a palaver discussion!

RUBBER TAPPING

Have you ever thought about what a tire, or the soles of your shoes, is made from? The answer is latex, which comes from rubber trees that grow in Liberia. A sticky, milky fluid, latex is "tapped" and collected from rubber trees. It is highly waterproof and very stretchy.

GELA MASKS

Worn by the mysterious Bassa people from the region of Buchanan, *gela* masks are warrior headdresses used to contact ghostly spirits and dead ancestors; wearing a mask is said to give the wearer special powers and to protect them from evil spirits. *Gela* means "ancient one."

CÔTE D'IVOIRE

Burkina Faso

Ghana

Liberia

Yamoussoukro

N

Africa

100 miles

Pop. size	20,316,086	(58TH)
Landmass (sq mi)	124,500	(69TH)
Life Expectancy	58.01	(179TH)

This is a soccer-crazed country famous for its chocolate, beaches, and the Akan people, as well as 60 other ethnic groups.

Named after its huge ivory trade in the past century, Côte d'Ivoire (Ivory Coast) was also the location of a grim civil war in 2002, which tore the nation in two. Peace is returning now, and bringing travelers with it.

THE DANCE IS ON
A national source of pride, the *coupé décalé* ("cut and run") dance movement is one of the most important musical styles to emerge from Côte d'Ivoire. Upbeat, crazy, and rebellious, the *coupé décalé* was a vital form of escapism during the civil war.

ABLE APES
Fancy interacting with the smartest chimpanzees in the world? Take a trip to Taï Forest. The chimps you'll find there are very intelligent, using stone tools to break nuts and sticks to help forage for food. They also chew leaves to use as sponges!

COCOA CRAZY
Côte d'Ivoire supplies 30 percent of the world's cocoa—it's the largest producer of the sweet stuff on earth! A key ingredient of chocolate, cocoa beans are one of the world's most traded crops; research suggests that people in Switzerland eat up to 240 chocolate bars each per year. How many have you eaten today?

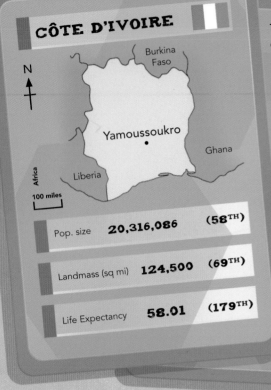

Basilica of Our Lady of Peace

ONE BIG BASILICA!
Côte d'Ivoire is the proud home of the largest church in the world! The enormous Basilica of Our Lady of Peace was inspired by St. Peter's Basilica in Vatican City, but this one is 86,000 sq. ft. (8,000 m²) bigger!

IVORYBALLS
Côte d'Ivoire has long been considered to be the best soccer team in Africa to play on an international stage. Didier Drogba, from Côte d'Ivoire, is also believed to be the best player to emerge from Africa.

Didier Drogba

ALOKO YUMMY
One of the Ivory Coast's national street food favorites is *aloko*: fried plantain served with onions and chilies. Sounds delicious—why not try it today?

SCRAMBLE FOR AFRICA

In 1884, powerful European nations met in Berlin to split and divide Africa for colonial rule—without even asking Africans. When there were no clear borders, like mountains or rivers, the Europeans simply drew a line on the map. Before this colonial division, which affects the continent to this day, Africa was comprised of more than 10,000 states, each with their own distinct languages and customs.

Colonized by France during the "scramble for Africa," Burkina Faso is considered the heart of West Africa, because of its geographical location near the Equator.

It's also very hot and very dry, with the nation struggling through the worst drought and famine in human history.

BURKINA FASO

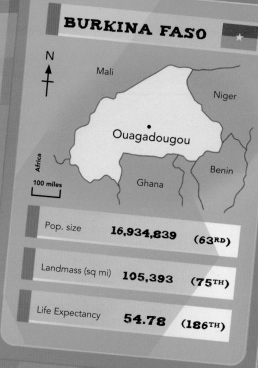

N

Mali

Niger

Ouagadougou

Africa

Ghana

Benin

100 miles

Pop. size	16,934,839	(63RD)
Landmass (sq mi)	105,393	(75TH)
Life Expectancy	54.78	(186TH)

WELCOME HOME

In the Móoré dialect, Ouagadougou, the name of the nation's capital, means "You are welcome here at home with us." Burkina Faso means "Land of the Honorable People," and native Burkinabés are considered as the most honest and welcoming people in Africa.

SNEAK-A-PEAK

The Peaks of Sindou, near Banfora, are a region of sacred interest and one of Burkina Faso's most spectacular natural landmarks. The craggy sandstone rock formations stick out like a sore thumb from the flat savanna.

PAINTED HOUSES

The Kassena people in the village of Tiebele in the south of the country are famous for their highly decorated houses. The dwellings are built from mud and straw, and then the women of the tribe paint elaborate geometric murals on the outside of the walls using colored mud and white chalk.

MOST OF THE MOSSI

The country's largest ethnic group is the Mossi, making up over 40 percent of the population. More than six million Burkinabés are Mossi. Wooden masks are very sacred to the Mossi, especially those carved like antelopes.

Mossi wooden mask

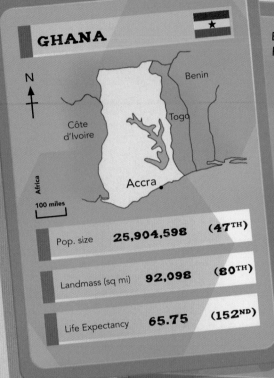

GHANA

N

Africa

100 miles

Côte d'Ivoire

Benin

Togo

Accra

Pop. size	25,904,598	(47TH)
Landmass (sq mi)	92,098	(80TH)
Life Expectancy	65.75	(152ND)

Baking in the day's heat, Golden Ghana deserves its place in the sun, for its future as a beacon of hope for other African countries burns bright.

Ghana is revered as a traveler's heaven and has been dubbed "Africa for beginners" by those who have been there.

VOLTA = VOLTAGE

The world's largest artificial reservoir, Lake Volta, provides almost all of Ghana's electrical needs. The lake was formed when the White Volta and Black Volta rivers were merged by human construction. The force of the water flowing into the Akosombo Dam now generates vast quantities of electricity that Ghana exports to Togo and Benin.

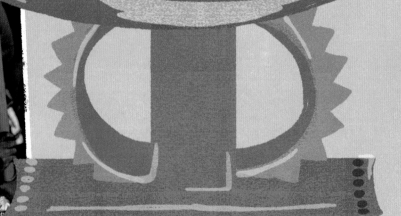

Members of the Ashanti tribe wearing colorful Kente cloth.

THE GOLDEN STOOL

Wearing their iconic and patented pattern of Kente cloth, the Ashanti are the largest group of the Akan people. The Ashanti believe that a golden stool (made from pure gold) floated down from the sky and landed in the lap of Osei-tutu, the first Ashanti king. The soul of the Ashanti people resides in this sacred stool, which has bells to warn the king of incoming danger! Only a few people know the location of the Golden Stool.

SUCCULENT SNAILS

Snails are a popular snack in Ghana and you'll find slimy, salty snail skewers on sale from market traders across the country.

PALACE OF PAGA

Painted in the traditional style of the Pio area, the Palace of Paga was built in 1670 and was the residence of the paramount chief Paga. When Paga died his royal stool was painted black, a ritual that happens with all of Ghana's Akan tribal chiefs.

Gnassingbé Eyadéma

THE EYADÉMA DYNASTY

Togo's "president for life," Gnassingbé Eyadéma, ruled the land from 1967 until his death in 2005, and was one of Africa's longest-serving rulers, although he was rather strange. Eyadéma once published a comic book about a plane crash that he survived to prove that he was a superhero, and he created a wristwatch that flashed a picture of his face every 20 seconds!

On bumpy roads a few miles off the beaten track is Togo, an upright sliver of a country, sandwiched between Ghana and Benin.

A land beating to the sound of drums, voodoo, over 30 tribal groups, mud castles, bats, and even more drums, Togo is the place to go.

TOGO

Ghana · Benin

Africa

100 miles

Lomé

Pop. size	6,816,982	(103RD)
Landmass (sq mi)	21,925	(125TH)
Life Expectancy	64.06	(158TH)

GROTTES DE NANO

Hidden in the village of Nano is a cave system built into the cliffs of Mount Semoo by the Moba people, to protect them from foreign invaders.

VOODOO MARKET

In Togo's capital, Lomé, you can buy all sorts of spooky, strange, and supernatural stuff. Here you can see dead heads, hands, feet, and bones of crocodiles, cats, and monkeys for sale. The black magic of voodoo rituals are still practiced in Togo today, and the heads of animals—crushed into powders—are believed to help with fertility, good luck potions, and warding off evil spirits!

Animal skulls on sale at the voodoo market.

MUD FORTRESS

Built more than 400 years ago in the Koutammakou region, the Batammariba people live in mud-tower houses that look like castles, called *takienta*. The structures helped fend off invasions by neighboring tribes. The buildings are constructed using no tools—only clay, wood, and straw.

Takienta

RHINO BEETLES

Growing as large as an adult's hand—more than six inches long!—*Dynastinae*, or rhinoceros beetles, are an unwelcome pest in the Togo grasslands. The beetles are the largest species of their kind and are famous for the large black horn on their heads.

WRESTLEMANIA

One of the 37 tribes of Togo are the Kabye people, who live on the northern savanna plains. The Kabye continue the initiation ritual of Evala, a famous rite of passage. Young men on the verge of adulthood must wrestle others to prove their strength and bring good fortune to the family name.

BENIN

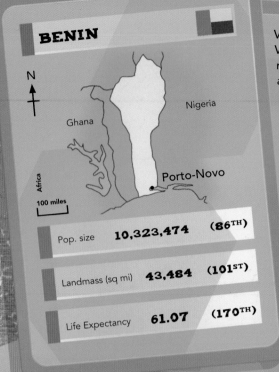

N

Ghana

Nigeria

Africa

100 miles

Porto-Novo

Pop. size	10,323,474	(86TH)
Landmass (sq mi)	43,484	(101ST)
Life Expectancy	61.07	(170TH)

Voodoo. Voodoo. Voodoo. If you only remember one thing about Benin, it should be that it is the birthplace of the world's most feared black-magic rituals.

Of course Benin has many other amazing things going for it: one quarter of the land is outstanding national parks, which teem with wonderful wildlife.

WE DO VOODOO

Benin is the origin point of voodoo. Not to be confused with voodoo as it is shown in Hollywood movies, "Vodun"—as it is known locally—is an official religion of the country and is taken very seriously. Voodoo followers believe that the Earth is ruled by divine elements—*vodun* means "spirits."

LAND ON STILTS

Take a trip to Ganvie, a village on Lake Nokoué. The villagers of Ganvie built their homes on stilts to protect them from the Dahomey tribe—who believed a water demon guarded the lake. The Dahomey were a bloodthirsty bunch: they would appease dead kings with human sacrifices to ensure their ancient spirit rulers had servants in the afterlife!

GO TO PAGE 82
In which European city would you have to paddle to your front door?

The rare Saharan cheetah

WHAT A CHEETAH!

The rarest large mammal on earth is the northwest African cheetah, or Saharan cheetah. It is believed only 200 still exist. Very camera shy, this incredible creature—which has paler fur and fewer spots than your average cheetah—has only been photographed a handful of times.

BRUSH UP YOUR FACTS!

In 2013, 300,000 Nigerian students broke the record in tooth brushing when public schools in the city of Lagos united to brush their teeth simultaneously for one minute.

FOUR-DAY FISHING FESTIVAL

Beginning in 1934, Nigeria's most famous event is the Argungu Fishing Festival. Every year, more than 40,000 hopefuls leap into the Matan Fada River in Kebbi and try to catch the biggest fish. The person who does wins one million naira—or US$5,500!

NIGERIA

More than 170 million people live in Nigeria, making it the most populated country on the continent.

This giant of a nation is not only full of people, but also full of promise for the future. With more than 250 ethnic groups (each with their own language and way of life), there is no end of culture and lovely landmarks.

Pop. size	173,615,345	(7TH)
Landmass (sq mi)	356,669	(32ND)
Life Expectancy	52.62	(192ND)

NOLLYWOOD — 2,000+ FILMS MADE!

Nigeria boasts the world's third-largest movie industry. Every year more than 2,000 films are made, compared to 800 in the United States. The U.S. has almost 40,000 movie theaters though, whereas there are only 100 in Nigeria.

SACRED FOREST

In Oshogbo there is a sacred forest, believed to be the 400-year abode of the fertility goddess Oshun. The shrine is seen as a symbol of the Yoruba identity and contains statues and artworks designed to please the gods.

YORUBA!

With a population of 35 million, Nigeria's Yoruba people are one of the largest ethnic groups in Africa. The Yoruba are known for their colorful dress, the *aso oke*, as well as their wooden masks, which are worn every year between March and May during masquerade festivals, called Gelede.

Wooden Yoruba mask

CAMEROON

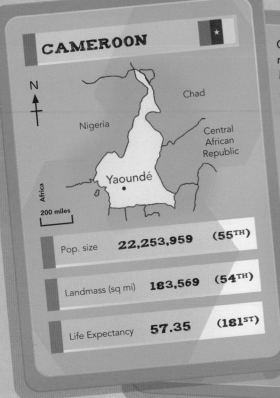

N

Nigeria

Chad

Central African Republic

Yaoundé

Africa

200 miles

Pop. size	**22,253,959**	**(55TH)**
Landmass (sq mi)	**183,569**	**(54TH)**
Life Expectancy	**57.35**	**(181ST)**

Cameroon is a nation of highs and lows. More than 250 languages are spoken here, including "Camfranglais," a slang created by Cameroonians that mixes French, English, and local dialect.

It is also one of the soggiest countries on earth, with the annual rainfall drenching that of many other nations.

MUSGUM MUD HUTS

North Cameroon's Musgum people live in conical huts made of mud and grass. These structures are 32 ft. (10 m) tall and help to keep people cool on hot sunny days.

GLOBAL KILLER

The world's deadliest virus, HIV, has its origins in Cameroon, and has claimed the lives of millions of Africans and many other people worldwide. HIV is an infectious disease that traveled from animals to humans via a process called zoonosis.

BAMILEKE PEOPLE

With their famous beaded clothing, drum headwear, and colorful elephant masks, the Bamileke people from North Cameroon are one of the nation's most famous ethnic groups. Their *tsamassi* dance is just one of Cameroon's 200 known traditional dances.

EXPLODING LAKE!

The world's most feared exploding lake is Cameroon's Lake Nyos. Harmful carbon dioxide gas leaks into the water from a nearby volcano. In just one night in August 1986, around 2,000 people and 3,500 animals were killed by a gigantic cloud of the poisonous gas that was released into the air.

RED, WHITE AND BLUE MONKEY

You've never seen a monkey quite like a mandrill. With red, white, and blue markings all over their bottoms, bellies, and faces, these exotic creatures can be found in southern Cameroon. They're the world's largest monkeys!

WET WET WET!

Visitors to San Antonio de Ureca on Equatorial Guinea's Bioko Island need to be prepared for a downpour. With more than 411 inches of rain a year, it wins the award for "wettest place in all of Africa!"

FERNANDO POO

It was a Portuguese explorer named Fernão do Pó who discovered Equatorial Guinea's Bioko Island in 1472. After his death, Po became known as Fernando Poo!

Mbolo! With its capital city Malabo on its own little island, Equatorial Guinea is the only nation in Africa where a country and a capital are not on the same landmass.

Living in poor conditions, the Equatoguineans struggle to enjoy a good quality of life.

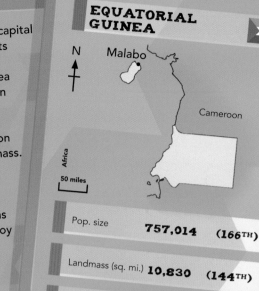

EQUATORIAL GUINEA

N

Malabo

Cameroon

Africa

50 miles

Pop. size	757,014	(166TH)
Landmass (sq. mi.)	10,830	(144TH)
Life Expectancy	63.49	(163RD)

BONGOS

Not a drum, but an antelope! With white stripes and long horns, the bongo lives among Equatorial Guinea's lush and dense forests.

SLIPPERY WHEN WET

The goliath frog—the world's largest—originates from the Monte Alen National Park area of Equatorial Guinea. They can grow larger than 11 in. (30 cm)—almost as big as a ruler!—and weigh as much as two bags of sugar. They are also very tasty, according to the locals.

ERIC THE EEL

At the 2000 Sydney Olympics, Eric Moussambani became an international celebrity and the most famous Equatoguinean. Nicknamed "Eric the eel," he placed last in the 100-meter freestyle race. His opponents swam the same distance in half the time, but the world loved him . . . and he set a new Equatorial Guinea record, so it wasn't all bad!

Goliath frog. Ribbit!

CENTRAL AFRICAN REPUBLIC

N

Chad

South Sudan

Bangui

DR Congo

Africa

200 miles

Pop. size	4,616,417	(121ST)
Landmass (sq mi)	240,534	(44TH)
Life Expectancy	51.35	(198TH)

Weighing in at twice the size of Poland, the Central African Republic (CAR) is located in the middle of the continent and, as such, is often regarded as the "real" Africa.

Nomadic tribes live in grass huts here, and it's teeming with a bonanza of wildlife, from gorillas to butterflies.

AKA PEOPLE

The wandering tribes of the Aka have their own language and are known for their close parenting, especially between child and father. The tribe is also known for teeth sharpening—a mating ritual where Aka teenagers' top and bottom front teeth are filed to a point.

Hypolimnas salmacis

FLUTTERBYS

The Central African Republic is famed for its butterfly population, with many hundreds of brightly colored, unique, and very large species. Sadly, butterfly hunters in the Bangui region catch and kill these tender insects and sell their wings to artists, who use them for mosaics. The wings of rare butterflies can be sold for hundreds of dollars.

Female Colotis danae

CANNIBAL DICTATOR

Jean-Bédel Bokassa gave himself such a lavish coronation ceremony that he almost bankrupted the entire country! If that wasn't bad enough, he was accused of being a cannibal and was said to have murdered—and eaten—his opponents, as well as feeding them to his pet crocodiles and lions!

Mylothris chloris

GORILLAS IN THE MIST

CAR has the largest lowland gorilla population in the world. The exact number is unknown, but it is believed that more than 2,000 reside in the Sangha Forest Reserve. These animals weigh 400 lb. (at least twice the weight of your dad!) and can grow over five and a half feet tall! The word "gorilla" comes from the Greek *gorillai*, meaning "tribe of hairy women!"

Jean-Bédel Bokassa

THAT'S RELATIVITY!

It took 6 minutes and 51 seconds to prove that Albert Einstein's world-changing theory of general relativity was correct. This was the duration of a total solar eclipse—the longest solar eclipse recorded—that was witnessed by Sir Arthur Eddington on Príncipe on May 29, 1919. The bending of light around the sun, as predicted by Einstein—and observed by relative positions of "nearby" stars—proved the genius physicist correct.

Once known as the Chocolate Isles, thanks to the Portuguese who started to farm cocoa beans here 500 years ago, Africa's second-smallest country is actually two small islands floating off the coast.

But it isn't just the chocolate that puts this island nation on the map—it's the wildlife too.

SÃO TOMÉ AND PRÍNCIPE

★ ★

N

Africa
20 miles

São Tomé

Pop. size	192,993	(183RD)
Landmass (sq mi)	372	(179TH)
Life Expectancy	64.22	(157TH)

WILD ORCHIDS

Due to its isolation from mainland Africa, São Tomé and Príncipe has many unique species of flora and fauna. The most exotic are the 129 species of orchid that grow among São Tomé's rainforest—dense jungle that covers 28 percent of the country.

THE BIG DOG

São Tomé's Cão Grande, or Big Dog, is a towering block of rock that was once part of a volcano. Rising out the jungle floor like a big thumb, Big Dog is 2,132 ft. (650 m) tall and is often shrouded in cloud.

CATCH A MARLIN

One of the more spectacular fish that swim in the salty seas surrounding São Tomé and Príncipe is the blue marlin. These fishies can weigh up to 1,985 lb. (900 kg) and each has a long spear pointing out of its head.

AUTO DE FLORIPES

Every August 10, the entire population of Príncipe—around 5,000 people—takes part in a dramatic performance that depicts the colonial battle between the Portuguese Christian invaders and the indigenous Moors. Everyone assumes a role and character and dresses up accordingly.

LEVE LEVE

It's not surprising that the residents of a beautiful island nation such as São Tomé and Príncipe—with its golden beaches, coconut trees, neon-blue lagoon and very warm waters—have a motto to live their life by. *Leve leve*, or "take it easy," is a maxim that all the islanders take seriously!

Blue marlin

GABON

N

Equatorial Guinea

Libreville

Africa

Congo

100 miles

Pop. size	1,671,711	(155TH)
Landmass (sq. mi.)	103,347	(77TH)
Life Expectancy	52.06	(194TH)

Historians have recorded that Gabon, covered in more than 85 percent rainforest, has been the hiding spot for humans for more than 400,000 years, and no wonder.

With amazing wildlife around every corner and some seriously lush landscapes, Gabon is the perfect place to get close to nature.

CIRQUE DE LECONI

Gabon's most famous natural landmark is the Cirque de Léconi—a red-rock canyon with a striking circular shape and a deep red color, which dates back many millions of years.

Sun-tailed monkey

GODZILLA!

What do you get if you cross an anteater with a lizard? A pangolin! These monster creatures don't eat humans, just ants and termites. Their scaly backs and giant size (5ft./1.5m in length), give them the appearance of a mini Godzilla!

Iboga plant

IBOGA

One of the three recognized religions of Gabon is Bwiti, practiced by the forest-dweller group, the Babongo. As part of the Bwiti initiation ceremony, young men ingest the root of an iboga plant for the first time. Iboga is said to cause powerful hallucinations that can last up to four days—the forest elephants are known to eat it too!

UNIQUE WILDLIFE

Gabon is famous for its unspoiled rainforest, which is filled with an incredible array of animals and birds. Some of these species are endemic to Gabon, which means they can't be found anywhere else in the world. One such creature is the sun-tailed monkey. This rare animal with its bright tail was only discovered in the 1980s.

CATCHING THE WAVES

Gabon is one of the only places in the world where you might be lucky enough to see a hippo frolicking in the surf! These hefty creatures love the waves and have been filmed bodysurfing at the beach of Loango National Park.

SPITTING DISTANCE
The Republic of Congo's capital city, Brazzaville, sits on the northern bank of the Congo River.

Brazzaville

CONGO RIVER

Kinshasa

On the other side of the river lies Kinshasa, the capital city of the Democratic Republic of Congo. This is the only example in the world where two capital cities are situated on the opposite sides of a river, facing one another.

Never to be confused with the Democratic Republic of Congo (see page 120), the Republic of Congo is surrounded by five neighboring nations.

Famously described as the "heart of darkness" by British writer Joseph Conrad, the Congo is a wild place indeed.

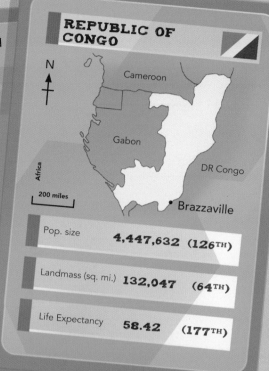

REPUBLIC OF CONGO

N

Cameroon

Gabon

DR Congo

Africa

200 miles

Brazzaville

Pop. size	4,447,632	(126TH)
Landmass (sq. mi.)	132,047	(64TH)
Life Expectancy	58.42	(177TH)

FUNKY ZOMBIE MAMBO
The Congo's largest ethnic group are the Kongo. The Kongans speak Kikongo, the language that gave the world the wonderful words "zombie," "funky" and "mambo!"

BUSHMEAT
A controversial type of dinner in the Congo is bushmeat. This is, basically, any type of mammal, insect or amphibian that can be hunted in tropical forests and eaten by those who don't have access to a regular supply of livestock. Bushmeat has been linked to the spread of the life-threatening viruses HIV and Ebola.

NGOMA
For the Kongo people drums—known as *ngoma*—are very important. Special and unique rhythms and beats are played on drums to signify death, birth or marriage.

Ngoma like this one are made of carved wood and have cowhide stretched across the top.

BOAT TO SCHOOL
How do you get to school? In the Congo, children skillfully glide past the crocodiles lurking in the Congo River in well-crafted, home-made wooden canoes.

SWIMMERS BEWARE!
Mokèlé-mbèmbé, or "one who stops the flow of waters," is a feared water monster that haunts the depths of the Congo River. This legendary long-necked, dinosaur-esque beast is a creature of sacred local mythology and can kill elephants who stand too close to the river's edge.

Mokèlé-mbèmbé

DEMOCRATIC REPUBLIC OF CONGO

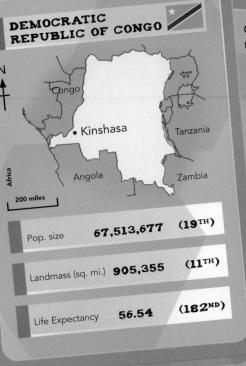

N

Congo

• Kinshasa

Tanzania

Africa

Angola

Zambia

200 miles

Pop. size	67,513,677	(19TH)
Landmass (sq. mi.)	905,355	(11TH)
Life Expectancy	56.54	(182ND)

Once known as Zaire, the Democratic Republic of Congo is home to 250 ethnic groups and 700 languages and is the most biodiverse region in the entire continent.

More than 60 percent of the mighty Congo River passes through this magical land.

IT'S BIG!

At almost one million square miles, this nation is huge. It's larger than the following countries combined: Spain, France, Germany, Sweden, and Norway!

THE GUNGU FESTIVAL

Held every July, the Gungu Festival promotes the traditional cultures of the forest-dwelling tribes, such as the Bapende, who dance in their tribe's carved wooden masks.

720 FT. DEEP

THE CONGO

The one and only Congo River gives life to a whopping 1.4 million sq. mi. (2.3 million km²) known as the Congo Basin. The Congo is almost 3,000 mi. (4,900 km) long and is the deepest river in the world. In places, it reaches 720 ft. (220 m) deep: you could stack two Statues of Liberty on top of one another and they'd still be completely submerged!

BONOBO-NO-MORE-NO

Bonobos, along with chimpanzees, are one of the closest primate relatives to human beings. This peaceful, intelligent and highly endangered creature is native to the Democratic Republic of Congo, where the world's only bonobo sanctuary, Lola Ya Bonobo, looks after orphaned bonobos. Human beings share 98.7 percent of our DNA with bonobos—we are more closely related to bonobos than they are to gorillas!

Statue of Liberty
305 FT.

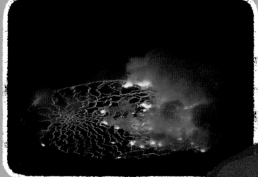

Okapi

BLOWING ITS TOP

Mount Nyiragongo is one of the planet's most active volcanoes. Its famous feature is its massive peak, whose center is a boiling lake of lava, constantly bubbling and over 1970 ft. deep!

FAMOUS FIGHT

The world's most famous boxing fight, between American boxers Muhammad Ali and George Foreman, took place in Kinshasa, on October 30, 1974. Billed as the "Rumble in the Jungle," the two fighters duked it out for the Heavyweight Championship of the World.

HALF ZEBRA, HALF GIRAFFE

The okapi lives nowhere else on Earth. With stripy legs (and butt!) and the head of a giraffe, these rather confused creatures can only be found in the Ituri Rainforest of the DRC.

DINNER IS SERVED

A popular Ugandan delicacy, sold at most markets, is a plate of crunchy grasshoppers! It is rude to say no if offered this treat, known locally as *nsenene*, so make sure you take a nice big handful!

The former British prime minister Winston Churchill once famously described Uganda as the Pearl of Africa. He's not wrong!

From gorillas to grasshoppers, wild water and even more gorillas (there are loads here!), Uganda is a gem.

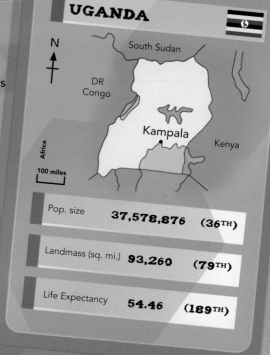

UGANDA

Pop. size **37,578,876** (36TH)

Landmass (sq. mi.) **93,260** (79TH)

Life Expectancy **54.46** (189TH)

WATER JET

Considered the most exciting part of the mighty Nile River, Murchison Falls is the 19-ft. (6-m.) gap where the river converges. This bottlenecking of the river causes a huge volume of water to shoot over the small gap with an explosive force—enough to blow your socks off!

MUZUNGUZUNGU

If traveling through Uganda—or any area of Central and Southern Africa, where the Bantu peoples dominate—you may hear the word *muzunguzungu*. Translated as "the look of a dizzy person," the word originally described the first European settlers, confused by their new surroundings. These days, the word has been adapted, and a *muzungu* is an affectionate term for someone with white skin.

EATS SHOOTS AND LEAVES

Known by scientists as *Gorilla beringei beringei*, mountain gorillas are a fascinating bunch. More than half of the world's mountain gorilla population call Uganda's Bwindi Impenetrable National Park home. The adult males are called silverbacks and they beat their chests with their fists when threatened.

Gorilla beringei beringei

Muzungu!

BILITA MPASH

Conjured up by the Bantu people, the state of *bilita mpash* refers not just to a really, really good dream, but a state of total bliss—a dream that makes you so happy you can never forget it. Have you had one of those lately?

TOMBS OF DEAD KINGS

The Tombs of Buganda Kings at Kasubi, with their large thatched roofs, are a sacred site in Uganda. Located here are the burial grounds for four kings of the Buganda Kingdom, known as Kabaka. For many centuries, ancient Buganda rituals, such as sacrifices and spirit conjuring, have been performed here.

KENYA

N ↑

Ethiopia
Uganda
Somalia
Nairobi
Africa
Tanzania

200 miles

Pop. size	44,353,691	(31ST)
Landmass (sq. mi.)	224,081	(49TH)
Life Expectancy	63.52	(160TH)

Everything in Kenya is jumbo. From its wildlife safaris to the height of the leaping Maasai people, and the greatest animal migration on earth to Africa's largest lakes and giant crocodiles.

In Kenya, size matters. It's big, but also beautiful.

LOTS OF LAKES

Due to the Great Rift Valley running through Kenya, the country is famous for its landscapes and lakes, including Lake Turkana—the world's largest permanent desert lake. But it is the colorful residents who are most famous. Bright pink flamingos wade in and out of Kenya's lakes, and can be seen in huge groups at Lake Bogoria and Lake Nakuru.

Think pink at Lake Nakuru!

ENDLESS PLAINS

Every year, the world's largest mammal migration occurs in the vast plains of the Serengeti. Between April and October, one million wildebeest, and hundreds of thousands of zebra travel across the Serengeti and through Kenya's Masai Mara—an epic odyssey that sees the animals search for food and fend off attacks from lions, leopards, and cheetahs.

LEAPING FOR JOY

The Masai Mara's Maasai warriors have a famous jumping dance ritual, known as *adumu*, which is performed at coming-of-age ceremonies when young men reach adulthood. This ceremony includes up to ten days of celebration . . . and jumping!

HOW DO YOU DO?

When members of the Maasai tribe greet an elder, or an important person from another village, they spit on their palm before shaking hands. It has also been observed that men spit on newborn babies and say they are "bad," in the belief that if they praise a baby, it will be cursed!

CIVIL WAR

Since the 1980s, millions of people have been affected by the Somali Civil War and famines. Many hundreds of thousands of refugees now live in makeshift huts built from any available material, struggling to survive.

YE BE PIRATES

Somalia is well known, and feared, for its pirates. Once fishermen, these ruthless figures have taken to seizing control of cargo ships in international waters and taking people on board hostage for large ransoms. In an effort to defend the Somalian coastline, the Royal Navy blasts Britney Spears' hit song *Oops! . . . I Did It Again*, hoping to scare them off!

Britney Spears

Often perceived as the least peaceful nation on earth, Somalia is plagued by bloody wars and disastrous droughts.

With Africa's longest coastline—over 1,879 mi. (3,025 km)—there is also much beauty to this controversial region known as the Horn of Africa.

SOMALIA

Ethiopia

Kenya

Africa

200 miles

Mogadishu

Pop. size	10,495,583	(83RD)
Landmass (sq. mi.)	246,199	(43RD)
Life Expectancy	51.58	(197TH)

LAND OF LEGEND

More than 5,000 years ago, the ancient Egyptians referred to Somalia as the Land of Punt. They valued its trees, which produced frankincense and myrrh: oils and spices that were presented as gifts at the birth of Jesus Christ. Ancient Romans called Somalia "Cape Aromatica" for its fragrances.

Frankincense and myrrh

HIDDEN GEM

Located in Somaliland, the Laas Geel cave paintings are the nation's outstanding cultural artifacts. More than 10,000 years old, the Neolithic rock art is the oldest in Africa and depicts humans worshipping animals. Due to its hidden location and lack of tourists, this cave art has remained in excellent condition.

NICKNAMES

Somalis love a good nickname, usually thought up by taking a physical attribute and identifying someone by it, i.e., big belly, strong muscles, or blond hair. The Somali word for "president" (*Madaxweyne*) literally means "Big Head," and the candidate with the biggest head usually wins!

Madaxweyne

ETHIOPIA

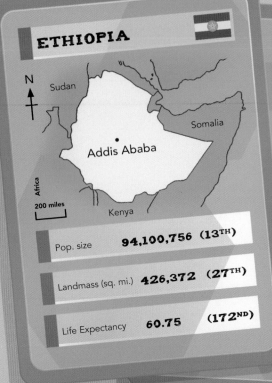

N

Sudan

Somalia

Addis Ababa

Africa

200 miles

Kenya

Pop. size	94,100,756	(13TH)
Landmass (sq. mi.)	426,372	(27TH)
Life Expectancy	60.75	(172ND)

Imagine France and Spain put together—that's the size of Ethiopia. It's gigantic.

More than 84 languages, 200 dialects, and 94 million people fill this region that breathed life into our earliest ancestors, earning it the name the 'cradle of humankind'.

THE ORIGINS OF SPECIES

Human life as we now know it began in Ethiopia. The earliest human fossils, dating back 200,000 years, have been found here, as well as the bones of Lucy—a member of the earliest hominid (human-like) species—which date back 3.2 million years. Stone tools, from 2.5 million years ago, have also been discovered.

THE COFFEE CEREMONY

The coffee plant, *Coffea arabica*, originates in Ethiopia and the drink is celebrated each day with a ritual known as the Coffee Ceremony. Occurring at breakfast, noon, and dinnertime, the ritual can take a few hours to perform, with the coffee beans roasted and then poured in ornate, ancient coffee pots. The Ethiopian saying *Buna dabo naw* means "Coffee is our bread."

HAMER TIME

In the Ethiopian Hamer tribe, young boys must take part in an iconic coming-of-age ritual. They must run, jump and land on the back of a bull and then run across the backs of several bulls in order to prove their manhood. They do this multiple times, usually wearing no clothes. If they are successful, they are permitted to choose a wife.

THE ETHIOPIAN CALENDAR

Ethiopia is the only country in the world to celebrate 13 months in a year! Not only that, but their calendar is different as well—the country is around 7.5 years behind the rest of the world.

HOLY ROCK

The cave churches in the sacred city of Lalibela are carved straight into one massive piece of rock. The doors and windows have also been skillfully carved so you can go inside, too!

LIVE AID

In 1985, Ethiopia's drought and famine became world news. To raise awareness for the millions of people living in these desperate conditions, singers Bob Geldof and Midge Ure created the charity Live Aid. Today, the charity still raises money for Africans in need by releasing the single *Do They Know It's Christmas*, featuring many of the world's most famous artists.

BABOON HEART

Ethiopia is home to a strange species known as bleeding-heart baboons. Known by monkey scientists as *gelada*, these creatures have a bright red patch on their chest and live only in the country's Simien Mountains.

WHERE YOUR SALARY COMES FROM

The lowest point in Africa, found deep in a crater 490 ft. below sea level, is the world's second saltiest lake, Lake Assal. When the water evaporates away in the dry season due to the suffocating heat, a thick crust of salt is left behind on the shoreline—the world's largest salt reserve. For centuries the Afar people of Djibouti would trade salt blocks, called *amole*, as currency. The word *salary* actually comes from *salurium*, meaning salt money!

It was dubbed the "Valley of Hell" by Europeans in the 18th century, because it is unbelievably hot and dry, but Djibouti is a mysterious and underappreciated land, boasting some of East Africa's most dramatic and bizarre landscapes.

Say *tasharrafna*, or "pleased to meet you," to Djibouti!

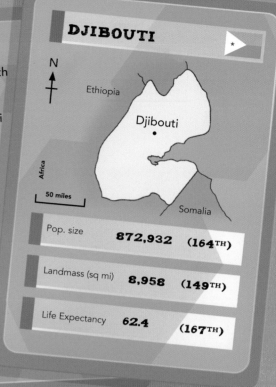

DJIBOUTI

N

Ethiopia

Djibouti

Africa

50 miles

Somalia

Pop. size	872,932	(164TH)
Landmass (sq mi)	8,958	(149TH)
Life Expectancy	62.4	(167TH)

MOONSCAPE

Lake Abbe is one of the hottest places on earth. Vast columns of rock called limestone chimneys emerge from the flat plains, giving the eerie feeling that you could be standing on the moon.

KHAT'S GOT THEIR TONGUE

Khat, or qat, is an important—if unhealthy—part of local culture. This addictive plant, legal in Djibouti, is chewed by most of the male population and leaves its consumers in a heightened state of euphoria and hyperactivity.

AFAR PEOPLE

Many of the Afar people have a distinctive Afro hairstyle, know as *gunfura*, created using butter. This not only protects their heads from the blistering sun, but also makes them look cool too! Sometimes men will spit on the *gunfura* of other tribesmen—a blessing, not a rude gesture.

WHAT A FISH!

The world's largest fish, the whale shark, swims in the oceans of the Djibouti Gulf and near the Bay of Tadjoura. These gentle monsters of the sea can grow up to 46 ft. (14 m) long—about the same as a double-decker bus! They live for more than 70 years and only eat tiny organisms called plankton.

Whale shark

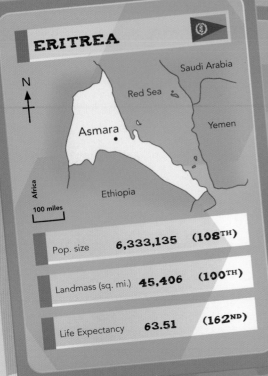

ERITREA

Saudi Arabia
Red Sea
Asmara
Yemen
Africa
Ethiopia
100 miles

Pop. size	6,333,135	(108TH)
Landmass (sq. mi.)	45,406	(100TH)
Life Expectancy	63.51	(162ND)

Eritrea and Ethiopia became independent from each other in 1993.

While the two nations share many customs, Eritrea is actually ten times smaller than its neighbor and, in recent years, has become one of the most isolated nations on earth.

The venomous titan triggerfish has been known to attack and bite divers.

THE RED SEA

Featured in the biblical story of Moses, the very warm and salty Red Sea is the 190-mile-wide dividing line between Africa and Saudi Arabia in Asia. The body of water is home to many neon-colored coral fish, including the dangerous titan triggerfish, scorpionfish, and rabbitfish, as well as up to 44 species of shark.

TIGRINYA PEOPLE

Eritrea's largest ethnic group is the Tigrinya people, making up more than 50 percent of the population. Females in the Tigrinya are famous for having very large, golden-colored nose rings!

MAD MEDEBAR

One of the capital city's largest markets is Medebar, and it's a pretty unusual place. Here you can find the recycling market—lots of tiny workshops where all sorts of things are turned into other things! Old tires are made into sandals, olive cans become little coffeepots, and even used artillery shells find new lives as combs! Nothing goes to waste.

THE RED SEA

ERITREA

BLACK MAMBA

Africa's most poisonous snake, the black mamba is also the world's fastest snake! With a top speed of over 12 mph. and a length of 13 ft. (4 m), you don't want this guy chasing after you! Two drops of a black mamba's venom can kill a person; a mamba can have as much as 20 drops in its fangs, ready to inject.

TUTSIS AND HUTUS

In 1994, the genocide (a term to describe the eradication of an entire race or group of people) of the Tutsi, a Rwandan ethnic group, by Hutu extremists, made international headlines. In just three months, thousands of people from both tribes were killed. Following the war, Rwanda—once defined by its tribal divisions—began asking its people to come together as one, no more Tutsis or Hutus—just Rwandans.

As part of Africa's Great Lakes region, Rwanda is known as the Land of a Thousand Hills—a country that is geographically at the center of Africa, but a nation torn in two by recent civil wars.

In the 21st century, Rwanda is on the road to peace and prosperity.

RWANDA

N

DR Congo · Uganda

· Kigali

Africa

Tanzania

Burundi

50 miles

Pop. size	11,776,522	(74TH)
Landmass (sq. mi.)	10,169	(147TH)
Life Expectancy	59.26	(176TH)

INTORE DANCERS

Moving to the beat of an *igoma* (drum), Rwanda's iconic Intore dancers were once warriors who performed the "Dance of Heroes" for their Tutsi king upon returning from war. Wearing long skirts and twirling spears, the dancers scream battle cries and stomp their feet aggressively while shaking their long blond hairpieces about!

BASKET MAKERS

Rwandan women are famous for their basketwork, a major source of income, tradition and pride. With a typical zigzag design, a nod to the country's hilly geography, the baskets have served many purposes in Rwandan history, most notably for carrying around secrets!

FANCY A DRINK?

Don't expect to see many Rwandans using glasses or cups. At traditional local bars, people tend to drink their homemade beer from cans and hollowed-out gourds—pumpkin-like fruits from the calabash tree—often using a straw.

IMIGONGO

Rwanda's *imigongo* is the country's most popular, and ancient, form of art—made from cow dung! Patterns and shapes are painted onto freshly made cow poo and then brightly colored using chalk and clays. The paintings highlight Rwandan love of local flora and fauna—but don't stand too close!

A zig-zag example of *imigongo*

BURUNDI

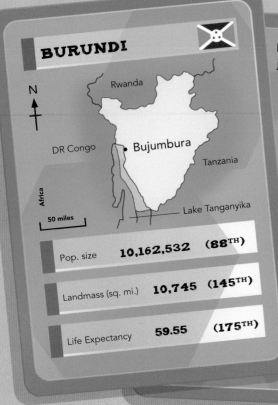

Rwanda

DR Congo

Bujumbura

Tanzania

Africa

Lake Tanganyika

50 miles

Pop. size	10,162,532	(88TH)
Landmass (sq. mi.)	10,745	(145TH)
Life Expectancy	59.55	(175TH)

Burundi is one of just two African nations colonized by Belgium.

This tiny nation, sandwiched between the Democratic Republic of Congo and Tanzania, is one of the world's poorest nations. Nonetheless, it boasts some amazing people and spectacular sights.

EUREKA TANGANYIKA!

The world's longest freshwater lake, Lake Tanganyika, is part of the African Great Lakes region. Its length is a whopping 410 mi. (660 km), making it longer than Ireland! It is home to 350 species of fish, including this guy, the Giant Nile Perch, which can grow to 6 ft. in length.

Giant Nile Perch

HERE COME THE DRUMS

Burundi's internationally famous Royal Drummers are loud and proud. Playing drums made from hollowed-out tree trunks covered in animal skins, the drummers choreograph complex and athletic rhythms with energetic dancing. The drum-playing skills are passed down from father to son; the drums themselves are a Burundi tradition symbolizing fertility and rebirth.

Lake Tanganyika is bordered by four countries: Burundi, Tanzania, Democratic Republic of Congo, and Zambia

DR. LIVINGSTONE, I PRESUME?

In the mid 1800s, Dr. David Livingstone traveled to Africa and, by doing so, became the first European to extensively explore the continent. Before he left, Livingstone's goal was to study the African people, the land and, most importantly, to see an end to the slave trade. His famous disappearance in 1865—when he got very lost—hit headlines all over the world. What had become of Dr. Livingstone? In 1871, newspaper journalist Henry Stanley set out on a quest to find the doctor. After eight months, he found his man and uttered the celebrated phrase, "Dr Livingstone, I presume?" The Pierre de Livingstone et Stanley is a large rock in Burundi that commemorates the visit the two explorers made to the country after they had found each other.

Henry Stanley

La Pierre de Livingstone et Stanley

Dr. David Livingstone

THE ROOF OF AFRICA

Mt. Kilimanjaro is the highest mountain in Africa as well as the planet's tallest mountain not part of a mountain chain. Standing at 19,341 ft. (almost 10,000 ft. less than Mt. Everest), the weather at the bottom of Kilimanjaro is tropical—hot, sticky, and humid—while the weather at the top is arctic—cold, snowy, and windy.

Tanzania is one of Africa's big hitters, featuring some of the continent's icons, from the plains of the Serengeti to the peak of Kilimanjaro.

A nation twice the size of California, Tanzania is not only huge in size, but it's an absolute goldmine of geographical beauty, wildlife, and local customs.

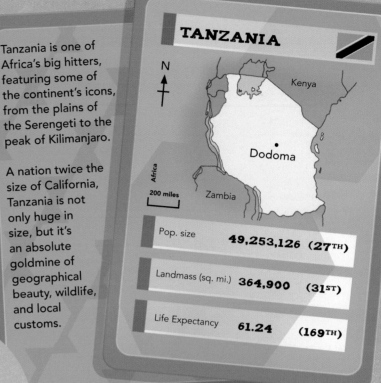

TANZANIA

Kenya

Dodoma

Africa

200 miles

Zambia

Pop. size	49,253,126	(27TH)
Landmass (sq. mi.)	364,900	(31ST)
Life Expectancy	61.24	(169TH)

LONG STORY SHORT

The shortest war ever fought was between Zanzibar, in Tanzania, and Britain, on August 27, 1896. It lasted 38 minutes.

WILD WILDLIFE

Tanzania's parks have some of the largest concentrations of wildlife per square kilometre anywhere on the globe, with more than four million wild animals from 430 species, including zebras, elephants, hippos, giraffes, buffaloes, and wildebeest.

SHIKAMOO

Greetings are important in Tanzania and are respected. Tanzanian children are trained from an early age to greet their elders with the word *shikamoo*, literally translated as "I hold your feet," followed by a bow or curtsy.

Giraffes

DIK-DIK

One of Tanzania's smallest residents is the dik-dik—a type of antelope no bigger than 16 in. (40 cm). When these baby creatures are in trouble, they whistle for help.

GOT THE GIGGLES

In 1962, a laughter epidemic tickled Tanzania's funny bone—for a whole year! The epidemic caused several thousands of people to laugh uncontrollably non-stop, and the giggles spread to many villages.

WEIGHT LIFTERS

Tanzania's dung beetles are the strongest insects on the planet. These crafty critters can pull more than 1,141 times their own body weight. That's the equivalent of a human pulling six double-decker buses!

MOZAMBIQUE

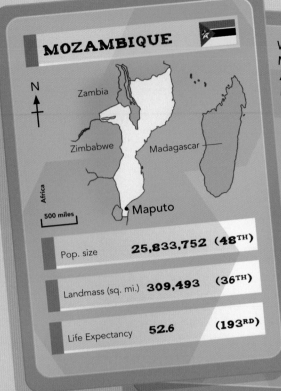

N

Zambia

Zimbabwe

Madagascar

Africa

500 miles

Maputo

Pop. size	25,833,752	(48TH)
Landmass (sq. mi.)	309,493	(36TH)
Life Expectancy	52.6	(193RD)

Welcome to Mozambique, East Africa's land of sky-blue seas, swamps, and sand.

It's a fusion of Portuguese, African, Indian, and Arabic cultures; a nation of dancers and dugongs; and a tropical paradise where the mysterious Madagascar is only a boat ride away. . .

DOING THE MAPIKO

The most well-known example of a local ceremony in Mozambique is the *mapiko* dance of the Makonde people. The men cover themselves with cloth and wear oversized, carved wooden masks of male faces. The dance is designed to frighten the local females and has grown out of male attempts to challenge the power of their women, because the Makonde are a society ruled by the mothers.

FACE MASK

The Musiro face mask is more than just a beauty regime in northern Mozambique. Made from the branch of a ximbuti tree, the medicinal (and cosmetic) paste is applied to women's faces to keep their skin looking young, protect them from the sun's rays and to signify their social status. You'll often see women walking around with the paste on!

HOT AND SPICY

When the Portuguese came to conquer Mozambique in the 16th century, they brought chili peppers with them. Known in the local tongue as *piri-piri* ("pepper pepper"), these hot additions to the local meals have, centuries later, become part of the national cuisine.

DHOW STREAM

Mozambique is famous for the giant (and delicious) Lourenco Marques prawns that swim in the coastal waters. Prawn fishermen use simple sailboats called *dhows* to transport their catch of the day from the coast inland via the mangrove swamps.

Lourenco Marques prawn

A lioness surveying her territory

PRIDE OF LION

Lions are one of the proudest and most dramatic symbols of Africa, although there are only around 35,000 of them left in the wild. Mozambique's Niassa Reserve is working hard to increase the population of these incredible creatures. Male lions defend their territories, which can be as large as 155 sq. mi. (250 km^2), and protect their cubs, while the females do most of the hunting. Lions mark their territory with very smelly pee.

LAKE MALAWI

One of the African Great Lakes, Lake Malawi has more kinds of fish than any other freshwater system on Earth, with more than 850 species. Explorer David Livingstone called it The Lake of the Stars because the fishing boats' lanterns, reflected in the crystal-clear water, mirrored the stars in the sky.

Let's start off by saying *zikomo* ("thank you") to Malawi. The people here are known as the friendliest and most polite in all of Africa.

The locals' hospitality has earned the country its nickname the Warm Heart of Africa.

MALAWI

N

Tanzania

Zambia

Mozambique

Lilongwe

Africa

100 miles

Pop. size	16,362,567	(65TH)
Landmass (sq. mi.)	45,747	(99TH)
Life Expectancy	59.99	(173RD)

SAY IT RIGHT

Malawians have a saying: *chimanga ndi moyo*, or "corn is life." For 80 percent of all Malawians, life revolves around growing enough corn, also known as maize, to feed the family.

THE CHEWA TRIBE

The Chewa Tribe—one of Malawi's main ethnic groups—performs the traditional *gulu wamkulu*, or "Great Dance," for special ceremonies. Dancers move as if possessed by the spirits of the masks they wear. The Chewa people believe that these spirits are animals called *nyama* and *mizumi* and are the spirits of their dead ancestors.

MALAWISAURUS

With a length of 30 ft. (9 m), the Malawisaurus (Malawi lizard) was a type of sauropod (long-necked dinosaur) that roamed the savannas of Malawi 140 million years ago. Fossils of this great lizard were discovered in Karongo.

BIRD-SPOTTING PARADISE

Malawi is home to more than 650 bird species, including the beautifully colored African pygmy kingfisher. This tiny bird flashes through the air and snaps up insects and spiders for its dinner.

ZAMBIA

N

DR Congo

Lusaka

Africa

Zimbabwe

200 miles

Pop. size	14,538,640	(70TH)
Landmass (sq. mi.)	290,585	(39TH)
Life Expectancy	51.83	(196TH)

Zambia is one of Africa's top safari destinations. It's packed with amazing wildlife and friendly people who make great guides.

From roaring big cats and thundering waterfalls to busy copper mines and colorful local customs, Zambia is a must-visit for any explorer.

TOP SPOT FOR LEOPARDS

Zambia's South Luangwa National Park is one of the best spots to spot a leopard's spots. The strongest species of Africa's big cats, leopards can climb trees, swim across lakes, and purr when they're happy.

THE LOZI KING

The remarkable Kuomboka ceremony takes place every year when the plains around Mongu become flooded. The tradition's name means "get out of the water"; it follows the Lozi king as he directs his tribe to higher ground to escape the flood. Spectators watch the king's black-and-white painted barge travel up the Zambezi River, accompanied by over 100 rowers. The barge has a large black replica of an elephant on top!

BRIDGE OVER TROUBLED WATER

The Victoria Falls Bridge connects Zambia with neighbor Zimbabwe, and serves as the border between the two nations. The bridge is almost 656 ft. (200 m) in length and was constructed in 1905. For many years it was the site of the world's longest bungee jump, with many bungee jumpers diving off the bridge and dunking their heads in the Zambezi River below!

SPLASH DOWN

Zambia's most iconic natural landmark is Victoria Falls. It has a brilliant local nickname: the Smoke That Thunders. It's the largest waterfall in the world, with more than 500 million liters of water pouring over the edge every minute! That's enough water to fill 200 Olympic Swimming pools every minute!

GOING BATTY

If you thought the wildebeest migration across the Serengeti was impressive, then you'll go batty about Zambia's fruit-bat migration. Every November more than eight million fruit bats flock to Kasanka's National Park. They come to Zambia to give birth and fill up on essential foods.

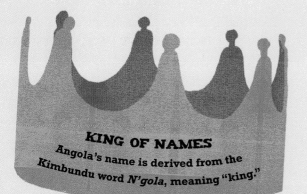

KING OF NAMES

Angola's name is derived from the Kimbundu word *N'gola*, meaning "king."

MWILA TRIBE

In southern Angola, women in the Mwila tribe, from the Huila region, wear brightly colored headdresses and beaded necklaces. They put them on when they enter maturity and never remove them for the rest of their lives. The colors of the necklace relate to the person's marital or social status.

Angola's history is a million miles away from its potential future, but it has left the country scarred and underdeveloped when compared to its neighbors.

However, when it comes to people and their traditions, Angola is home to some of the most fascinating and beautiful tribes on the planet.

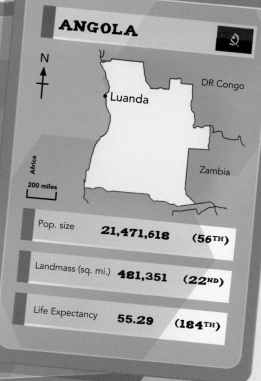

ANGOLA

N

Luanda

DR Congo

Zambia

Africa

200 miles

Pop. size	21,471,618	(56TH)
Landmass (sq. mi.)	481,351	(22ND)
Life Expectancy	55.29	(184TH)

GHOST TOWN

Africa's first "ghost town," Kilamba New City, is the largest of several satellite cities being constructed by Chinese firms in Angola. It was designed to be a state-of-the-art city for 500,000 local people, with over 750 eight-story apartment blocks. However, Angolans cannot afford to live there, and for the past four years the entire city has been almost empty!

IMBONDEIRO

Angola's national tree is the awesome imbondeiro. According to legend, the imbondeiro tree was the first tree ever planted, but after it grumbled about the majesty of other trees being planted nearby, the gods picked up the imbondeiro tree and planted it upside down just to keep it quiet . . . and it kept on growing like that!

SHIPWRECK BEACH

Around the world, there are more than three million shipwrecks on the ocean floor, but on Angola's Shipwreck Beach, a 1.5-mi. (2.4-km) stretch of golden sand, there are more than 20 rusting and abandoned vessels of different types, from cargo ships to massive tankers to tiny tugs.

NAMIBIA

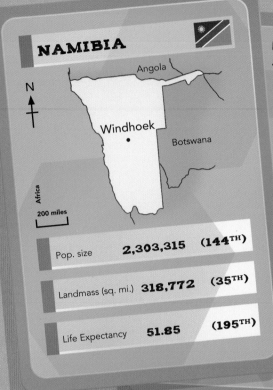

Angola

Windhoek

Botswana

N

Africa

200 miles

Pop. size	2,303,315	(144TH)
Landmass (sq. mi.)	318,772	(35TH)
Life Expectancy	51.85	(195TH)

Namibia is one of Africa's most striking countries. Home to the mammoth Namib and Kalahari Deserts, this southeastern African nation is a very hot and sandy place!

But that's not all. From sand dunes to scorpions and skeletons, Namibia is a place full of special secrets.

HOLY MOLY HOBA METEORITE!

Around 80,000 years ago, the largest meteorite to ever crash land on earth smashed into Namibia. Weighing around 66 tons, the Hoba meteorite, as it is known, is made of pure iron and was discovered by a farmer in 1920. Scientists believe that the meteorite skipped across the surface of Earth's atmosphere like a stone skipping on water, before being sucked in by gravity!

SPECIAL K

The Kalahari Desert has many inhabitants, from gazelles to giraffes, lions, and elephants, but it is the Kung people, a nomadic tribe of hunter-gatherers, that are the most fascinating. To pronounce "Kung" correctly you must make a clicking sound before the *k*. This click is usually expressed in writing with an exclamation mark: !Kung.

BRIGHT RED HIMBA

The nomadic Himba people of northern Namibia glow a bright red! By covering their skin and hair in ochre (a natural earth pigment containing iron oxide) and butter, they protect themselves from the unrelenting desert sun.

ZEBRA ON THE MENU

One minute you may see a gang of zebra taking a dip in a cool lagoon in the Etosha National Park, the next a zebra steak may end up on your plate. Zebra is a popular delicacy in Namibia. Could you eat it?

THE GREAT THIRST

Namibia's Kalahari Desert is one of southern Africa's iconic deserts. In the Tswana language, the Kalahari is known as "the great thirst." It is thought that the desert is more than sixty million years old!

Namib dune
1148 FT.

A STING IN THE TAIL

Many scorpions, such as the black hairy thick-tailed scorpion, live in the Namib and Kalahari deserts. They are the most poisonous of all scorpions found in Africa.

Spring Temple Buddha, China
502 FT.

Big Ben, London
315 FT.

Statue of Liberty, New York
305 FT.

SAND DUNES

The Namib Desert has the world's largest sand dunes and is believed to be the world's oldest desert. Many of the sand dunes are more than 1148 ft. high! People from all over the world come to ride the dunes—a bit like snowboarding but much, much hotter!

COMPARE THE MEERKAT

The world's cutest animal roams the dry dunes of the Kalahari Desert. Yes, Botswana is one of the places meerkats call home. Living in groups called mobs, meerkats survive this harsh climate by sniffing out spiders, snakes, grubs and lizards. A mob member always stands guard as other meerkats eat.

Covered by the great lake of sand known as the Kalahari Desert, Botswana is a flat and arid country with some strange inhabitants!

With wild dogs who hunt people; the native San who speak with clicks; "earth pigs" such as aardvarks; and mongooses known as meerkats, Botswana is a place you can't miss!

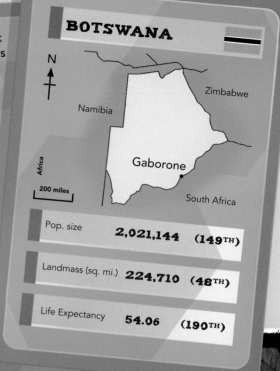

BOTSWANA

Namibia
Zimbabwe
Gaborone
South Africa

Africa
200 miles

Pop. size	2,021,144	(149TH)
Landmass (sq. mi.)	224,710	(48TH)
Life Expectancy	54.06	(190TH)

THE SAN PEOPLE

With a culture dating back more than 100,000 years, the nomadic San people of Botswana are as ancient as the Kalahari. Using wood made from quiver trees, these highly skilled hunters shoot poisoned arrows to kill prey, such as zebra. The heat in Botswana can be so fierce that the San people collect water in large ostrich eggs, which they then bury in the sand and come back to later on. The sand keeps the water fresh and cool.

A NEW CANOE

One of Botswana's most popular tourist trips is taking a trip in a traditional canoe, known as a *mokoro*, down the Okavango Delta, often believed to be the wildest part of Africa. The water in the delta never reaches the sea, nor does it rejoin the Okavango River; instead, it either sinks into the desert or evaporates away due to the blistering heat of the sun.

LOUVRE OF THE DESERT

4,500 rock paintings have been found at Tsodilo in Botswana. This small part of the Kalahari Desert has been given the nickname the Louvre of the Desert, after France's famous Louvre art gallery in Paris.

KALAHARI ELEPHANTS

Standing out like a sore thumb against the bright gold background, you'll find the dark grey hide of African elephants at Chobe National Park. There are more African elephants in Botswana than anywhere else—around 130,000! The largest-ever African elephant weighed ten tons—the same weight as 135 average-sized people!

ZIMBABWE

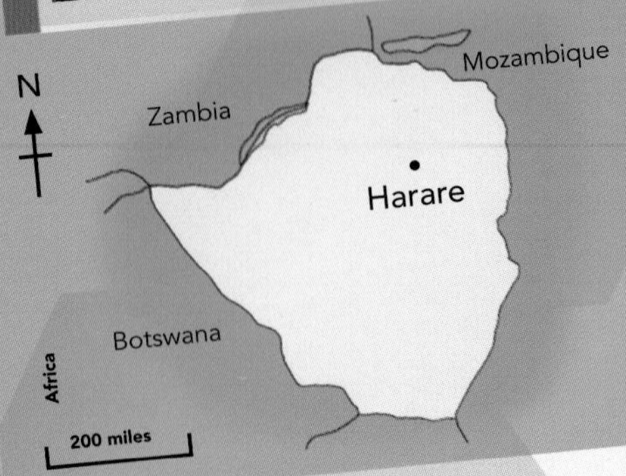

Mozambique

Zambia

N

Harare

Botswana

Africa

200 miles

Pop. size	14,149,648	(71ST)
Landmass (sq. mi.)	150,872	(61ST)
Life Expectancy	55.68	(183RD)

Zimbabwe has been through its fair share of financial and political troubles, but things are getting better and better for this beautiful country.

Visitors are starting to return to Zimbabwe to experience its incredible wildlife, breathtaking scenery and colorful traditions.

HOLD ON TO YOUR PADDLE!

With the world's largest sheet of falling water, Victoria Falls, as a backdrop, the mighty Zambezi River is the best place to make a splash and go whitewater rafting. With over 22 types of dangerous, fast-flowing rapids, the Zambezi River's twists and turns are the biggest in the world, and they include several Class 5s – the most dangerous! The rapids' names are also spectacular: the Devil's Toilet Bowl, Oblivion, Morning Glory and Stairway to Heaven.

SHINE A LIGHT ON THE SHONA

Zimbabwe's largest ethnic group is the Shona. They believe in ancestral spirits, and they are well known for their stone sculptures and totems, using the multi-colored serpentine stone, a type of rock that is more than 2.5 billion years old.

TRILLIONAIRES

A trip to Zimbabwe might make you a trillionaire. The 100-trillion-dollar banknote was introduced to cope with the country's financial crisis and hyperinflation of the nation's currency, the Zimbabwean dollar, which was abandoned in 2009. Today, the 100-trillion-dollar banknote can be bought on eBay!

ONE HUNDRED TRILLION DOLLARS

RESERVE BANK OF ZIMBABWE

NO LAUGHING MATTER

Hyenas, or *Crocuta crocuta*, are Africa's most common carnivore, and can be spotted in the savanna and grasslands across Africa. Hyenas are known for their distinct "laughter," a sound that can be used as an alarm to warn other hyenas of predators from over three miles away.

ART ROCKS!

Zimbabwe's Matobo National Park is the place to see sacred balancing rocks—naturally forming rock shapes made out of pure granite. Pictured here is the mother and child kopje—a fantastic rock formation created not by man but by mother nature!

TABLE MOUNTAIN

Shaped flat like, well, a table, Table Mountain is one of the oldest mountains in the world. Often covered in thick white cloud, known as Table Cloth, the mountain sits at more than 3,280 ft. (1,000 m) above sea level. At the top of the mountain, vervet monkeys steal tourists' snacks from out of their hands!

Halfway between the equator and Antarctica sits South Africa, the southern tip of the African continent.

From great white sharks to table mountains, apartheid to Zulu warriors, cheetahs to peacemakers, South Africa is no longer a country that sees things in black and white.

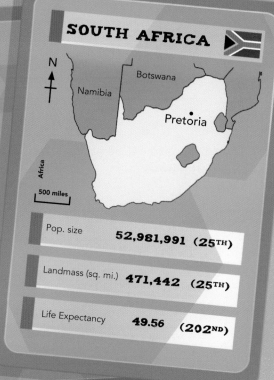

SOUTH AFRICA

Namibia · Botswana · Pretoria · Africa

500 miles

Pop. size	52,981,991	(25TH)
Landmass (sq. mi.)	471,442	(25TH)
Life Expectancy	49.56	(202ND)

SPEEDY GONZALEZ!

The planet's fastest land mammal, the cheetah, can run over 70 mph. (112 km/h)—faster than most cars on a highway! These magnificent creatures with golden fur and black spots never fully retract their claws, helping them to run more quickly.

Cheetah

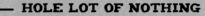

HOLE LOT OF NOTHING

South Africa may be known for its diamonds . . . but it's just as famous for its diamond mines. The world's biggest manmade hole, known (imaginatively) as the Big Hole, can be seen at the site of the now-abandoned Kimberly diamond mine. Some 50,000 miners dug up more than 22 million tons of earth by hand. The hole is 705 ft. (215 m) deep and yielded more than 14,500,000 carats of diamonds from 1871 to 1914.

GREAT WHITE

Off the coast of Gansbaai, at South Africa's most southerly tip, is Shark Alley: a strip of water between two rocky islands where thousands of seals become lunch for the great white sharks that lurk beneath the waters. Every year, tourists come to swim in the waters with the sharks. They are protected by a cage, but it's still an experience that's not for the faint-hearted

ZULULAND

The Zulu were once great warriors feared by everyone and are perhaps the most famous of all Africa's indigenous tribes. Shaka Zulu, who died in 1828, was the king of the Zulus, a respected military genius who created new battle and warfare techniques, and who united the separate tribes of Southern Africa to found the Zulu Kingdom.

Nelson Mandela

REVOLUTION!

After spending 27 years in prison for fighting for equal rights for black South Africans, the national hero, Nelson Mandela, became South Africa's first freely elected president in 1994. He died in 2013 and was mourned by millions of people all over the world.

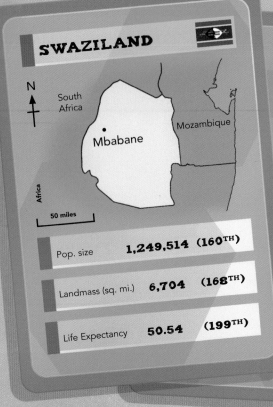

SWAZILAND

N

South Africa

Mbabane

Mozambique

Africa

50 miles

Pop. size	1,249,514	(160TH)
Landmass (sq. mi.)	6,704	(168TH)
Life Expectancy	50.54	(199TH)

Swaziland still embraces its own traditional cultures and customs and has largely yet to move forward into the modern world.

Surrounded by Mozambique and South Africa, the Kingdom of Swaziland has had human inhabitants for 200,000 years.

UMLHANGA CEREMONY

The reed dance ceremony, or *umlhanga*, is an eight-day-long event that brings together tens of thousands of the country's young, unmarried and childless women. They gather at the queen mother's residence, where they cut down tall reeds and fix up the fence around the royal village. Once that task is complete, the women dance for the royal family and a feast begins. The purpose of the *umlhanga* is to unite the nation's women . . . and also to fix the queen's fence!

INCWALA CEREMONY

Another of Swaziland's ancient traditions is the *incwala* ceremony, an event to celebrate renewal and a new season, and to praise the king. This six-day event sees thousands of Swazi people dance, feast, and perform rituals while wearing battledress and traditional robes. On day four, the main day, the king emerges and throws a sacred gourd onto a black shield.

INTO THE WILD

Critically endangered, black rhinos are on the verge of extinction. This generation may be the last to see this majestic creature in the wild. Believed to be more than 50 million years old, black rhinos can weigh up to 2,976 lb. (1,350 kg)!

WITCH DOCTORS

Swaziland's *sangomas*, or spirit doctors, play a respected role in traditional culture, especially at the Mantenga Village. Here the *sangoma* will bring balance between the living and the dead, protect warriors, perform ritual and animal sacrifices and heal the sick with the supernatural powers of ancient spirits.

YOU HAVE BEEN WARNED

If you ever find yourself tucking into a meal in Swaziland, only use your right hand to eat your food. Using your left hand is rude; that's normally the hand you wipe your butt with! The commonly used SiSwati language has no words for "right" or "left." So, if you want to tell someone to turn left, you say "the side of the hand with which you do not eat!"

CLOSE TO THE EDGE

Lesotho's Matekane is a notorious airport landing strip, where a 1,300 ft. (400 m) runway extends over the edge of a 2,000 ft. (600 m) cliff! It's a scary place to land—or take off—but the views are fantastic!

Buried within the borders of South Africa is the tiny country of Lesotho. Sometimes called the Kingdom of the Sky, it's the only country on earth located 3,280 ft. (1,000 m) above sea level.

Lesotho is the cold, mountainous (and sometimes snowy) cousin of Africa's main desert countries.

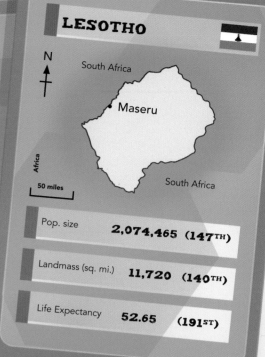

LESOTHO

Maseru

South Africa

South Africa

Africa

50 miles

Pop. size	2,074,465	(147TH)
Landmass (sq. mi.)	11,720	(140TH)
Life Expectancy	52.65	(191ST)

HATS OFF TO THE BASOTHO

Basotho hats are the national symbol of the Basotho people. Shaped like cones and made from straw, the hats are topped off with a knot.

THABA BOSIU

Lesotho's magical Thaba Bosiu (Mountain at Night) is a flat-topped sandstone plateau that provided a perfect lookout spot, and natural fortress, for Chief Moshoeshoe in the 19th century to spot invading Ndebele people. Being 394 ft. (120 m) higher than the surrounding area gave the chief a great vantage point. It is called the Mountain at Night because enemies believed the mountain looked bigger at night!

LIZARD FROM LESOTHO

Looking like a tiny T. Rex, with little hands that would not have been able to pick up anything properly, a Lesothosaurus was a small dinosaur discovered in Lesotho in 1978. Fossils date this mini-dino back 200 million years.

Lesothosaurus

BURIED UPRIGHT

Basotho people are buried in a sitting position, with their bodies facing toward the east and the rising sun. This is so the bodies can be ready to leap up if called upon by the ancient spirits in the afterlife.

WOW WATERFALLS...

Just a few miles away from the village of Semonkong is one of the planet's most fascinating fast-flowing high waterfalls: Maletsunyane Falls. Frothing white water cascades 630 feet over the edge of a V-shaped cliff into a lush, green canyon.

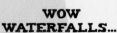

MADAGASCAR

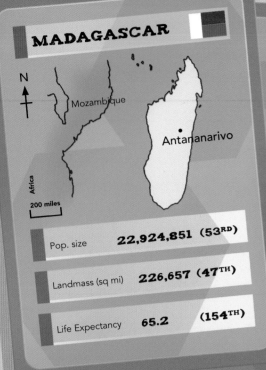

N

Mozambique

Antananarivo

Africa

200 miles

Pop. size	22,924,851 (53RD)
Landmass (sq mi)	226,657 (47TH)
Life Expectancy	65.2 (154TH)

160 million years ago, the land of Madagascar tore away from coast of Mozambique and drifted hundreds of miles from the African mainland.

This isolation has resulted in an explosion of incredible geographical and natural wonders.

MALAGASY PEOPLE

Madagascar isn't all about the exotic wildlife. The people are fascinating too. Divided into 20 ethnic groups, the Malagasy people are the indigenous residents of the island. The Sakalava tribe, who live on the western edge of the island, are well-known for the colorful custom of painting their faces for ceremonies.

ALLÉE DES BAOBABS

One of Madagascar's most striking landmarks is the Allée des Baobabs, an alley of 25 majestic baobab trees. These 98-foot-tall trees, with their fat trunks and sparse leaf foliage, can store 26,396 gallons of water (120,000 liters) in order to survive dry season.

WONDERFUL WILDLIFE

Over 70 percent of the 250,000 wildlife species in Madagascar are found nowhere else in the world. An estimated 90 percent of the 14,000 plants native to Madagascar are also found nowhere else.

VANILLA ICE CREAM

The majority of the world's vanilla comes from Madagascar. The sweet flavor is found in the seedpods of a vanilla orchid. Did you know that vanilla is the second most expensive spice in the world after saffron?

TOMATO FROG

Endemic to Madagascar, *Dyscophus antongilii*, or tomato frogs, look a lot more like giant tomatoes, than green frogs! As a unique survival tactic, they puff their body up to twice its size and secrete a snotty glue that causes their predator's lips and eyes to stick together.

LEMUR SELFIE

101 species of Lemur live on the island of Madagascar, the only place in the world they can be found in the wild. Some lemurs are known to have a mating call that sounds just like a police siren! In 2014, lemur named Bekily, living in London Zoo, made headlines when he snapped one of the first animal selfies to go viral!

C-C-C-C-CHAMELEON

Madagascar is home to a rainbow of chameleons—almost half the world's chameleon species can be found on this incredible island. The chameleon's super power is that its skin changes color depending on its surroundings, mood and body temperature.

COCO DE MER

The world's largest seed is the coco de mer coconut or "double coconut." You can only find it in Seychelles. It can weigh as much as 50 lb. (23 kg) and is famous for its resemblance to a human butt!

ALDABRA ATOLL

Aldabra Atoll is the world's second-largest raised atoll, uninhabited by humans and known as the "crown jewel" of the Indian Ocean. It is also home to 150,000 Aldabra giant tortoises, which can grow up to four ft. in length – perhaps as big as you!

Bonzour! Welcome to the paradise of Seychelles—Africa's smallest country! This group of 115 tiny islands floats happily in the Indian Ocean, 1,000 mi. (1,600 km) east of the African continent.

Seychelles is home to a fusion of Indian and East Asian cultures as well as the several thousand visiting Western tourists.

SEYCHELLES

N

Africa

Victoria

10 miles

Pop. size	**89,173**	**(192ND)**
Landmass (sq mi)	**174**	**(189TH)**
Life Expectancy	**74.25**	**(92ND)**

FEATHERED FRIENDS

Bird Island is so named for the whopping 750,000 pairs of sooty terns that flock there every year to breed. They hover above the beaches in clouds and the noise of their wings and chirping calls is deafening!

Aldabra giant tortoise

Where in the world would you find a famous exploding atoll?

GO TO PAGE 202

COTTON CANDY SAND

Wash ashore on the island of La Digue, and on the Anse Source d'Argent Beach you'll find billions of grains of pale pink sand, a phenomenon that is caused by the colorful coral reefs nearby.

Olivier Levasseur

BILLION DOLLAR PIRATE

You may have never heard of him, but famed French pirate Olivier Levasseur was known to have terrorized the Indian Oceans in the 18th century, plundering European trade ships for their cargo. When he was hanged for piracy in 1730, it was believed he had buried a treasure worth a billion dollars somewhere on the island of Mahe in the Seychelles. The only clue Levasseur left behind as to the location of the buried treasure was a cryptogram that was tied around his neck on the day of his execution.

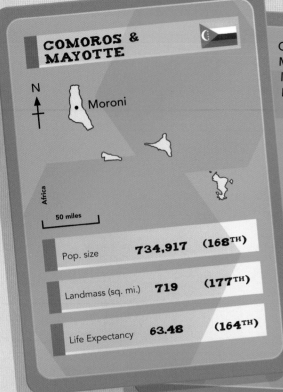

COMOROS & MAYOTTE

N

Moroni

Africa

50 miles

Pop. size	734,917	(168TH)
Landmass (sq. mi.)	719	(177TH)
Life Expectancy	63.48	(164TH)

Comoros is a country, Mayotte is not. The latter is part of France and is under French authority, but belongs to the Comoros Island region. The former is comprised of three other islands called Grande Comoro, Moheli, and Anjouan.

Confused? Don't worry, these gorgeous islands have lots of ways to distract you.

DOUBLE BARRIER REEF

Mayotte's colorful double barrier coral reef is 100 miles long and stretches around the entire island. One barrier reef can be seen about 9.5 mi. (15 km) off the coast, with another barrier reef ring about 984 ft. (300 m) off the coast.

GRAND MARIAGE

Known as a *grand mariage*, a wedding on Comoros can last nine days. Female wedding guests attend wearing brightly colored traditional gowns and smear yellow wood powder called *bwe la mssitzanou* on their faces.

Barreleye fish

SPOOK FISH

One of the world's strangest tropical fish, the spook fish, or barreleye, swims off the shores of Mayotte and the island's coral reefs. The freaky fish has a black body, large telescopic eyes, and a transparent head!

YLANG-YLANG

This tiny island in the Indian Ocean is the world's greatest producer of the ylang-ylang plant. Contained within the plant's yellow flower is an oil that is used in many perfumes and has many stress-relieving and mood-elevating properties.

NEVER BORED WITH BAO

Comoros locals can be seen whiling away the hours playing Bao—a local traditional board game. A mixture of checkers, backgammon, and chess, Bao uses "seeds" to sow and capture an opponent's seeds on a wooden board that has circular holes or "pits."

DEAD AS A DODO

The national bird of Mauritius is the dodo, a funny-looking and flightless animal that disappeared from the face of the Earth in the 1600s. It is believed the reason dodos became extinct was because, unlike most other animals, they weren't afraid of humans and never ran away. This, of course, made them easy to catch! No doubt this is the reason why the Portuguese settlers who discovered them called them dodos, or "simpletons!"

The esteemed American author Mark Twain was once quoted as saying: "You gather the idea that Mauritius was made first, and then heaven, and that heaven was copied after Mauritius."

We think this sums up the island nation rather well!

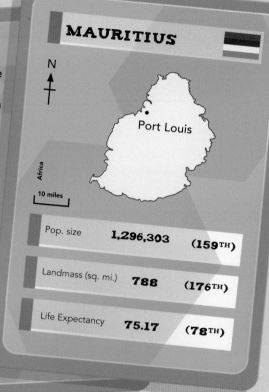

MAURITIUS

N

Africa

10 miles

Port Louis

Pop. size	1,296,303	(159TH)
Landmass (sq. mi.)	788	(176TH)
Life Expectancy	75.17	(78TH)

THE SEGA DANCE

The *sega* is the Mauritian national dance. Women twirl their brightly colored dresses and sway their bodies to the beat, while men shuffle and bang the beat out on drums made from goatskins.

UNDERSEA WALK

One of Mauritius's most famous tourist attractions is the underwater walk. Visitors put on special breathing helmets and walk along the sea floor and around the coral reefs.

MAHA SHIVARATRI

Every year, 500,000 Hindu pilgrims—about half the total population of Mauritius—travel to the holy lake of Grand Bassin to offer food praises to the god Shiva for the Maha Shivaratri festival. The celebration extends to three days and is one of the most important annual Hindu celebrations.

EUREKA HOUSE!

Mauritians are descended from African, Indian, Chinese, Dutch, and French settlers—with many of those nations having ruled over the land since the 1600s. Much of Port Louis's colonial architecture remains from when the French settled in the 18th century. The most famous building is the Eureka House.

GEORGIA

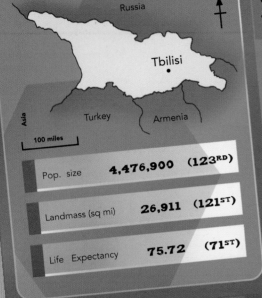

Russia

Tbilisi

Asia

Turkey

Armenia

100 miles

N

Pop. size	4,476,900	(123RD)
Landmass (sq mi)	26,911	(121ST)
Life Expectancy	75.72	(71ST)

Welcome to Georgia, a nation that sits at the crossroads of Europe and Asia.

Georgia has a unique and ancient cultural heritage. With enchanting forests, architectural styles that bridge Europe and Asia, and three alphabets, Georgia is a place you will never forget.

WHAT'S IN A NAME?

Remember that Georgia isn't called Georgia by Georgians! They call their country Sakartvelo, which in the Georgian alphabet looks like this:

საქართველო

GEORGE'S DRAGON

The Freedom Monument can be found in the historic old town of the capital city Tbilisi. This 115 ft. (35 m) tall golden statue of St. George slaying a dragon is the most famous landmark in Tbilisi's central square. St. George is Georgia's patron saint, and the national flag featuring his red cross on a white background can be seen everywhere!

A FEAT OF FEASTS!

Like most countries, Georgians like to enjoy a tasty feast, or *supra*, with family and friends. The national dish of delicious meaty dumplings called *khinkali* is seen on many families' tables, and the traditional head of the table, the *tamada*, is responsible for giving speeches, telling stories and jokes, and making sure everyone has a good time.

SPACE AGE

There is an incredible amount of futuristic architecture in many of Georgia's cities. The country's Parliament Building is shaped like a giant marble that is 328 ft. (100 m) tall!

KARTLIS DEDA

In 1958, the year that Tbilisi celebrated its 1,500th anniversary, an aluminum statue measuring 66 ft. (20 m) was erected. The statue shows a Georgian woman, known as Kartlis Deda, in traditional clothing holding a bowl of wine in her left hand (for friends of Georgia) and a sword in her right hand (for any enemies). The statue can be seen from miles away, and is a powerful symbol of national identity.

16,627 FT.
(5,068 M)
Shkhara

15,770 FT.
(4,807 M)
Mont Blanc

THE CAUCASUS

What's the highest mountain range in Europe? The Alps? Wrong!

The highest range is the Caucasus Mountains, marking the border between Georgia and Russia. Georgia lays claim to the third-highest, Shkhara, which at 16,627 ft. (5,068 m) beats Mont Blanc in the Alps by over 820 ft. (250 m). These dramatic mountains, with their terrifying hairpin roads and hidden villages, are the stuff of legend. In Greek mythology, they were one of the pillars holding up the world.

CAUCASIAN

The word "Caucasian" meaning "Europeans with white skin," originates from Georgia's Caucasus Mountains. The Caucasus have been the dividing line between the Caucasians of Europe and the residents of Asia for many centuries.

FIVE-FINGER MOUNTAIN

A sacred site in Azerbaijan is Besh Barmag mountain. Every year, thousands of the country's residents make pilgrimages to the solid-rock shrine to kiss the craggy stone.

Azerbaijan is known as the ancient "land of fire," where fire worshipping, folklore, superstition, and wild horses are part of everyday life.

It's also—according to some scholars—the location of the biblical Garden of Eden resides.

AZERBAIJAN

N

Georgia   Russia

Armenia

Asia

Baku

100 miles

Pop. size	9,416,598	(92ND)
Landmass (sq mi)	33,436	(113TH)
Life Expectancy	71.91	(120TH)

CARPET MUSEUM

Stunningly woven carpets are one of Azerbaijan's most important and beautiful cultural traditions. In recognition of this, the country's new Carpet Museum—shaped like a rolled-up carpet!—opened in 2014. It displays the world's largest collection of Azerbaijani rugs.

MUD VOLCANOES!

Azerbaijan is home to more than half of the world's mud volcanoes, nearly 400 of them! Mud volcanoes squelch out stinky gases that are brewed many miles underground every second of the day. Famously, in 2001, the Lok-Batan Mud Cone erupted, shooting out red-hot flames!

THE BURNING MOUNTAIN

The Burning Mountain, or Yanar Dag, is a rare natural-gas fire and a sacred phenomenon in Azerbaijan's Absheron peninsula. The hilltop is lit up with eternal flames—that can reach a height of 10 ft. (3 m)—all year round due to a steady seeping of natural gas escaping from the ground. Yanar Dag has been burning for centuries, and the fire shows no signs of ever going out.

WE LOVE HORSES

Azerbaijani people have a great love and respect for horses. The national animal is the ancient, and sadly endangered, Karabakh horse, a breed with a reputation for its speed, elegance, and good temper. One of the nation's favorite and oldest sports, *sur papaq*, is played on horseback.

Karabakh horse

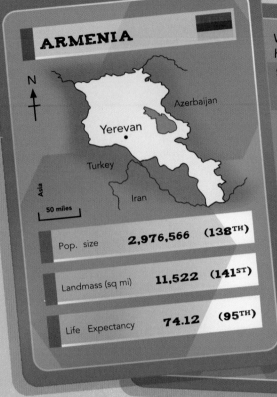

ARMENIA

N

Azerbaijan

Yerevan

Turkey

Asia

Iran

50 miles

Pop. size	2,976,566	(138TH)
Landmass (sq mi)	11,522	(141ST)
Life Expectancy	74.12	(95TH)

When it comes to history, folklore, geography, and wine, it's hard to beat Armenia—a culturally rich country famous for its mythology and monasteries.

The nation was the first place ever to adopt Christianity; and has fought for its independence several times, finally winning when it broke free of the Soviet Union in 1991.

ETERNAL FLAME

Tragically, during World War One, around 1.5 million Armenians died at the hands of the Ottoman Empire. To honor the victims, a complex called the Armenian Genocide Memorial and Museum was built, where an eternal flame burns. Every April, thousands of Armenians gather there to remember those who died.

ZVARTNOTS CATHEDRAL

With mighty Mount Ararat, in present-day Turkey, as a backdrop, it's easy to see why Zvartnots Cathedral was once referred to as the most beautiful church in the world. Built around 642, a deadly earthquake sadly demolished the cathedral in 930 and it has never been rebuilt.

3.5 MILES!

Tatev Monastery

WORLD'S OLDEST LEATHER SHOE

We all take our shoes for granted these days. But imagine owning the first pair of shoes ever. Dating back 5,500 years, the world's oldest leather shoe was discovered in an Armenian cave in 2010. It had been preserved in sheep poop—a very smelly shoe!

THE WINGS OF TATEV

In 2010, the Wings of Tatev was officially recorded by Guinness World Records as the world's longest nonstop double track cable car. Traveling at a speed of 23 mph (37 km/h), the cable car can carry 25 passengers from Halidzor to the Tatev Monastery 1,050 ft. (320 m) above the ground. Its total length is 3.5 mi. (5.7 km) and the scenery is amazing—just don't look down!

GRAND BAZAAR

Turkey's most famous city, İstanbul (formerly known as Byzantium and Constantinople) is the world's only city to span two continents. Another of its many claims to fame is its busy and fragrant Grand Bazaar—one of the world's oldest and largest indoor shopping markets. It has 64 streets and over 4,000 shops, where visitors haggle for spices, carpets, lanterns, and other exotic goods!

Lanterns at the Grand Bazaar

A bridge between the continents of Europe and Asia, Turkey has been an important geographical and cultural hotspot for humanity for thousands of years.

With stunning architecture and bustling cities, some truly amazing beaches and breathtaking mountains, not to mention fabulous food, Turkey is a magical place.

TURKEY

Pop. size	74,932,641	(18TH)
Landmass (sq mi)	302,535	(37TH)
Life Expectancy	73.29	(102ND)

COTTON CASTLE

Pamukkale, or Cotton Castle, is one of Turkey's biggest natural tourist attractions. The cascading of geothermal mineral water has left calcium-rich deposits that form stone waterfalls, and created pools full of bubbling, neon-blue waters.

AYA SOFYA

Arguably one of the most impressive buildings ever constructed, over the past 1,500 years the dome-shaped Aya Sofya has been a cathedral, a mosque, and a museum. The mosaic pattern that covers the inside of the domed roof is made up of 30 million gold tiles.

THE BIRD

Did you know in Turkey the word "turkey" means "Indian bird"? The Indian word for "turkey" means "Peruvian bird." In Greece, the word "turkey" means "French bird." The Malaysian word for "turkey" means "Dutch chicken." Confusing!

One seriously fluffy bunny!

ANGORA RABBIT

Angora rabbits look nothing like normal rabbits. These giant fluffballs, originating from Ankara, are one of the oldest species of rabbit on the planet. They are bred very large for their special angora wool, which covers their entire body and is world renowned as a clothing material.

CAPPADOCIA

Turkey's most lunar-like landscape, Cappadocia, is not only a collection of strangely shaped giant volcanic rock formations that have been eroded by wind and rain— they are also people's cave houses. Buried 278 ft. (85 m) underground in this region are several ancient city complexes, such as Derinkuyu, believed to be more than 5,000 years old.

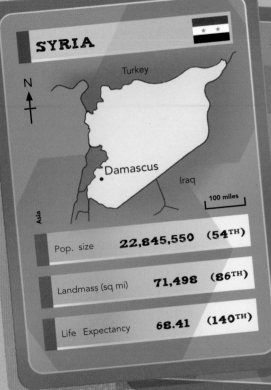

SYRIA

Turkey

N

Damascus

Iraq

Asia

100 miles

Pop. size	22,845,550	(54TH)
Landmass (sq mi)	71,498	(86TH)
Life Expectancy	68.41	(140TH)

Syria is an archaeologist's dream. Packed with ancient temples, beautiful mosques, and abandoned fortresses, this is a country with stunning sights.

Tragically, it's best known for the devastating civil war that is tearing the nation apart and currently making it one of the most dangerous places on Earth.

WATER WHEELS

Hamah's giant waterwheels, or *norias*, are not only an eye-catching sight along the Orontes River, they are also reminders of Syrian farmers' engineering intelligence in the 12th century. The wheels scoop up water from the river below and drop it into man-made canals that supply water to areas with crops. Clever!

SYRIAN HAMSTERS

Raise your hand if you have a hamster. Syrian hamsters, also called golden hamsters, are the most popular species kept today as pets. Unbelievably, almost all pet Syrian hamsters can trace their ancestry back to a mother and her 12 pups caught in Aleppo, Syria, by Professor Aharoni in 1930.

DAMASCUS STEEL

Damascus steel has long been revered as a legendary—and unbreakable—choice of metal for weapons such as swords, blades, and spears. It was said that a Damascus sword could slice a falling scarf in midair! For years, modern blacksmiths puzzled over how ancient sword-makers could fashion a metal so strong without modern technology. One of the techniques that made the blades so strong was heating the metal until it was blisteringly hot and then cooling it rapidly—sometimes, so legend says, by plunging it into the pee of red-headed boys!

Syrian hamster

THE CONFLICT RAGES ON

Syria's civil war has been called "the worst humanitarian disaster of our time." Since 2011, more than 10 million people have become refugees, and an estimated 200,000 people have died.

PALMYRA

Two thousand years ago, the ancient city of Palmyra was thriving. With a population of 100,000, hundreds of temples, and almost 700 nearby towns, it was a vital stopover in Syria's desert for traders en route to Persia, India, China, and the Roman Empire. However, in the 16th century, the city was mysteriously abandoned. Now all that remains are ruins.

WORLD'S LARGEST RESTAURANT

There is a restaurant in Damascus called Bawabet Dimashq (Damascus's Gate). It can serve more than 6,000 people at a time and hires 1,800 waiters per shift! It is officially the largest restaurant in the world. Inside there are waterfalls and replicas of Syria's archaeological ruins. The chef can produce up to 25 plates of food in one minute!

1,800 waiters per shift!

HEALTHFUL HUMMUS

The Lebanese people are in love with hummus—a dip made out of blended chickpeas. It's delicious with warm pita bread and olive oil. The world's largest serving of hummus weighed in at 23,043 lb. (10,452 kg) and was achieved by Lebanese chef Ramzi Choueiri and 300 student chefs at Al-Kafaat University in Beirut, on May 8, 2010.

The far-reaching Roman Empire once occupied a quarter of the whole world, and made it as far as Lebanon.

Four-thousand-year-old Lebanon is one of the oldest countries in the world—its name even appears several times in the Old Testament of the Christian Bible.

LEBANON

N

Beirut

Asia

Syria

50 miles

Pop. size	4,467,390	(125TH)
Landmass (sq mi)	4,036	(166TH)
Life Expectancy	77.22	(51ST)

TOE TAPPING!

If a Lebanese bride steps on a single girl's foot on the day of her wedding, it is believed that it will bring the girl luck and that she, too, will get married soon!

STONE OF THE PREGNANT WOMAN

This massive monolith, located at Lebanon's Baalbek archaeological site, weighs 1,100 tons— that's more than five blue whales! It's the largest stone ever carved by mankind! Its purpose is a mystery; many historians think the stone was due to be turned into a giant trilithon rock shape (like Stonehenge in England), but it was never completed.

TREE OF GOD

The national symbol of Lebanon is the cedar, and it is proudly represented on the flag. This tree is mentioned in the Bible, with many Christians believing that the cedar forests were planted by God's own hands, which is why they're called the "Cedars of God" (and why Lebanon is called "God's Country on Earth").

OCCUPIED

Lebanon is no stranger to war. Between 1975 and 1990, the nation was embroiled in a disastrous civil war between Christians and Muslims that separated east and west Beirut. Throughout history, more than 16 countries have occupied Lebanon.

PHOENICIAN EMPIRE

Between 1200 B.C. and 300 B.C. the Phoenicians, the original people of Lebanon, built an empire that rivaled those of the ancient Greeks, Romans, and Egyptians. They were the race that was responsible for seeing humans set sail on a grand scale. It is believed that the Phoenicians became the first seafaring peoples, building the first ancient trireme warships out of strong cedar wood ("trireme" means "with three banks of oars").

A trireme warship

THE COLOR PURPLE

The word Phoenicia, the ancient name for Lebanon, means "land of the purple." Indeed, the Phoenician Empire was built on the trading of Tyrian dye, a purple dye that was squished out of a rare type of sea snail. If you wore the color purple, like many Roman emperors and generals did for centuries, it usually meant you were a VIP!

FISHES AND LOAVES

Jesus Christ's most iconic miracle, the multiplication of five loaves of bread and two fish to feed 5,000 people, is believed to have happened at Tabgha, on the Sea of Galilee. Galilee is also the site of Jesus's many other miracles, including his resurrection, turning water into wine, and walking across the water.

ISRAEL

Pop. size	**8,059,400**	**(98TH)**
Landmass (sq mi)	**8,019**	**(152ND)**
Life Expectancy	**81.28**	**(16TH)**

N

Jerusalem

Syria

Egypt

Jordan

Asia

100 miles

The world's most contested country, Israel is also one of the newest. Created in 1948, this Holy Land is a sacred spot for Jews, Christians, and Muslims.

Both Israelis and Palestinians believe it to be their home, and the conflict between the two sides rages on. But Israel is more than just a war zone. Here's the proof . . .

ISRAEL'S TOP BIBLICAL PLACES

This country is jam-packed with important religious sites. Here are just a few of them:

Garden of Gethsemane

The Garden Tomb

Church of the Holy Sepulchre

Mount Zion

Mount of Olives

Via Dolorosa

WORLD'S LOWEST POINT

It's impossible to dive in. . . but you can float! The Dead Sea lies at the bottom of the Syrian-African Rift Valley. It's 1,312 ft. (400 m) below sea level and is the lowest point on Earth. The Dead Sea has almost 10 times more salt in it than oceans and gets its name from the fact that no animals can survive in the hypersaline (supersalty) conditions.

The Dead Sea

THE WESTERN WALL

Located on the site of the once-great King Solomon's Temple, Jerusalem's Western Wall has been a site for Jewish pilgrimages for more than 2,000 years. It is believed that more than one million prayer notes are left in the cracks of the wall each year.

DON'T LOOK DOWN!

Overlooking the Dead Sea is an ancient fortress. . . with a difference. Masada sits right on top of a remote rocky plateau 1,312 ft. (400 m) high, and was controlled by Herod the Great, more than 2,000 years ago.

TEMPLE MOUNT

Sitting atop a sacred hill within the Old City of Jerusalem is the most important holy site for those who follow Judaism, Temple Mount. Built 1,000 years before the birth of Jesus Christ, Jewish people believe that it is the place where God gathered the dust to create the first human, Adam. For those who follow the Muslim faith, Temple Mount is the place where the Prophet Muhammad ascended to heaven, as described in the Quran.

IRON DOME

Due to Israel's ongoing conflict with Palestine, Israel's government, with help from the U.S., became the only country in the world to employ a high-tech missile defense system. It intercepts—and destroys—short-range rockets headed into populated areas of Israel. The system works by detecting a rocket launch and firing its own special rockets into the air to blow up the missile en route to its target. Iron Dome, as it is known, has helped save many lives and can shoot down as many as 15 rockets simultaneously!

THE NATIVITY

The birthplace of Jesus Christ (the son of God on Earth, according to followers of the Christian faith) was in Bethlehem. It was here that the three wise men with their gifts of gold, frankincense, and myrrh followed a star from the east to a stable, to pay their respects to the newborn baby Jesus.

With several of the Bible's holiest sites, including Nazareth and Bethlehem, it is little wonder that Palestine and Israel have been fighting over this land since Israel was created in 1948.

Palestine, often called a "country-in-waiting," has no official capital city and is divided into two regions—the West Bank and the Gaza Strip.

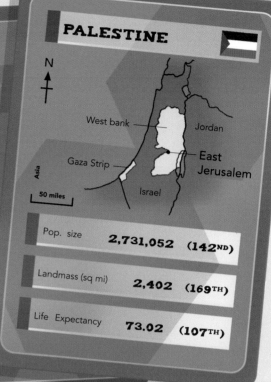

PALESTINE

West bank
Jordan
Gaza Strip
East Jerusalem
Israel
Asia
50 miles

Pop. size	2,731,052	(142ND)
Landmass (sq mi)	2,402	(169TH)
Life Expectancy	73.02	(107TH)

OLIVE HARVEST

Palestine is described as "the land of olives and vines" due to the olive trees and vineyards that punctuate its landscape. The olive harvest is an important event in many Palestinians' calendars, and there is evidence that olive oil has been produced in this region for more than 4,000 years!

LET'S GO FLY A KITE

On July 28, 2011, at Al-Waha beach in the Gaza Strip, the world record of the most kites flown simultaneously was achieved, when a staggering 12,350 took to the skies! In order to promote peace in the region, children of the Gaza Strip, assisted by United Nations Relief, came together to show the world what happens when people work together.

WADI QELT

Carved into the steep cliffs of the Wadi Qelt river gorge that runs between Jerusalem and Jericho is the stunning St. George's monastery, built in the year 420. In order to reach the monastery, pilgrims must walk across a narrow bridge that spans the gorge.

Keffiyeh headscarf

HEADS UP

An icon of Palestinian solidarity, the *keffiyeh* is a black-and-white checkered headscarf. Once worn only by men—most famously by former Palestinian leader Yasser Arafat—it has become gender neutral in recent years.

THREE IS THE MAGIC NUMBER

Christmas comes once a year, right? Not if you live in Bethlehem. This Palestinian town celebrates Christmas three times a year.

1) December 25, like many other Western traditions

2) January 6, as per the Greek Orthodox Church

3) January 18, as per the Armenians

DEC 25

JAN 6

JAN 18

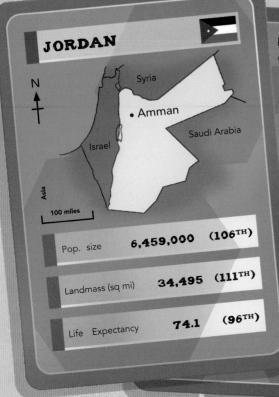

JORDAN

N

Syria

• Amman

Israel

Saudi Arabia

Asia

100 miles

Pop. size	6,459,000	(106TH)
Landmass (sq mi)	34,495	(111TH)
Life Expectancy	74.1	(96TH)

Located in the heart of the Middle East, Jordan is officially known as the Hashemite Kingdom of Jordan, after the Arab dynasty that has lived and ruled in the area since 1916.

It's an often-overlooked land, full of magical sights. *Ahlan wa sahlan* ("welcome") to Jordan!

WHAT A FALAFEL!

In 2012, a team of 10 chefs in Amman created a new world record—the largest falafel ever made! A traditional Arabian dish, falafel is squished chickpeas shaped into a disc and then deep fried. This world-beating whopper contained 176 lb. (80 kg) of chickpeas, 11 lb. (5 kg) of onions, and 4.5 lb. (2 kg) of fresh parsley and coriander! It was so big it stuffed the stomachs of 600 hungry diners.

AMMAN CITADEL

In Arabic, the Amman Citadel is called Jabal al-Qal'a. It's an L-shaped hill that is one of the world's oldest continuously inhabited places. Over thousand of years, the citadel has been occupied by many great civilizations, including the Romans, the Babylonians, and the Persians. The most famous archaeological find here is the ruins of the Temple of Hercules.

PETRA-FIED!

Known around the world as the "Rose City," Petra is truly incredible. The city was carved into the sandstone rock 2,000 years ago and, following a huge earthquake in 700, remained "lost" until Europeans uncovered it in 1812. The most famous of all the city's architecture is Al Khazneh, which was the ancient treasury.

MANSAF

The national dish in Jordan is called *mansaf*, a dish that is associated with Bedouin traditions. To make it yourself, all you need are rice, chunks of stewed lamb, and a yogurt sauce called *jameed*.

A SEA OF RED

One of the youngest oceans on Earth, the Red Sea began filling with aquatic life 30 million years ago and is full of amazing fish, including the grumpy-looking bearded scorpionfish!

DESERT POLICE

Jordan's deserts are guarded by an army known as the Desert Patrol. Riding on camels, and wearing a red-and-white *keffiyeh*, the Desert Patrol protects Jordan from drug and gun smugglers and keeps watch over valuable archaeological sites.

TALLEST FOUNTAIN

The Jeddah Fountain, or King Fahd's Fountain as it is known in Saudi Arabia, is the tallest fountain in the world. Spraying salt water from the Red Sea 1,024 ft. (312 m) into the air at a speed of 233 mph (375 km/h)—roughly the same speed as the fastest sports car ever made—the fountain lights up at night and can be seen from miles away!

The birthplace of the Islam faith, Saudi Arabia is also one of the most modern countries in the Middle East.

Financially wealthy due to the huge quantity of oil it produces, this nation is also one of tradition—a place where you'll find supershiny skyscrapers as well as desert nomads.

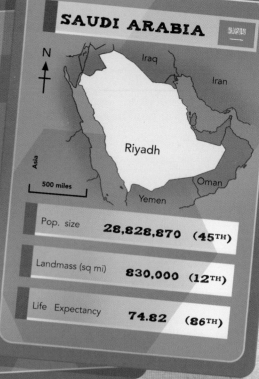

SAUDI ARABIA

N

Iraq
Iran
Riyadh
Asia
Oman
Yemen

500 miles

Pop. size	28,828,870	(45TH)
Landmass (sq mi)	830,000	(12TH)
Life Expectancy	74.82	(86TH)

MUD HOMES

Not far from the space-age skyscrapers of Riyadh lie the mud homes of Najran. Today, more than 200 mud homes still exist and are built in a traditional style that highlights how Bedouin people used to live hundreds of years ago.

HOLY PLACE

The Kaaba, a black cuboid building at the center of the al-Masjid al-Haram mosque in Mecca, is the holiest place in all of Islam. It is towards this that Muslims from all over the world face during their daily prayers. Muslims believe Mecca to be the birthplace of the last messenger of God, Muhammad.

BIG FEAST

Three animals are used for the main dish at the wedding feasts of the Bedouin people. The dish is a roasted camel stuffed with a whole roasted sheep, stuffed with a chicken, stuffed with eggs. It's the Russian doll of cuisine!

OIL RICH

With an estimated 268 billion barrels' worth of oil buried deep underneath its deserts, Saudi Arabia owns roughly 18 percent of the world's oil. The average barrel of oil is worth around $55, making the country's oil reserve worth trillions!

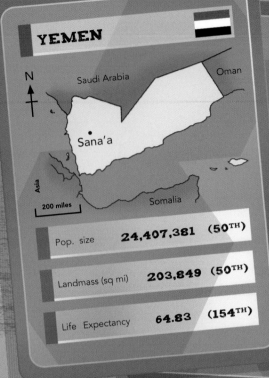

YEMEN

N

Saudi Arabia
Oman

Sana'a

Asia

Somalia

200 miles

Pop. size	24,407,381	(50TH)
Landmass (sq mi)	203,849	(50TH)
Life Expectancy	64.83	(154TH)

Yemen is packed with date palm trees, sand, and cities made of mud.

With the Arabian Sea knocking on its door, Yemen also enjoys some spectacular coastline. Socotra island, 220 mi. (354 km) off the coast, is known as one of the best places on the planet to go surfing.

DRAGON BLOOD TREES

Located solely on the island of Socotra, dragon blood trees may look like upside-down umbrellas, but they get their sinister name from the blood-red sap that they produce, a substance that has been highly prized for thousands of years.

MANHATTAN OF THE DESERT

More than 1,700 years ago the town of Shibam, Wadi Hadramawt, was founded and it is now famous for the 500 narrow houses that were built out of mud bricks in the 16th century. Known as "Manhattan of the desert," the buildings are the tallest mud structures in the world, The town is often called the "oldest skyscraper city in the world." Take that, New York!

328 FT.
drop from bridge!

SHIHARA BRIDGE

Constructed in the 17th century, the Shihara Bridge connects two villages in the Jabal Sharara mountain range. Built to keep Turkish invaders away, the bridge-makers ensured that the crossing could be destroyed in a matter of seconds so that no invaders could enter Yemeni territory! Below the bridge is a 328 ft. (100 m) plummet to the canyon floor.

FASHIONABLE DAGGERS

It is customary for men in Yemen to wear a *jambiya*, a type of short, curved dagger. The dagger's handle indicates a man's social status—and the sight of it reminds Yemeni men not to pick fights with one another! *Jambiyas* also play an important part in special ceremonies— young boys often dance with daggers during a wedding ceremony.

KEEP COVERED

Many Muslim women in Yemen wear a long black cloak called an *abaya*, with a veil called a *niqab* that keeps their face and hair hidden at all times from male strangers, in accordance with Islamic faith. Another covering worn by Muslim women across the world is called the *hijab*, a veil that covers the hair but not the face.

THREE-DAY WEDDINGS

Yemenis take much pride in their wedding traditions. An average wedding feast lasts three days. In traditional Yemeni weddings, the bride is adorned with many trinkets, colorful headwear, and herbs.

SINBAD THE SAILOR

Sohar, a once-great maritime port and former capital city of Oman, is also the birthplace of Sinbad the Sailor. Sinbad, a fictional hero of the Middle East, traveled in search of fortune in seven magical voyages that are now told to children all over the world. One of the sailor's most famous adventures sees him carried away in the claws of a giant mythical bird called a roc.

Sinbad carried away in the roc's talons

Sitting at the top of the big toe of the boot of the Persian Gulf, Oman can be found sunbathing on the shores of the Arabian Sea.

The legendary location of the lost treasure city of Ubar (the "Atlantis of the Sands"), Oman's coastline is now chock full of ultraluxurious five-star hotels and resorts!

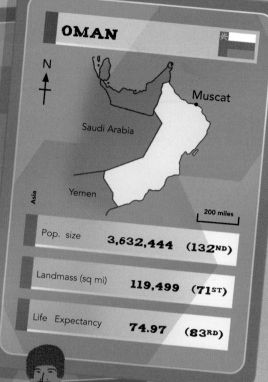

OMAN

N

Muscat

Saudi Arabia

Yemen

Asia

200 miles

Pop. size	**3,632,444**	**(132ND)**
Landmass (sq mi)	**119,499**	**(71ST)**
Life Expectancy	**74.97**	**(83RD)**

WAHIBA SANDS

The Wahiba Sands region of Oman is not as barren or uninhabited as you might think. The nomadic Bedouin people have adapted to live and thrive in this often harsh landscape, and while traveling through the dunes you might see a Bedouin woman in traditional dress and a peaked veil, standing out as a splash of color against the golden sand.

DISHDASHA

The male national dress, as dictated specifically by Sultan Qaboos, Oman's king, is the *dishdasha*, a white ankle-length robe with long sleeves, with a *wazar* wrapped around the waist. The Omani *dishdasha* is complemented with either a *kuma* hat (worn after working hours) or a *mussar* headdress.

GIANT INCENSE BURNER

Look up in awe at Oman's Giant Incense Burner in Muscat. The three-story incense burner is a national symbol of Oman and a tribute to the frankincense trade that defined the nation's early trading wealth.

SCARY SANDSTORMS

Oman, along with many arid states in the Middle East, frequently gets hit by sandstorms, meteorological phenomena that look superscary. Sandstorms occur when a strong wind (known in Arabic as a *haboob*) blows loose sand and dirt together, forming a giant cloud of sand, often 328 ft. (100 m) high and traveling as fast as a speeding car.

UNITED ARAB EMIRATES

Qatar
Abu Dhabi
Oman
Saudi Arabia

N

Asia

100 miles

Pop. size	9,346,129	(93RD)
Landmass (sq mi)	32,278	(115TH)
Life Expectancy	77.09	(52ND)

In the past 25 years, the UAE has raised the stakes of high-life, modern living in the 21st century, breaking a wave of world records as it grows.

For example, Dubai now boasts 10 of the world's tallest 50 buildings, including the world's first seven-star hotel—and has 448 skyscrapers. In 1991, it had just one.

BIG FRIENDLY GIANT

Ladies and gentlemen, this is the world's tallest building: the Burj Khalifa. With construction completed in 2010, the Burj is so big that you can witness a stunning sunset on the top floor for two minutes longer than you can on the ground floor!

Leaning Tower of Pisa, Italy—183 ft. (56 m)
Big Ben, U.K.—315 ft. (96 m)
CCTV Headquarters, China—768 ft. (234 m)
The Shard, U.K.—1,010 ft. (308 m)
Eiffel Tower, France—1,063 ft. (324 m)
Empire State Building, U.S.—1,453 ft. (443 m)
Petronas Towers, Malaysia—1,483 ft. (452 m)
Freedom Tower, U.S.—1,791 ft. (546 m)
Shanghai Tower, China—2,073 ft. (632 m)
Burj Khalifa, Dubai—2,716 ft. (828 m)

Burj Khalifa, Dubai
2,716 FT.
(828 M)

Eiffel Tower, France
1,063 FT.
(324 M)

LET THERE BE LIGHT!

The Festival of Lights in Sharjah turns light into an art form. For the nine-day festival in February, the buildings are illuminated with beautiful colors so the city becomes one big gallery.

SEVEN BECOME ONE

The seven separate emirates that join hands to form the United Arab Emirates are:

1) **Abu Dhabi** (the capital)
2) **Ajman**
3) **Dubai**
4) **Fujairah**
5) **Ras al-Khaimah**
6) **Sharjah**
7) **Umm al-Quwain**

SPEEDY POLICE

With the UAE being one of the world's largest oil producers, gasoline is very cheap. To stop road accidents caused by speeding in superquick sports cars, the Dubai police drive around in supercars, too, including Lamborghinis, Ferraris, and Bentleys! This allows them to catch speeders who think they can outrun them!

POLICE

WORLD ISLAND

Currently being built 2.5 mi. (4 km) off the coast of Dubai, the World Islands will feature the most luxurious living accommodations in the world. Three hundred artificial islands have been created in the shape of the globe, and each one will have many private homes and resorts, to become an exclusive playground for the rich and famous. Richard Branson, the British billionaire, owns the island shaped like Great Britain.

BANG, BANG!

It's official, the record for the world's largest-ever fireworks display goes to Dubai! To celebrate the New Year in 2014, 479,651 fireworks were fired into the air in just six minutes—that's an incredible 1,332 fireworks per second!

PEARL QATAR

Located in Doha, the luxurious-looking Pearl Qatar is an artificial island built on top of Qatar's once world-renowned pearl-diving sites. The island cost $15 billion to make and is quickly becoming known as the Arabian Riviera.

After many years of watching the UAE and Saudi Arabia grow into the most luxurious Arab nations on Earth, the tiny state of Qatar decided to join in.

The third-largest oil and natural-gas supplier, Qatar is the world's richest country and has the fastest-growing economy on Earth!

QATAR

N

Bahrain

Saudi Arabia

Asia

Doha

50 miles

Pop. size	2,168,673	(145TH)
Landmass (sq mi)	4,473	(162ND)
Life Expectancy	78.38	(38TH)

TORNADO TOWER

One of Qatar's most iconic buildings is the Tornado Tower. Built in 2008, the skyscraper is built to look like its whirling, windy namesake. It has 52 floors, and while it's an office building during the day, it lights up at night with a display of over 35,000 colored lights.

PHENOMENAL FLAG

In 2013, Qatar created the world's largest flag. The maroon and white flag was the size of 14 soccer fields and weighed 9.8 tons! The flag was recycled into 200,000 backpacks for schoolchildren across 60 countries, after the record was verified.

FIRST-CLASS FALCONS

Falconry is a popular sport in Qatar. The birds are trained to hunt prey and return to the falconer's outstretched glove. These noble birds are high flyers in more ways than one—you can find them sitting in first class with their handlers on Qatar Airways flights!

ARCH OF SWORDS

Take a stroll down Grand Hamad Street in Doha and you'll come across the Arch of Swords. The national emblem of the country shows two crossed swords. A respected Qatari sword dance, known as an *ardah*, is an important part of a traditional Qatar wedding ceremony.

BAHRAIN

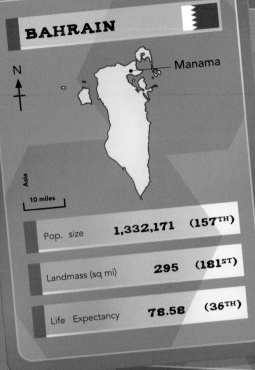

N

Manama

Asia

10 miles

Pop. size	1,332,171	(157TH)
Landmass (sq mi)	295	(181ST)
Life Expectancy	78.58	(36TH)

Bahrain may be tiny, but it packs a punch!

As the smallest Arab nation on Earth, Bahrain is actually made up of 33 islands, of which 92 percent of the available land is desert.

GRAND PRIX

In 2004, Bahrain hosted the first-ever Formula One Grand Prix in the Middle East, at the ultra-high-tech Bahrain International Circuit. Due to Bahrain being a Muslim country with a strict no-alcohol policy, race winners—who usually enjoy spraying their defeated opponents with champagne on the podium—are instead handed fizzy, non-alcoholic rose and pomegranate water, called *waard*.

SUNDAY BLUES

Up until September 1, 2006, Bahrain's weekend was Thursday and Friday. Today, the nation takes Friday and Saturday off, in order to have a day of the weekend shared with the rest of the world. Sunday, however, is not a day of rest—it's the first day of the week.

ARABIAN SAND CATS

They may look super cute, but Arabian sand cats are tough cookies. As the only known cat to live in a desert, these sandy-colored felines have thick fur on their feet and eat poisonous snakes for dinner.

PEARLING

Pearl diving in Bahrain has been occurring for 4,000 years. Bahrain's name means "two seas," due to the freshwater wells that bubble up in the middle of the salt water, which has encouraged such beautiful pearls to grow in the oyster beds under the sea. Up until 200 years ago, pearls were more valuable than diamonds! Traditional pearl diving takes place without any specialist equipment. Divers just hold their breath and are lowered into the water on the end of a weighted rope.

TREE OF LIFE

Bahrain's famous mesquite tree is known as the Tree of Life, or *Shajarat-al-Hayat*. At 400 years old, the 26 ft. (8 m) tree stands proudly all on its own in the vast swathes of Bahrain desert. The fact that the water source of the tree is a mystery attracts 50,000 pilgrims each year. Many tree experts believe it to have one of the deepest-known root systems of all the trees on the planet.

KUWAIT TOWERS

The country's most famous landmark—and stunning example of architecture in modern Kuwait—is the three Kuwait Towers, built in 1979. On the main tower, 614 ft. (187 m) tall, the bottom "bulge" is a water tank, and the top "bulge" is a restaurant. Their blue mosaic design is meant to reflect the look of a historic mosque.

Like its neighboring Persian Gulf nations, Iran, Iraq, and Saudi Arabia, Kuwait's wealth and modern history are built on sales of its mega oil reserves.

With its cool sea breezes and amazing architecture, Kuwait City stands out as an oasis amid the harsh desert surroundings.

KUWAIT

N

Iraq

Iran

Asia

Saudi Arabia

Kuwait City

50 miles

Pop. size	**3,368,572**	**(135TH)**
Landmass (sq mi)	**6,880**	**(156TH)**
Life Expectancy	**77.64**	**(48TH)**

ROBOT JOCKEYS

Camel racing has been popular in Kuwait and large parts of the Middle East for centuries—it is one of the few competitive ways the nomadic Bedouin people could entertain themselves in the vast oceans of desert. In 2006, child jockeys—who were primarily used to ride the camels—began to be replaced by robots. Kuwait was the first country to introduce them, with many robots designed to look like real humans!

EVEN MORE TOWERS

Kuwait is the only country in the world with no natural water supply from lakes or reservoirs, which means in an arid desert such as this, freshwater is as valuable as oil. Throughout the country, 33 striped water towers were strategically placed to collect as much rainwater as possible.

RAMADAN

During the ninth month of the Islamic calendar, Ramadan is celebrated. All Muslims around the world must take part. Throughout the month, eating or drinking is forbidden during daylight, and all bad habits must be given up. Muslims observe Ramadan because it is the month that, according to Islamic faith, God revealed the Quran to the Prophet Muhammad.

HOPPING RATS!

With its very strong back legs and tiny front legs, Kuwait's lesser Egyptian jerboa is one of the few rats that can jump! Spotted hopping all over the desert during the nighttime, jerboas have excellent hearing and can run as quickly as you can ride your bike!

Lesser Egyptian jerboa

THEY'RE LOVING IT!

When the first McDonald's opened in Kuwait in 1994, 15,000 people lined up! The traffic jam for the drive-thru was 7 mi. (11 km) long.

IRAQ

Pop. size	33,417,476	(38ᵀᴴ)
Landmass (sq mi)	169,235	(59ᵀᴴ)
Life Expectancy	71.42	(124ᵀᴴ)

Many wonderful things that have helped drive humanity forward happened right here in Iraq. It's often referred to as the "cradle of civilization".

From Noah's Ark supposedly being built here, to the city of Erbil, a contender for Earth's oldest city, there's plenty to see and do in Iraq. Check these out. . .

TELL-TALE SIGN

With a history dating back 6,000 years, Erbil claims to be the oldest city on Earth. Built upon a tall "tell," a mound of ground and soil that has grown over the centuries due to human development, the Citadel of Erbil rises 100 ft. (30 m) above the surrounding land.

LANGUAGE LESSON

Arabic is the language spoken by more than 200 million people around the world, and it is the language the Quran, the holy book of Islam. Arabic words are written down right to left—try writing that way for a day!

GREAT MOSQUE OF SAMARRA

Located almost 80 mi. (130 km) from capital city Baghdad is the spiraling cone minaret of the Great Mosque of Samarra. In the 9th century, when it was built, it was the largest mosque in the world, ascending 171 ft. (52 m) above the ground.

ZIG-A-ZIGGURAT

Ancient Egyptians liked to build pyramids. Ancient Sumerians and Babylonians liked to build ziggurats. These mammoth structures were constructed out of mud bricks as shrines to ancient gods. The most iconic is the 4,000-year-old Great Ziggurat of Ur.

THE HANGING GARDENS OF BABYLON

Though its real location has yet to be definitely established, it is thought that this Wonder of the Ancient World can be located in Hillah. Legend tells us of a Babylonian ruler called King Nebuchadnezzar II, who built this famous rooftop garden out of the ruined city of Babylon for his wife, Amytis, who missed her mountainous homeland. The gardens are described as "paradise on Earth."

FIVE TIMES FAST!

Try this Arabic tongue twister on for size:

Mishmishna mish mishmishkom w mishmishkom mish mishmishna, lamma mashmash mishmishkon, ma kan mashmash mishmishna.

(Our apricots are not the same as your apricots, and your apricots are not the same as our apricots. When your apricots were ripe, our apricots were not ripe yet.)

FREEDOM TOWER

One of Iran's most iconic modern landmarks is the Azadi Tower, an impressive marble structure built in 1971 to celebrate the 2,500th anniversary of when the Persian Empire ruled the world.

Azadi Tower, Tehran

THE PERSIAN EMPIRE

The largest empire the world has ever known was the Persian Empire. Around 480 B.C., it accounted for 50 million of the world's population—almost half! The empire was first established by Cyrus the Great and spread across central Asia, the Mediterranean, North Africa, and parts of Europe.

Khosh amadin (welcome) to Iran. You may have heard of it by another name—Persia—the first nation to cease being nomadic, settle down, grow crops, and raise livestock, 12,000 years ago!

The ruins of ancient Persepolis are 2,500 years old and are one of the country's must-visit attractions.

IRAN

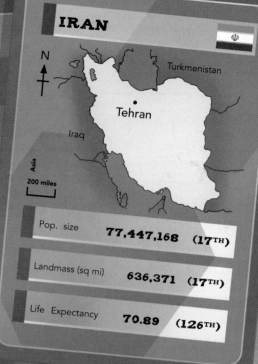

Turkmenistan

Tehran

Iraq

N

Asia

200 miles

Pop. size	77,447,168	(17TH)
Landmass (sq mi)	636,371	(17TH)
Life Expectancy	70.89	(126TH)

PERSIAN VERSE

Poetry is incredibly important to Iran and its people. Thousands of pilgrims travel to the tomb of Hafez, the most popular poet in Persian history. Every evening the structure is lit up, and pieces of Hafez's poetry are performed to the crowd among the orange trees and ornamental streams.

MAGIC CARPET RIDE

Persian carpets, or rugs, are world renowned and account for 30 percent of all the handwoven carpets sold worldwide. It is believed that Iran employs more than one million weavers, who design and make these iconic carpets with their intricate patterns. Each medium-sized rug can take up to a year to make!

THE CAT SAT ON A MAT

Iran is famous for both its Persian cats and its Persian carpets. With their iconic long hair and cute, flat faces, Persian cats are even lazier than normal felines, often being called "furniture with fur."

TURKMENISTAN

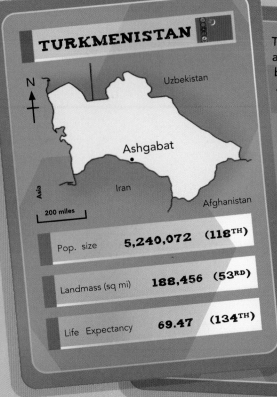

Uzbekistan

N

Ashgabat

Asia

Iran

Afghanistan

200 miles

Pop. size	5,240,072	(118TH)
Landmass (sq mi)	188,456	(53RD)
Life Expectancy	69.47	(134TH)

Turkmenistan is a land of record-breaking wonder and geographical splendor. Everywhere you look, something awesome is happening!

The country is 70 percent composed of the gigantic Karakum Desert, but that hasn't stopped life from growing abundantly in its mega cities.

TURKMEN WISDOM

A popular Turkmen phrase, "Water is a Turkmen's life, a horse is his wings, and a carpet is his soul," can often be heard uttered by *aksasals*—Turkmen with white beards respected for their wisdom, who often wear big, black shaggy hats, known as *telpeks*.

EARTH SHATTERING

On October 6, 1948, an earthquake measuring seven on the Richter scale devastated Turkmenistan's capital city, Ashgabat, killing two-thirds of the population—more than 150,000 people. The city has been rebuilt in white marble, giving Ashgabat the world's highest density of white-marble-clad buildings—more than 500—and sending it into the *Guinness World Records* book.

YANGYKALA CANYON

As far from the beaten path as you're ever likely to get on planet Earth, Yangykala Canyon is a mesmerizing site—and one worth the trip! The canyon is made up of all shapes, sizes, and colors, with bands of pink, red, and yellow rock standing out from the desert floor.

Derweze (Door to Hell)

THE DOOR TO HELL

Known locally as Derweze, this man-made 230 ft. (70 m) crater was set on fire by Soviet geologists to burn off the natural gas they discovered there when drilling for oil. They thought that the flames would die after a few days, but the crater has now been burning for 40 years! The site is known as the Door to Hell.

SUPER STAR

If you ever want to see the world's largest star, you don't need to buy a telescope—just buy a ticket to Ashgabat. Built in 2011, and measuring 692 ft. (211 m) tall, the Turkmenistan Broadcasting Center Tower incorporated the "Star of Oguzkhan" into the design.

JURASSIC PARK

One hundred and fifty million years ago, Turkmenistan was the best place to see dinosaurs. Known as the "Plateau of the Dinosaurs," the country has the most awesome collection of fossilized dinosaur tracks anywhere on the planet. Discovered in the 1950s, more than 483 footprints have been preserved in the muddy ground of the Köytendag National Park. It is one of the most valuable dinosaur fossil sites anywhere in the world.

SURROUNDED

Surrounded on all sides by neighboring countries such as Kazakhstan and Tajikistan, Uzbekistan doesn't have any sea coasts. In fact, it is "double landlocked," meaning it is two whole countries away from the sea!

Only one other country on the planet is double landlocked, but which one is it?

SEE PAGE 81

Formerly part of the Soviet Union, this Central Asian nation is now famous for its blue-domed mosques and mighty minarets.

But, in the 14th century, Uzbekistan was an important location along the Great Silk Road, and thus the epicenter of the new, expanding, modern world.

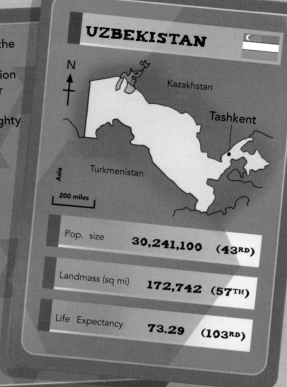

UZBEKISTAN

Kazakhstan

Tashkent

Asia

Turkmenistan

200 miles

Pop. size	30,241,100	(43RD)
Landmass (sq mi)	172,742	(57TH)
Life Expectancy	73.29	(103RD)

BREAKING BREAD

According to an ancient Uzbek tradition, whenever family members go on a journey, they have to take a bite from a small piece of *lapioshka,* a type of flat, unleavened bread. The remaining bread is then buried somewhere safe until the family member comes home.

MARCO! POLO! MARCO! POLO!

The esteemed Venetian explorer Marco Polo may be the inspiration for the classic children's hide-and-seek game, but more importantly, he was one of the most famous merchants who traveled along the entire length of the Silk Road. Polo's journey took three years, and his experiences were published in 1300 in a book called *Livre des merveilles du monde (Book of the Marvels of the World).* The book inspired other travelers to see the world, including a certain Mr. Christopher Columbus.

MORNING PLOV

One of the signature dishes of Uzbekistan is *plov,* sometimes called pilaf. It's a savory rice dish with meat, onions, and carrots. The head of the household traditionally makes *plov,* and there are so many cherished family recipes throughout the country that some say there are over 1,200 ways to make the dish! *Plov* is traditionally cooked in a large cauldron and served to guests on the morning of a wedding celebration.

GREAT SILK ROAD

More than a thousand years ago, the Great Silk Road—less a road and more an unmarked trading route—connected Europe and Asia, two different worlds at the time. Merchants from Europe traveled the 4,000 mi. (6,437 km) route, making connections with traders from exotic lands, swapping gold, silver, and food for silks, fabrics, medicines, and spices, items that were of great value and scarcity back home.

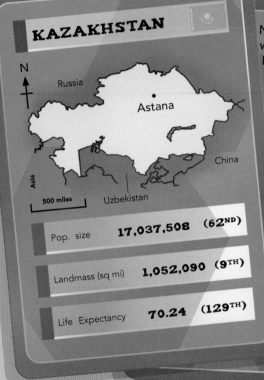

KAZAKHSTAN

N

Russia

Astana

Asia

China

Uzbekistan

500 miles

Pop. size	17,037,508	(62ND)
Landmass (sq mi)	1,052,090	(9TH)
Life Expectancy	70.24	(129TH)

Never to be confused with smaller sister Kyrgyzstan, Kazakhstan is a transcontinental nation that is one of a kind. Indeed, *kazakh* is a Turkic word meaning "independent."

Geographically located in both Europe and Asia, it is a huge country that equals the size of Western Europe.

STAN AND DELIVER

Turkmenistan, Uzbekistan, Kazakhstan, Kyrgyzstan, Pakistan, Afghanistan, Tajikistan all have something in common. What is it? Yes, their names all end in "stan," a word meaning "land of."

ROCKETS AT THE READY

Currently operated by Russia but located in Kazakhstan, the Baikonur Cosmodrome is the world's first and largest space-launch facility. Russian space flights take off from here, either sending payloads of equipment and cosmonauts to the International Space Station or rocketing satellites out of the Earth's atmosphere and into orbit.

THE CASPIAN SEA

Known as the largest inland body of water anywhere on Earth, the semisalty Caspian Sea is where the beluga sturgeon swims around. The eggs of this particular fish are known as caviar, a delicacy that takes 35 years to mature and can cost more than $300 for just a small 3.5 oz. (100 g) jar.

Beluga caviar

A IS FOR APPLE

The humble apple originates from the snowy hillsides of Almaty, Kazakhstan's biggest city, where they grew wild for thousands of years before humans started harvesting them. Now there are 7,500 varieties of apples grown around the world and they are the second most eaten fruit on Earth.

BIG TENT

The world's largest tent may not sound like a thrilling record to hold, but when you take a look at the neon wonder that is the Khan Shatyr ("Royal Marquee") Entertainment Center in capital city Astana, you'll know why it's such a big deal. Its completely transparent! At night, it lights up in bright neon colors, and the 492 ft. (150 m) tall tent can be seen from miles around. It was completed in 2010.

HIGH HORSE

Historians believe that Kazakhstan is where humans first started to tame and ride wild horses. The country is famous for its population of wild Kazakh horses, which are known as excellent riding animals. Horse meat is also considered a delicacy in Kazakhstan.

STEPPE INTO THE WILD

Most of Kazakhstan's geography is extremely flat and barren. Known as "steppe," the land is predominantly dry grassland with no trees and can get extremely hot in summer and very cold in winter.

EPIC OF MANAS

Though never really written down, the *Epic of Manas*, the world's longest poem, is the centerpiece of Kyrgyz culture and a monumental achievement. Recited in a semimelodic chant by elder statesmen and storytellers, known as *manaschi*, the oral poem is 500,000 lines long, making it 20 times longer than the next longest poems, Homer's *Odyssey* and *Iliad*, combined. The poem details epic battles and struggles of the ancient Kyrgyz people.

Kyrgyz manaschi

Never to be confused with its bigger brother Kazakhstan, Kyrgyzstan is a timeless land of mountain valleys, mountains, lakes, yurts, and did we mention mountains?

Kyrgyz translates as "forty"—a representation of the 40 nomadic tribes who were united as Kyrgyzstanis by the warrior Manas.

KYRGYZSTAN

Kazakhstan

Bishkek

Asia

Tajikistan   China

100 miles

Pop. size	5,719,500	(112TH)
Landmass (sq mi)	77,202	(85TH)
Life Expectancy	70.06	(132ND)

FIVE FINGERS

Kyrgyzstan's finest example of local cuisine is the national dish *beshbarmak*. Served in a bowl called a *kese*, and eaten with only your hands—hence the name of *beshbarmak*, or "five fingers"—this tasty broth is boiled sheep meat served with noodles in an onion sauce. The sheep's head is often served to the guest of honor.

HOT LAKE

Affectionately known as the Hot Lake, Issyk Kul Lake never freezes over, despite its high altitude and being surrounded by snowy mountains. It is the second-largest saltwater lake on Earth, and it's the salt that stops the water from freezing.

PRE-GLAMPING CAMPING

These days camping in a yurt—a type of big strong tent—is considered glamorous camping, or "glamping". But for thousands of years, the nomadic Kyrgyz people have taken shelter in yurts to protect them from the harsh weather of the steppe as they slept. Kyrgyzstanis are so indebted to traditional yurts as a way of life that one features on their national flag—the only flag to have a tent on it!

Yurt

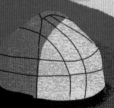

TAJIKISTAN

Uzbekistan
Kyrgyzstan
China
Dushanbe
Asia
Afghanistan

N

100 miles

Pop. size	**8,207,834**	**(95TH)**
Landmass (sq mi)	**55,251**	**(94TH)**
Life Expectancy	**67.06**	**(145TH)**

Welcome to Tajikistan, one of the world's highest countries!

Famed for its dry fruit, for being covered by 90 percent mountains, and for being closed off to the world for an entire century by the Russians, this stunning state is finally spilling its secrets and opening itself up to the world. *Roh-i-safed—* safe trip!

WAVE THAT FLAG!

Tajikistan's Dushanbe Flagpole is 541 ft. (165 m) tall and was built to celebrate the nation's 20-year anniversary of independence from the Soviet Union.

BAA, BAA, MARCO POLO SHEEP!

Named after the intrepid Venetian adventurer Marco Polo, who first detailed them in his book, *Livre des merveilles du monde (Book of the Marvels of the World)*, Marco Polo sheep are the biggest species of sheep in the world.

Marco Polo sheep

WILD GAME

Regarded as the world's wildest game, *buzkashi* is a horse-mounted sport that has the same sort of rules as polo, but with one main difference: the ball is the body of a headless goat! The brutal game, translated as "goat dragging," is played at the March Navrus festival in Hissar and involves competitors trying to grab the goat from each other. The winner is the player who can drag the goat across the goal, sometimes known as the Circle of Justice.

NON BREAD RULES

A delicious and traditional type of bread served in Tajikistan is called *non*. There are rules when dealing with *non*, with which you must comply:

1) It is highly uncustomary to serve a Tajik person a meal with no **NON**.

2) **NON** is so highly respected that if a piece is dropped on the floor, you aren't allowed to eat it. A whole new **NON** must be freshly made.

3) Nothing is allowed to be placed on top of a **NON**, unless it is another piece of **NON**.

4) If a **NON** is placed upside down, it's bad luck.

THE PAMIR HIGHWAY

Tajikistan's most awesome natural landmark happens to be the place where the Himalayan, Hindu Kush, Karakoram, Kunlun, and Tian Shan mountain ranges meet. The Pamir mountain range—one of the highest collections of mountains—contains the M41 Highway, or the Pamir Highway, part of the Silk Road, a route that has been used for centuries to help transport goods across the country.

JAM-PACKED MINARET

The Minaret of Jam, Afghanistan's first World Heritage Site, stands alone in the remote and isolated mountain region of Ghor Province. This intricately decorated tower, with its beautiful geometric patterns, was constructed around 1190 and is made entirely of baked mud bricks. In 2014 it was reported that this revered 800-year-old minaret was in "imminent danger" of falling down.

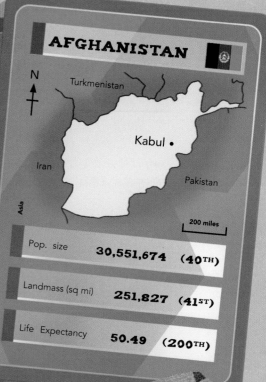

Modern history has not been kind to Afghanistan, as the country has faced decades of civil war, terrorism, and military presence.

Still, Afghanistan remains one of the world's greatest natural wonders and an ancient treasure trove.

AFGHANISTAN

Turkmenistan

N

Iran

Asia

Kabul •

Pakistan

200 miles

Pop. size	30,551,674	(40TH)
Landmass (sq mi)	251,827	(41ST)
Life Expectancy	50.49	(200TH)

BAMIYAN BUDDHAS

Built into the sandstone Bamiyan Cliffs were once two giant Buddha statues, decorated with gold and jewels. They were constructed in the mid-16th century to honor the teachings of Buddhism and were surrounded by the ruins of a Buddhist monastery carved into cliffs. Sadly, in 2001, the ruling Taliban government destroyed them with dynamite. All that remain are two empty holes.

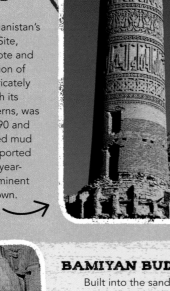

BLUE MOSQUE

The Shrine of Hazrat Ali, or the Blue Mosque, is located in Mazar-i-Sharif, one of Afghanistan's largest cities. Perhaps the country's most iconic religious site, the dual blue domes of the shrine were built in the 15th century. Five times a day, during prayer, hundreds of Muslims come to perform a *salat*, a ritual bowing, to worship the oneness of God.

The Shrine of Hazrat Ali

KITE FIGHTING

Kite flying is a gentle, relaxing hobby, a great way to pass the time and unwind with the wind. Not in Afghanistan! Kite fighting is a serious sport here and involves many kite flyers all competing at the same time, trying to "cut" the taut kite lines of their opponents. This is done by using an abrasive line—a string that is coated with powdered glass. The rules to kite fighting are simple: whoever keeps their kite flying the longest wins.

Afghan hound

GOOD DOG

Afghan hounds, with their thick, long fur, are one of the oldest-known breeds of dog. They are also one of the biggest. In 2005, the world's first scientifically cloned dog, Snuppy, was created using a cell from the ear of an Afghan hound. Snuppy is named after the initials of the Seoul National University (SNU), where she was cloned, and the word "puppy." Snuppy was named the world's most amazing invention in 2005 by *Time* magazine.

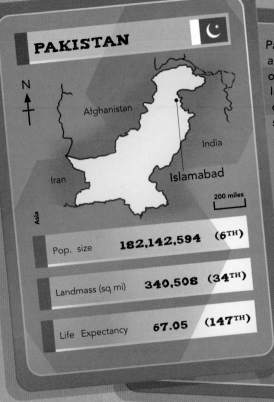

PAKISTAN

N

Afghanistan

Iran

India

Islamabad

200 miles

Asia

Pop. size	182,142,594	(6TH)
Landmass (sq mi)	340,508	(34TH)
Life Expectancy	67.05	(147TH)

Pakistan is known as the "crossroads of Asia," where Indian and Asian cultures fuse to form something entirely new and magical.

Contained within its borders are massive mosques, national mausoleums, phenomenal palaces, and friendly people. Pakistan is the "land of pure," for sure.

IT'S NOT CRICKET

Cricket may be the most popular obsession in Pakistan, but polo is a much more exciting sport to watch! Most people refer to polo as "hockey on horseback," which is a pretty accurate description. The name *polo* was invented in Pakistan—the word translates as "ball" in the local language. The most important local polo match of the year is played high up in the Hindu Kush mountains, at Shandur Top, the world's highest elevated polo field. It is played between the very best sportsmen and horses chosen for the Gilgit and Chitral teams by a panel of judges.

KARAKORAM HIGHWAY

It may well house the second-tallest mountain in the world, the mighty K2, but the Karakoram Highway is pretty spectacular all by itself. Often described as the "Eighth Wonder of the World," this iconic route meanders for 750 mi. (1,200 km), connecting Islamabad with China's Xingjiang province. It is officially the world's highest paved road, situated amongst the world's harshest terrain.

MOHENJO DARO

Now it's an archaeological site, but 4,000 years ago Mohenjo Daro (Mount of the Dead) was the place to be seen and home to one of the largest populations of humans of that period. Mohenjo Daro is also the first example of a city built using a grid pattern, a system that is used predominantly today in most town and city planning.

MARKHOR MY WORDS!

Ladies and gentlemen, we give you the markhor—the world's strangest goat! This peculiar creature is the national animal of Pakistan and has two corkscrew horns and a massive beard, which makes it looks rather odd. Imagine having one as a pet!

Markhor

JINGLE BUSES

Pakistan's jingle trucks and buses with their brightly colored decorations are a tradition as long and colorful as the trucks themselves! The custom first started out when bus drivers began taking reminders of their homes with them on long journeys. Over the years, drivers have decorated their trucks and buses with bright patterns and swirls, depictions of historical scenes, portraits, and chains that jingle when the truck moves. The more the truck jingles, the wealthier its owner.

Where else in the world might you find crazily colorful buses? SEE PAGE 19

Vishnu

HINDUISM—THE BASICS!
Eight out of ten people who live in India practice Hinduism. According to this faith, three gods ruled over the world. Brahma the creator, Vishnu the preserver, and Shiva the destroyer.

Shiva

Brahma

As the birthplace of two of the world's most-followed religions— Hinduism and Buddhism—it comes as no surprise that India holds many things in its own culture sacred.

From maharajas to mountains, tigers to temples (and tea!), cricket to cows, rivers to rice, —everything is *kamāla* ('amazing') in India.

INDIA

N

Pakistan   China

New Delhi

Asia

500 miles

Sri Lanka

Pop. size	1,252,139,596	(2ND)
Landmass (sq mi)	1,222,559	(7TH)
Life Expectancy	67.8	(143RD)

COLOR EXPLOSION
India's Holi Festival has traveled the world as the "Festival of Colors" and is celebrated across the country every year. The event welcomes spring and says goodbye to winter. Large sacks of colorful powder, flower petals, and balloons filled with colored water are handed out to the hundreds of thousands of attendees who then throw them all over each other!

MY, WHAT A MUSTACHE
Hailing from Jaipur, Ram Singh Chauhan is the proud owner of the world's longest mustache. After 32 years of uninterrupted growth, Mr. Chauhan's mighty 'stache is almost 16 ft. (5 m) long! Not surprisingly, he spends two hours a day grooming it!

A TRULY REGAL CAT
Panthera tigris tigris, or Bengal tiger, as it's more commonly known, is a majestic creature— though there are fewer than 2,500 left in the wild. The royal Bengal prowls proudly around grasslands of India, Bangladesh, Bhutan, and Nepal. It is the national animal of India, and its roar can be heard more than a mile away!

A NICE CUP OF TEA
India is the world's largest consumer of tea. Two of the most iconic places to go to pick tea are Darjeeling and Assam. Here, tea pickers select the very best black tea leaves, which are then dried, crushed, and, finally, put in your tea bags. Remember—the best tea is that which has been brewed in boiling water for more than four minutes.

Bengal tigers

WORLD'S MOST BEAUTIFUL
Twenty-eight different types of precious stone were used to build the Taj Mahal—often voted as the world's most beautiful building. Building began in 1653, and 20,000 workers toiled away over a period of 21 years, in honor of Mogul Emperor Shah Jahan's favorite wife, Mumtaz Mahal. During the day, the Taj Mahal appears in three different colors—pink in the morning, white in the evening, and golden at bedtime, when lit by the moon.

Taj Mahal

HOLY COW!
In Sanskrit, the language of Hinduism, the meaning of the word *gavisti* is "war," but the literal translation is "a desire for more cows." In Hinduism, cows are sacred. According to Hindu scripture—which believes in the reincarnation of human souls into animals—gods and goddesses live in the bodies of cows.

SRI LANKA

India
Asia
100 miles
Colombo
N

Pop. size	20,483,000	(57TH)
Landmass (sq mi)	25,332	(122ND)
Life Expectancy	76.35	(64TH)

Sri Lanka may be known as the "Teardrop of India," but it has no reason to be sad—the country's amazing.

With more sacred temples, tombs, and tea-pickers than you can shake a banyan branch at, as well as stunning lagoons and coastline, *ayubowan* (may you live long) in Sri Lanka.

ADAM'S PEAK

From Dambulla Cave Temple to Adam's Peak, when it comes to sacred places, Sri Lanka has it covered from top to bottom. Shooting out of the ground at a height of 7,359 ft. (2,243 m), Adam's Peak is a holy mountain for Buddhism, Hinduism, Islam, and Christianity. At the top, there is a rock formation known as Sri Pada, believed to be the footprint of Buddha (Buddhism), Shiva (Hinduism), and Adam (Islam and Christianity). Every year, millions of pilgrims trek to pray in front of the footprint.

Paintings decorating Sigiriya

MARRIAGE IS ALMOST THE END OF THE WORLD

Sri Lanka's most notorious beauty spot is called World's End. It's a sheer cliff rock face with a 4,000 ft. (1,219 m) vertical drop. In January 2015, a Dutch honeymooner, Mamitho Lendas, became the first person to survive the almighty drop when he slipped after taking pictures of his wife. A tree is believed to have broken his fall!

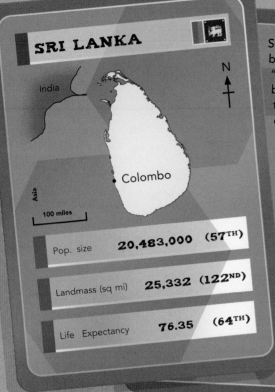

SEE PAGE 6

Where else in the world can you find a sheer mountain like this one?

PAWS FOR THOUGHT

An ancient palace built on top of a 656 ft. (200 m) tall rock, Sigiriya is a fortress like no other in the world. It has giant lion paws carved out of rock and hundreds of exquisite paintings of beautiful women on the face of the rock.

SWEET SMELL OF SUCCESS

Discovered more than 4,000 years ago by the Egyptians, cinnamon is one of Sir Lanka's greatest exports. Not only does this spice taste nice, it has brain-boosting functions, too. One smell of the stuff will help you stay alert for longer and make your memory work better.

JUMBO POOL PARTY

Each year, more than 7,000 wild Asian elephants arrive at a muddy reservoir at Minneriya National Park for a well-deserved drink of water after a long journey! This is the largest elephant migration in the world, and it's known as "the gathering."

UNDERWATER MEETING!

To raise awareness of the matter of the Maldives' possible disappearance underwater, President Mohamed Nasheed relocated a meeting with his staff to the bottom of the ocean! In 2009, the president and 13 government officials put on their scuba gear and sank to the bottom of the sea. They then sat at their desks and got to work!

You've arrived just in time. Well done! Many believe that in a few decades time, the islands of the Maldives will no longer exist.

As the flattest and lowest-lying nation on Earth, the rise in ocean levels could mean this tranquil island paradise could become wiped off the map.

MALDIVES

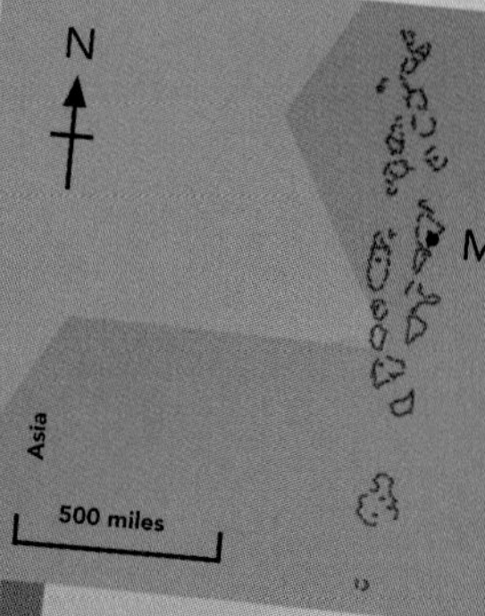

N

Asia

500 miles

Male

Pop. size	345,023	(177TH)
Landmass (sq mi)	116	(195TH)
Life Expectancy	75.15	(80TH)

NEMO FOUND

The Maldives is home to hundreds of funny-looking species, such as hammerhead sharks and hermit crabs, but the funniest of all is the clown fish. This orange-and-white fish protects its eggs by hiding them in the wispy tendrils of sea anemones.

BUNGALOWS OF THE SEA

Sitting on top of a crystal clear lagoon, the Maldives' water bungalows are the most luxurious way to kill some time! The coconut-palm tree, the national tree of the Maldives, is used from bark to branch, husk to root, to help construct these tranquil homes.

LIGHT OF A BILLION STARS

It may appear as if there are billions of stars in the water, but the tiny sparkling points of light in the sea near the beaches of Vaadhoo Island are actually a phenomenon called bioluminescence, caused by tiny marine microbes called phytoplankton.

NEPAL

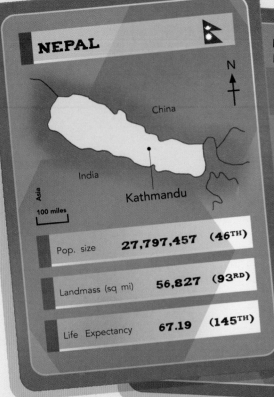

China

India

Asia

Kathmandu

100 miles

N

Pop. size	27,797,457	(46TH)
Landmass (sq mi)	56,827	(93RD)
Life Expectancy	67.19	(145TH)

Nepal is the birthplace of Buddha and home to the mysterious Yeti and the world's tallest mountain.

In 2015, the country was rocked by two devastating earthquakes, which damaged many buildings and caused landslides that destroyed villages. Many countries offered aid, but it will take years for Nepal to recover.

THE NATION'S FLAG

Nepal is the only nation on Earth with a non-quadrilateral flag. The flag's two triangles symbolize the Himalayan mountains that loom so large in the foreground of the country. They also represent Nepal's two major religions, Hinduism and Buddhism.

HOLY MEN

Nepal's Hindu holy men are called sadhus. With a deep belief in Hinduism, sadhus are revered throughout much of southern Asia for their spiritualism and rejection of material possessions. In their orange-and-yellow robes, they are often seen blessing special ceremonies, protecting villages from evil, and practicing meditation.

DON'T BE RUDE!

When meeting someone from Nepal, you must remember two things:

1) Don't touch anybody on the head—heads are spiritual parts of the body.
2) Don't offer your hand to greet a Nepalese person with a handshake or move in close for a kiss and a hug. Instead, put your palms together, bow your head, and say, *namaste* ("I salute the God in you").

WHEN IS IT?

Nepal is one of the last remaining nations to use the ancient Hindu Vikram Sandwat calendar. The calendar is 56.5 years ahead of the Gregorian one. The year starts in April, in the month of Baishakh. In Kathmandu, it's already the year 2070!

Namaste!

THE MIGHTIEST OF MOUNTAINS

The Nepalese call it Sagarmatha, "goddess of the sky." To the rest of the world, it is simply Mount Everest. At 60 million years old and 29,029 ft. (8,848 m) tall—just under the cruising altitude of a jumbo jet—Everest is 10 times higher than the tallest man-made structure ever constructed, the Burj Khalifa tower, in Dubai.

29,029 FT. (8,848 M)
Mt. Everest, Nepal

OTHER TALL MOUNTAINS AROUND THE WORLD

22,831 FT. (6,959 M)
Mt. Aconcagua, Argentina

20,322 FT. (6,194 M)
Mt. McKinley, U.S.

19,340 FT. (5,895 M)
Mt. Kilimanjaro, Tanzania

15,771 FT. (4,807 M)
Mont Blanc, France

12,388 FT. (3,776 M)
Mt. Fuji, Japan

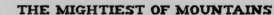

ROOF OF THE WORLD

Tibet is the highest place on Earth and home to the world's tallest mountains. Tibetan people have adapted to living at high altitudes. Tibet even has the world's highest train, the Qīnghai–Tibet Railway, which goes from Tibet's capital city, Lhasa, to Běijīng. Along the way, you can see huge salt lakes, plains dotted with yaks and herders' tents, and snow-capped mountain peaks.

"Roof of the world," the "land of snows," "Shangri-La"—this corner of Asia has been called dozens of beautiful names.

With its mountainous terrain, Buddhist monks, and ancient traditions, this land is so unlike anywhere else on Earth that only one word is really necessary: Tibet.

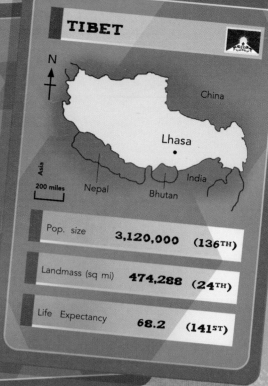

TIBET

N

Asia

China

Lhasa

200 miles

Nepal   Bhutan   India

Pop. size	3,120,000	(136TH)
Landmass (sq mi)	474,288	(24TH)
Life Expectancy	68.2	(141ST)

SELF-MADE MONKS

Dressed in handmade red robes, known as *kāṣāya*, Tibetan Buddhist monks are a national icon of Tibet. Monks carry out many rituals, such as meditation and mantras, and devote themselves to their "lamas"—types of wise teachers. A mantra is a word, or sometimes just a syllable, that Tibetan monks concentrate on, believing it to bring them inner wisdom, peace, and greater strength.

MASSIVE MASTIFFS

The Tibetan mastiff is one of the most expensive breeds of dog in the world. These furry canines have been sold in recent years for as much as $1.5 million per pup! The most famous of all is Big Splash—or *Hong Dong* in Chinese—a red Tibetan mastiff that looks like a big red cuddly bear!

TIBETAN PRAYER WHEELS

Tibetan prayer wheels are not to be toyed with. They consist of a metal cylinder on a handle, with a small weight attached. When the handle is flicked, the small weight hits the metal cylinder and makes a noise. Inside the handle is a written prayer, called *Om mani padme hum*, which means "O Jewel in the Lotus Hum" and is recited by Tibetan monks.

THE DALAI LAMA

Jetsun Jamphel Ngawang Lobsang Yeshe Tenzin Gyatso is better known by his other name, the Dalai Lama. Or, to be even more precise, the 14th Dalai Lama. The Dalai Lama is the revered "head teacher" of Tibetan Buddhism, a holy position held sacred for almost 1,000 years, with many Tibetans believing that when a lama dies, he is reincarnated in a baby born soon afterwards.

KING PALACE

Located in Lhasa, the former residence of the exiled Dalai Lama is Potala Palace, one of the grandest buildings in the world. Built in 637 by Lobsang Gyatso, the fifth Dalai Lama, Potala is made of thick stone walls, and it has copper foundations so it can withstand earthquakes. The palace has more than 10,000 shrines to its iconic lamas, as well as 1,000 rooms. Strangely for a building with 13 stories, the Potala Palace has only three very long staircases to get you from the bottom to the top!

BHUTAN

Tibet

• Thimphu

Asia

India

50 miles

N

Pop. size	753,947	(167TH)
Landmass (sq mi)	14,824	(135TH)
Life Expectancy	68.98	(137TH)

Look out of your nearest window. Can you see a fairy-tale, cliff-top monastery? Or a Buddhist monk paying respect to a demon? How about a blue poppy? Or a goat that looks like a cow?

Can you see any of these amazing things? No? Well, in Bhutan, you can!

LAND OF THE THUNDER DRAGON

Bhutanese people call their home Druk Yul, which means "the Land of the Thunder Dragons," because of the almighty thunderstorms that roar—and echo— through the Himalayan mountain range.

BE HAPPY

While most countries of the world worry about GDP (Gross Domestic Product)—how much they earn from selling things— Bhutan's king, Jigme Singye Wangchuck, strongly believes in Gross National Happiness (GNH). This philosophy strives to achieve a balance between the ancient and spiritual and the modern and material. As a result, Bhutan became one of the last countries to allow its people access to television and the Internet, which it did in 1999. King Wangchuck believes that television and the Internet could distract from and corrupt their traditions. He could be right!

TIGER'S NEST

Paro Taktsang Dzong (Tiger's Nest Monastery) is Bhutan's most iconic structure. It was carved into a cliff's edge in 1692 and is a site where monks travel to meditate and worship—and decorate it with hundreds of colorful prayer flags.

Kira

Gho

TSHECHU

Bhutan's main religious festivals, known as Tshechus, are a vital part of the Bhutanese calendar. Every year they unite the remote mountain villages at sacred monasteries. Colorful masks and ritual dances, such as the Gumpa dance, the Black Hat dance, and the Dance of the Terrifying Deities, have been preserved and honored for centuries.

THE BLUE POPPY

The nation's iconic flower, the blue poppy, is as rare as it is beautiful. It only grows at really high altitudes, 13,123 ft. (4,000 m) above sea level, where not even trees can grow or insects can fly! The flower can grow to more than 3 ft. (1 m) high but only flowers once before dying, so it's incredibly rare to see it in bloom.

GOAT? ANTELOPE? COW?

There are lots of strange animals wandering the Himalayas, but the animal that takes first prize is the takin—a goat-antelope that looks like a cow. Bhutan's national animal is so unusual that many Bhutanese believe it was created when Drukpa Kunley, the Divine Madman and a popular saint, visited Bhutan and magically fused a goat's head with a cow's bones!

GHO AND KIRA

The Bhutanese government—on orders from the king—has imposed a rule called *driglam namzha*, which dictates what citizens are allowed to wear, as well as how they should behave in order to keep their ancient customs alive and well in the modern age. Men wear *gho*. Women wear *kira*.

L IS FOR LUNGI

The iconic traditional dress of Bangladeshi men is the *lungi*—a patterned piece of fabric that is worn like a skirt and tied around the waist. *Lungis* are popular gifts for Bangladeshis who have just got married.

SEE YOU SOON, MONSOON

Every June to September, Bangladesh experiences its monsoon season, an intense period of strong winds and increased rainfall—often leading to large areas of flooding. In 1998, the Bangladesh monsoon left two-thirds of the country underwater and 30 million people without homes. It was described as the worst flooding in human history.

Striped man-eating tigers roam the largest mangrove swamps in the world, millions of people roam the most overcrowded city in the world, and monsoons bring storms and floods every year.

So hold onto your hats, and get ready for breathtaking Bangladesh!

BANGLADESH

N

India

Dhaka

India

Asia

100 miles

Pop. size	156,594,962	(8TH)
Landmass (sq mi)	56,977	(92ND)
Life Expectancy	70.65	(127TH)

THEY SURE LIKE RICKSHAWS

Rickshaws—bicycle taxis—are the most popular way of traveling in Dhaka. There are more than 300,000 of them on the streets! The word "rickshaw" comes from the Japanese word *jinrikisha*, which literally means "human-powered vehicle." Since 2000, Dhaka has become renowned as the rickshaw capital of the world and, as a result, traffic can stand still for more than seven hours a day!

Rickshaw

JAM-PACKED TRAINS

Every year, in honor of the Muslim festival of Eid al-Fitr, thousands of Bangladeshis pack themselves onto trains at Dhaka Station in order to travel home to their villages to be with their families. Eid al-Fitr is the biggest Muslim festival and marks the end of the holy fasting month of Ramadan.

WHAT A RICE SURPRISE!

Seven percent of all Bangladesh's agricultural land is used for producing rice—the country's most valuable source of economy, as well as food—producing 35 million tons of it a year! There are fields and fields and fields of it all over the place. Rice, in case you didn't know, is the seed of a grass species called ***Oryza sativa***.

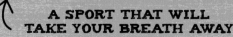

A SPORT THAT WILL TAKE YOUR BREATH AWAY

Bangladesh's national sport is *ha-du-du*, or *kabaddi*, as it is internationally known. "Raiders" from one team tag, tackle, and invade the playing area of the opposing team. One main rule: at all times the player who raids must repeat the phrase "Kabaddi, Kabaddi, Kabaddi, Kabaddi, Kabaddi," without running out of breath. If they do—they're out!

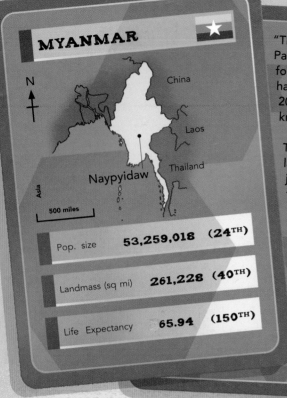

MYANMAR

N

China
Laos
Thailand
Naypyidaw

Asia

500 miles

Pop. size	53,259,018	(24TH)
Landmass (sq mi)	261,228	(40TH)
Life Expectancy	65.94	(150TH)

"The Land of Pagodas" is one name for Myanmar, but it has others, too. Until 2011, this nation was known as Burma.

This golden-tipped land of rubies and jade contains thousands of places of worship and temples, as well as the Road to Mandalay, described by the famous poet Rudyard Kipling.

SHWEDAGON PAGODA

Myanmar is packed with thousands of pagodas—cone-shaped structures that are sacred places for the teaching and practicing of Buddhism. The 2,500-year-old Shwedagon Pagoda is perhaps the most famous of them all. It is believed to house eight strands of Buddha's hair as well as other ancient Buddhist relics. At the very tip-top of the peak of the pagoda there are 5,448 diamonds and 2,317 rubies, as well as 1,065 bells made out of gold.

SNEEZY MONKEYS

Possibly the most adorable animal on the planet, the Myanmar snub-nosed monkey has upturned nostrils, which means it sneezes every time it rains! The monkeys end up having to spend rainy days sitting with their heads tucked between their knees to avoid this—otherwise their predators would know where they are.

GOLDEN ROCK

Dangling perilously close to the edge of a cliff sits the Kyaiktiyo Pagoda, also known as Golden Rock. Buddhists believe that the giant, gravity-defying boulder is balanced on a single strand of Buddha's hair, keeping it from rolling down the cliff. The pagoda is a popular site for Buddhist pilgrims.

LAKE LEG ROWERS

The Intha people who live around Myanmar's Inle Lake are renowned for their refreshing way of rowing their boats—they use their legs! This distinctive style evolved because the lake is covered in reeds, which makes it difficult to steer around them from a sitting position. Genius!

RINGS AROUND THE WORLD

The Kayan people, one of Myanmar's smallest ethnic groups, are world-renowned for the stacks of brass rings they wear around their neck. Though their neck always remains the same length, the rings push down their collarbone, making it look like their neck has stretched! Many women from the Kayan tribe begin wearing the rings at just two years old.

WELCOME TO

Krungthepmahanakhon Amonrattanakosin Mahintharayutthaya Mahadilokphop Noppharatratchathaniburirom Udomratchaniwetmahasathan Amonphimanawatansathit Sakkathattiyawitsanukamprasi

BANGKOK

The nation's beloved capital city is called Bangkok. But Bangkok is actually a simplified version of the City of Angels' formal name. Its full ceremonial name is the tongue-twisting Krungthepmahanakhon Amonrattanakosin Mahintharayutthaya Mahadilokphop Noppharatratchathaniburirom Udomratchaniwetmahasathan Amonphimanawatansathit Sakkathattiyawitsanukamprasi. It is the longest city name in the world!

Welcome to the "land of smiles," an affectionate nickname for the friendly people who are spread out across the country's diverse landscapes.

From the ultra-modern cities that glow neon bright, to the paradise islands that welcome millions of tourists every year, you would be *baa* (crazy) not to visit Thailand!

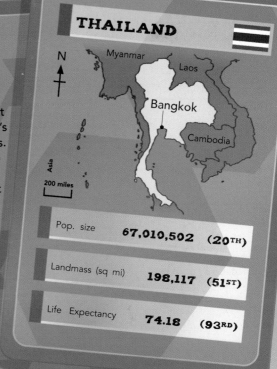

THAILAND

Pop. size	67,010,502	(20TH)
Landmass (sq mi)	198,117	(51ST)
Life Expectancy	74.18	(93RD)

WATER GOOD IDEA

Bangkok's floating markets, such as the one at Damnoen Saduak, are some of the most popular attractions in Thailand's capital city. Shoppers can hop from boat to boat and purchase fruits, vegetables, and spices in all sorts of different colors and sizes, from hundreds of different boats. If you're thirsty, buy some coconut juice—and drink it straight from the coconut.

LIGHT UP THE NIGHT

A lantern bug doesn't light up like a firefly, but it does come in many neon-bright colors. This stick insect is one of the most exotic creatures living in Thailand's tropical forests.

BIZARRE BUILDINGS

Architects in Thailand have created some of the strangest buildings in the world. One of the most iconic has been dubbed the Elephant Building. Can you guess why?

Lantern bug

COOL KARSTS

One of the most awe-inspiring of Thailand's tourist sites is the otherworldly landscape that surrounds the islets of Khao Phing Kan. Sticking out from the water like sore thumbs are tall towers called karsts. These have been captured in many famous films.

MONKEY SEE, MONKEY DO

Every November, people in Lopburi Province say thank you to the local monkeys for bringing tourists to the area—by putting on a Monkey Buffet Festival! More than 3,000 macaque monkeys come down from the trees to celebrate the event, which involves a feast of fruits, vegetables, and cakes for the monkeys to eat, as well as to steal from any person holding the food—cheeky monkeys! The festival also hosts plenty of monkey-related activities, with residents dressing up as monkeys, dancing like monkeys, and generally just monkeying around!

THAT'S A SMALL BAT, MAN

The world's smallest bat, the Kitti's hog-nosed bat, or bumblebee bat, lives in Thailand. It's about the size of a large bumblebee!

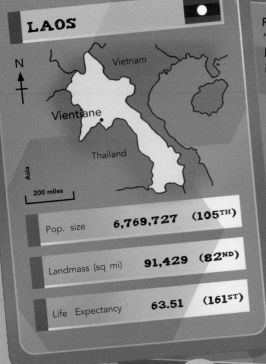

LAOS

N
↑

Vietnam

Vientiane

Thailand

Asia

200 miles

Pop. size	6,769,727	(105TH)
Landmass (sq mi)	91,429	(82ND)
Life Expectancy	63.51	(161ST)

Rhyming with "cow," not "house," landlocked Laos is a nation that is still feeling the aftereffects of the destructive Vietnam War that occurred in the 1960s and 1970s.

More than 80 million unexploded bombs remain undiscovered in this small but stunning country.

VOLLEYBALL WITH FEET

A popular sport in Laos is *kator*. It's like soccer and tennis mixed together, or volleyball that's played with your feet and a smaller ball! It has been played in Laos since 1100.

A high-kicking kator player

KING MEKONG FISH

Grows up to 10 ft.!

The mighty Mekong River flows through China, Burma, Laos, Thailand, Cambodia, and Vietnam, and it's home to the world's longest freshwater fish. The Mekong giant catfish can grow up to 10 ft. (3 m) long, and can weigh up to 660 lb. (300 kg).

FAST FOOD

Laos' night markets, such as the famous Luang Prabang market, sell all sorts of crunchy snacks—from fried rats and bats to toads and crickets, weaver ants, bamboo caterpillars, grasshoppers, wasps, termites, stinkbugs, beetles, waterbugs, worms, and dragonflies. If it moves, it can be eaten!

Fried rats!

BUDDHA PARK

Laos is full of religious *stupas*, *wats* (temples), and *pagodas*—places where Buddhists can go to meditate and study. Buddha Park takes a slightly different approach. Built in 1958, this sculpture park has over 200 Buddhist and Hindu statues, including a giant reclining Buddha, more than 394 ft. (120 m) long!

KING COBRA

With their forked tongue, deadly venom, and a length that reaches more than 13 ft. (4 m), the king cobra is one of the most dangerous snakes to ever slither around on Earth. Though it can kill elephants with just one bite, the king cobra usually finds its prey in other snakes and rats that live on the forest floor. If you see one raised off the ground and hissing in your direction, you'd better run. FAST!

BOOM!

The Bun Bang Fai (Rocket Festival) is an explosive event in the Laos lunar calendar. During the festival, bamboo rockets are fired into the air to let the god of rain, Phaya Thaen, know that it's time to send the rains to help that year's harvest be free from drought and pests. The higher a rocket goes, the bigger the praise that's heaped upon its builder.

A WAR OF THE WORLD

The Vietnam War was a conflict that saw North Vietnam (with the Viet Cong—their friends in the South) battle against South Vietnam and their ally, the United States. The war began in 1965 and ended when U.S. forces withdrew in 1973. More than two million Vietnamese people died during the conflict.

Nón lá

FANCY (T)HAT

The traditional and iconic headwear of the Vietnamese people is the *nón lá*, a conical hat made out of palm leaves. Along with the traditional female dress of *ao dai*, the hats have been worn for 3,000 years! Many people who travel to Vietnam bring back *nón lás* as souvenirs.

These days most people, upon hearing the word "Vietnam" instantly think "war." This is a natural response, considering the huge impact it has had on this nation ever since.

But, before modern history took its toll, Vietnam was the proud owner of an incredible heritage. It's an unforgettable place.

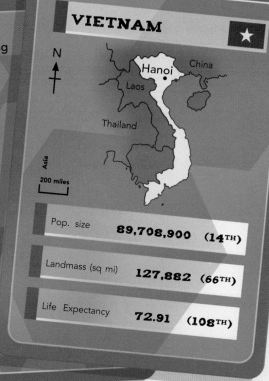

VIETNAM

N

Hanoi   China

Laos

Thailand

Asia

200 miles

Pop. size	89,708,900	(14TH)
Landmass (sq mi)	127,882	(66TH)
Life Expectancy	72.91	(108TH)

ONE WAY TO GET AROUND

Vietnam's mega cities, such as Hanoi and Hoi Chi Minh City, are bustling metropolises where people are in a hurry to get from A to B. The best way to travel is by bike—and you often see thousands of people on motorcycles or scooters waiting at traffic lights! Vietnamese people don't cycle light—it's not uncommon to see unusual items balanced very carefully on the back of their bikes. Cyclists can be seen carrying anything from fish traps, chickens, and goats to fruits, vegetables, and huge crates of bottled water.

A SOGGY TRADITION

Puppet shows are traditional the world over, but Vietnam lays claim to a special form of puppetry that's performed in a pool! Hanoi's famous water puppet shows feature large wooden puppets acting out traditional folktales accompanied by an orchestra. The puppeteers stand waist deep in water and use rods to make the puppets dance and splash about.

ROOM WITH A VIEW

Son Doong Cave is an incredible space. Formed around five million years ago, the cave system is more than 656 ft. (200 m) wide, 492 ft. (150 m) high, and 6 mi. (10 km) long!

FAT, ROUND, AND AWESOME!

Originating in Vietnam, pot-bellied pigs have become popular farmyard animals and pets all over the globe and can live for up to 20 years. They are by no means the largest of all pig species but they are always hungry. They have bad eyesight, but don't worry—they make up for it with good manners!

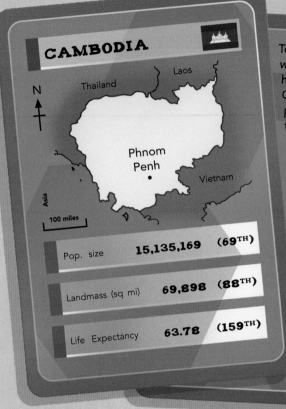

CAMBODIA

N

Thailand
Laos
Phnom Penh
Vietnam

Asia

100 miles

Pop. size	15,135,169	(69TH)
Landmass (sq mi)	69,898	(88TH)
Life Expectancy	63.78	(159TH)

Temples, known as *wats*, dominate the horizon in ancient Cambodia and provide some of the world's most breathtaking scenery.

It's a mystical place, where wild animals roam the streets, colorful *kramas* decorate people's heads, and fried tarantulas are on the menu!

GOOD KRAMA

Cambodians do not leave their houses without their *kramas*. A traditional, patterned garment, the *krama* has many uses: a scarf, a bandana, a sling to carry infant children, and even a hammock! Worn by men, women, and children, it traditionally comes in either red or blue.

Krama

HEAD START

In Cambodia, the head is regarded as the spiritually highest part of the body. Never touch or pat a Cambodian person on the head, as it's a sign of enormous disrespect!

KHMER ROUGE

The Khmer Rouge, led by dictator Pol Pot, took control of Cambodia by force in 1975. The repressive regime evacuated all the cities and forced everyone to work on farms. Those who protested and many educated people were killed. During their four-year reign, it is estimated that the Khmer Rouge executed three million Cambodians, many at the gruesome location now known as the Killing Fields. This tree was the site of many executions and now serves as a memorial to the children and babies who were murdered.

Fried tarantulas

CAVIAR OF CAMBODIA

Fried insects may be a strange delicacy to us, but to most Cambodians, they are a tasty, savory snack! Fried tarantulas, the "caviar of Cambodia," is on the menu at the Siem Reap Night Market, along with other creepy crawlies—roaches, locusts, and beetles.

ANGKOR WAT

Built more than 1,000 years ago, the temple complex of Angkor Wat has become the largest religious structure in the world. It is HUGE! It's reported to have taken 300 years to build and is known as the "city of temples" due to the fact that its ruins spread out over more than 200 square miles. Today, it is the primary tourist attraction in Cambodia.

TEMPLE OF TA PROHM

A stone's throw away from Angkor Wat is the temple of Ta Prohm. Abandoned five centuries ago, the temple site has been reclaimed by Mother Nature and the giant thitpok trees, with their huge trunks and eerie branches slouching over the once-sacred buildings.

SCRUMPTIOUS SATAY

Satay is a popular street-food snack throughout Malaysia. Chunks of chicken or beef are grilled on a skewer and covered in a sweet and sticky peanut sauce. Yum!

Borneo orangutan and baby

When it comes to being an exotic, mysterious, and ancient country, Malaysia doesn't monkey around. Though there are lots of monkeys!

From mega cities such as Kuala Lumpur to nomadic tribes deep in the jungles of Borneo, Malaysia has everything a traveler could wish for.

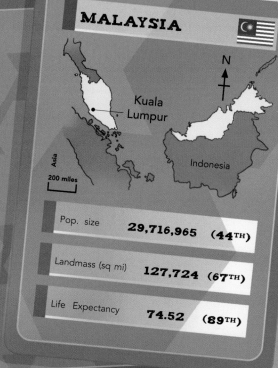

MALAYSIA

Kuala Lumpur

Asia

200 miles

Indonesia

Pop. size	29,716,965	(44TH)
Landmass (sq mi)	127,724	(67TH)
Life Expectancy	74.52	(89TH)

HANGING AROUND

The lush island of Borneo is one of planet Earth's only two places to see wild orangutans! Borneo orangutans are legendary—they are super smart, building nests high up in trees and using tools. Sadly, there are only around 12,000 left in the wild.

POWERFUL PETRONAS!

Kuala Lumpur's Petronas Towers are an iconic piece of the Malaysian city's skyline. Until 2004, the magnificent twin-tower structure was the tallest building in the world. It may have lost that status, but it's still one of the most amazing pieces of modern architecture on the planet!

Rafflesia flower

FLOWER POWER

Rafflesia is the largest flower species in the world, with blooms as large as 39 in. (100 cm)! But don't stand too close. The flower is notorious for its funky odor: a smell of rotting meat and stinky feet.

1,427 FT. wide

1,969 FT. long

377 FT. high

AWESOME CAVES

If you were to put your head into the Sarawak Chamber, a cave system in Borneo's Gunung Mulu National Park, you'd find yourself in the world's largest room! This "room" (think of it as a massive space underground) could fit eight jumbo jets on top of each other, with room to spare. It is 1,969 ft. (600 m) long, 1,427 ft. (435 m) wide, and 377 ft. (115 m) high.

MALAYAN TAPIR

Malaysia is one of 17 mega-diverse countries on Earth, with experts believing the land contains 20 percent of the world's total animal species. The most amazing of all is the Malayan tapir, an "odd-toed" mammal (it has four toes on its front legs and three toes on its back legs) and is half black, half white. When they're born, baby tapirs have black fur and white stripes, but as they grow older, their fur changes to help them blend into the moonlit jungles they hunt in at night.

BRUNEI

N

Bandar Seri Begawan

Asia

20 miles

Malaysia

Pop. size	417,784	(175TH)
Landmass (sq mi)	2,226	(170TH)
Life Expectancy	76.77	(56TH)

Surrounded by Malaysia and the South China Sea, the very tiny nation of Brunei is famous for its mosques, palaces, and the Bolkiah sultans (who have ruled the land for 600 years).

Despite its small size, it's the fourth-richest country in the world, thanks to its oil reserves.

QUITE A MOUTHFUL

The sultan of Brunei has a name as long as the zeroes in his bank account! Sultan Haji Hassanal Bolkiah Mu'izzaddin Waddaulah ibni Al-Marhum Sultan Haji Omar Ali Saifuddien Sa'adul Khairi Waddien is worth a reported $20 billion.

Sultan Haji Hassanal Bolkiah Mu'izzaddin Waddaulah ibni Al-Marhum Sultan Haji Omar Ali Saifuddien Sa'adul Khairi Waddien

PINOCCHIO MONKEYS

The proboscis monkeys that live in Brunei's thick, swampy rainforests have very long noses. They can walk upright, like humans, and live in colonies of about 20 members. Do you know how long a proboscis monkey's nose is? Have a guess. . .

A) 10 in. (25 cm)   **B)** 7 in. (18 cm)
C) 4 in. (10 cm)   **D)** 20 in. (50 cm)

Answer: C

FRESH PRINCE

The sultan likes the finer things in life, including the world's largest house! His palace, Istana Nural Iman, boasts 1,788 rooms, more than 250 bathrooms, and five swimming pools. Even the car park is massive—the sultan is believed to own more than 5,000 cars, worth more than $450 million! The most famous of them all is this gold-plated Rolls-Royce, made with 24-karat pure gold.

What a nose!

STICK OUT LIKE A SORE THUMB

Bruneians don't point with their index fingers; this is considered very rude. They point with their thumbs instead. Remember that if you're ever asked for directions.

MARINA BAY

Completed in 2011, at a cost of $6 billion, Marina Bay Sands—with its distinctive architectural design—is one of the most complex buildings ever constructed! The Sands SkyPark, which crosses the three buildings, contains the world's largest elevated swimming pool—492 ft. (150 m) long and 57 stories high!

Marina Bay Sands

Singapura, the "Lion City," doesn't have any lions, but it is one of only three city-states in the world.

As one of the busiest metropolises on Earth, Singaporeans—with their uber-long skyscrapers and giant ferris wheel—are living the high life. Come join them. . .

SINGAPORE

Malaysia

N

Asia

Singapore

10 miles

Pop. size	5,399,200	(116TH)
Landmass (sq mi)	276	(184TH)
Life Expectancy	84.38	(3RD)

IM-PORT-ANT PORT

With around 90 percent of the world's shopping transported by sea, those who control the world's biggest ports can become very wealthy indeed. So it is with Singapore, home to the world's busiest transshipment port. On any day of the year, there are more than 1,000 cargo ships in the port. One such ship—the world's largest in fact—the *Emma Maersk* often visits Singapore and is able to carry 11,000 cargo containers at once. If these containers were stacked end to end, they would go on for an eye-bending 42 mi. (68 km)!

HARD TO SWALLOW

**Q: What's big, round, spiky, smells of poop, and tastes delicious?
A: A Durian.**

That's right, this "King of Fruits," as it is known in Singapore, may smell like a spoonful of sewage, but to the locals it tastes great. The smell has been described as so off-putting that many Singapore hotels, restaurants, and public-transport authorities have banned it, with strict fines of up to $500 if you're caught eating it. No durians allowed!

GARDENS BY THE BAY

Singapore has lots of parks, but the king of them all is Gardens by the Bay. This "superpark" is home to a grove of giant "supertrees" that light up in magical colors every evening, and an indoor "cloud mountain" with its own thundering tropical waterfall!

RAINBOW TEMPLE

Built in 1827, the rainbow-colored Sri Mariamman Temple is Singapore's oldest Hindu temple. It is decorated with colorful statues of sacred Hindu deities such as Krishna, Murugan, Rama, and Mariamman, the Hindu goddess of rain. Every year, to celebrate the Hindu event of Diwali (the festival of lights), many thousands of Hindus travel to the temple to take part in a firewalking ceremony known as *Theemithi*. It is thought that by walking across white-hot coals you prove your devotion to your faith.

INDONESIA

Philippines
Malaysia
Asia
Jakarta

N

500 miles

Pop. size	249,865,631	(4TH)
Landmass (sq mi)	735,358	(14TH)
Life Expectancy	72.17	(116TH)

Indonesia is the world's largest island nation—over 17,500 islands unite this country together.

As a result, Indonesia is a wildly diverse region of the world. With so much to do, you may feel worn out just after reading this page!

Komodo dragon

BOROBUDUR

The Borobudur Mahayana Buddhist Temple in Magelang is 300 years older than Cambodia's Angkor Wat, and was built over a 70-year period in the 9th century. It is the largest Buddhist temple in the world; 504 Buddha statues sit on top of the structure, keeping a protective watch over it.

BALI KITE FESTIVAL

The island of Bali is one of the tropical treasures of Earth. But it isn't just the sandy beaches, coral reefs, and crystal blue waters that entice millions of travelers each year. The Bali Kite Flying Festival has also become one of the island's highlights. On Sanur Beach every July, thousands of competitors arrive to fly their strangely decorated and bizarre kites, shaped like anything from great white sharks and giant turtles to pirate ships and octopuses.

Where else in the world were hundreds of kites flown on a beach? SEE PAGE 151

THERE BE DRAGONS

Dragons might only exist in stories, but their close relatives are alive and well on the islands of Komodo, Rinca, and Flores. The Komodo dragon is the planet's largest lizard—10 ft. (3 m) long. They don't breathe fire, thank goodness, but they do have teeth that secrete venom into their prey whenever they take a big bite! CHOMP!

VOLCANO

When you think of volcanoes, you imagine red-hot lava, right? Well, Indonesia's volcano Ijen might just surprise you. In the crater of this volcano is a bright-turquoise lake and steaming yellow geysers. If you get there while it's still dark, you can see the volcano spewing lava covered in otherworldly neon-blue flames, due to the high sulphur content.

BOOM, BANG, AND BLAST

At 10:02 A.M. on August 27, 1883, the greatest volcanic explosion the planet had ever experienced occurred. When the mighty Krakatoa volcano erupted, it produced a sound wave that was heard 3,000 mi. (4,828 km) away, a sound so loud that it circled the Earth four times, a noise so BIG that it caused a devastating tsunami. This sound is often said to be the loudest ever made in the history of the world. Imagine standing in New York and being able to hear sound coming from the west coast of Ireland—that's how loud it was!

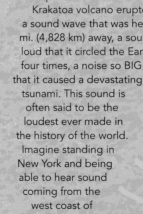

Krakatoa

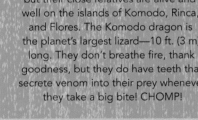

CAT POOP COFFEE

If your pet cat—let's call her Fluffy—ate a type of coffee bean, then pooped it out, would you roast that bean, grind it down, filter it with hot water, and then drink it? Probably not, right? Well, people do, and it's called *kopi luwak*. It is the most expensive and rarest coffee in the world and the only variety made from the poop of a cat-like creature called a civet, found on the Indonesian island of Sumatra. The coffee beans are eaten by the civets, then pooped out and collected to turn into coffee. Yum?

POLE POSITION

To celebrate the island's independence from Indonesia, the liberated people of Timor-Leste take part in the ancient tradition of *Panjat Pinang*, a unique way of celebrating. Every year, in villages all around the country, tall nut trees are chopped down and their trunks placed vertically in the center of each village. At the top of each trunk is a wheel of prizes, such as food and clothing. The trunk is then covered with slippery oil, and young men are encouraged to try and climb the pole and claim the prizes. It's often considered an impossible task, but a climber can seek the help of other villagers, working together and then splitting the rewards if they are victorious!

In 2002, the "land of the sleeping crocodile," Timor-Leste, became the first new nation of the 21st century after after having fought for its independence since the 16th century.

The word *timur* is the word for "east" in Indonesian and Malay, so this very tiny nation is, technically, called East-the East.

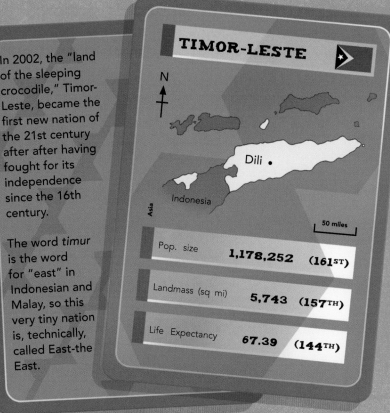

TIMOR-LESTE

N

Dili

Asia   Indonesia

50 miles

Pop. size	1,178,252	(161ST)
Landmass (sq mi)	5,743	(157TH)
Life Expectancy	67.39	(144TH)

Uma lulik ↓

MAGIC HOUSE

The word *lulik* is sacred, but very common, in Timorese culture. It means "holy." Many Timorese people believe that the country's peace and prosperity can be achieved through a balance between the real world and the spiritual world. An important place of worship of the Fataluku tribe is the *Uma lulik*, a type of traditional "sacred house" that can be found scattered everywhere. It is within these four walls that magical rituals—often the sacrificing of a buffalo—are held every year, calling upon the ancestors for wisdom. In return, the spirits guard and protect the houses.

CRISTO REI OF DILI

After an exhausting walk up 500 steps, you will be able to see a bird's-eye view of the Fatacuma Peninsula, as well as a dizzying view of Dili, Timor-Leste's capital city. Right next to you is an 89 ft. (27 m) statue of Jesus Christ, standing on top of a metal globe and facing out to sea. The statue was erected in 1996 and was an independence gift from Indonesia.

Where else in the world does a statue of Christ look out over the city to the sea? SEE PAGE 35

WONDERFUL WEAVING

Tais are the traditional woven cloth made by the women of Timor-Leste. Brightly colored and covered with intricate patterns, these are worn as clothing or used as wall hangings. The weavers are so skillful that they can incorporate letters or bespoke pictures into the cloth to make tourists their own personal *tais*.

MANU FULUN

A traditional headdress of many Timor-Leste tribes, including the Fataluku tribe, is the *manu fulun*. Made of rooster feathers, the ceremonial hat is worn by tribe elders during special events.

PHILIPPINES

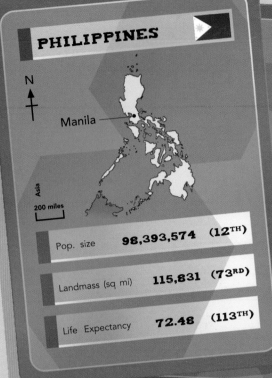

N

Manila

Asia

200 miles

Pop. size	98,393,574	(12TH)
Landmass (sq mi)	115,831	(73RD)
Life Expectancy	72.48	(113TH)

The Philippines is a collection of more than 7,000 islands north of Malaysia. They were named after King Philip II of Spain, during the Spanish colonization in the 16th century.

These sun-drenched idyllic islands mix mega cities such as Manila with beaches and stunning geographical landmarks.

MONSTER MYTHS

The Philippines' scariest mythical creature is known by several names. "Tik Tik," "Wak Wak," or "Aswang" is a half vampire, half werewolf that, unlike vampires, can feast on its prey—usually small children—during the day! Many newborn Filipino babies are given an orange-and-black bracelet to ward off the evil Aswang.

RICE TO MEET YOU

The 2,000-year-old Banaue rice terraces have been skillfully carved into the mountains of Ifugao by the hands of the indigenous ancestors. The terraces are supplied with water by an ingenious irrigation system that filters water down from rainforests above the terraces.

HANGING COFFINS →

An ancient Filipino tradition, the hanging coffins of Sagada are world famous and a custom that continues to this day. Filipinos have observed this ritual for centuries, believing that the higher they hang the coffins of their deceased family members, the closer they are to the heavens.

FIESTA TIME!

Celebrated every January, the Sinulog Fiesta is one of the biggest religious festivals of the year. It culminates in the Grand Parade, a never-ending procession of brightly clothed, masked performers parading through the streets of Cebu City, dancing the ritual *sinulog* dance and rejoicing!

MAWMAG THE GREAT

The Philippine tarsier, known locally as a *mawmag*, lives here and nowhere else. They grow to around 6 in. (15 cm) in height, roughly the size of an adult human hand. They are one of the world's smallest primates and are renowned for their big, bulging eyes. Their eyes are so big, in fact, that they cannot move them around in their sockets. Instead, the tarsiers have specially adapted so that their necks can rotate 180 degrees.

ROOSTER RUCKUS!

Often claimed to be the world's oldest spectator sport—dating back 6,000 years—cockfighting is a popular pastime in the Philippines and a national sport, known as *sabong*. The rules are simple: two roosters are placed at the center of a fighting arena, or stadium (known as the cockpit), and claw and stab each other in a gruesome fight to the death. Whichever rooster is left standing at the end wins, and the owner often receives large sums of money. Though a very controversial sport, it is still legal in many parts of Asia, with more than 30 million roosters killed every year in battle.

PANDAMONIUM AND PANDAMANIA

In recent years, a cultural and trade relationship between Taiwan and China has begun. To promote a more prosperous relationship between the two lands, in 2008, China sent Taiwan two giant pandas, known as Tuan Tuan and Yuan Yuan. *Tuan yuan* translates as "reunion" in Chinese, and the two pandas became instant celebrities and a popular attraction at Taipei Zoo, where they live. In 2013, the notoriously shy animals had a baby called Yuan Zai.

Yuan Zai

The island of Taiwan was christened Ilha Formosa (the Beautiful Isle) by the Portuguese, and they weren't wrong!

Despite some tricky politics, Taiwan is blossoming with green mountains and valleys, amazing architecture, and delicious food.

TAIWAN

N

Taipei

Asia

50 miles

Pop. size	23,329,772	(51ST)
Landmass (sq mi)	13,974	(136TH)
Life Expectancy	79.84	(30TH)

DRAGON AND TIGER PAGODA

Located near the beautifully named Lotus Lake are two iconic buildings reflecting traditional Taiwanese culture—the Dragon and Tiger Pagodas. Seven-stories high, the temple towers were built in 1976 and are ornately decorated with bright paintings of religious symbols and deities.

MADE IN TAIWAN

When it comes to tall towers, everyone in Taipei talks about Taipei 101 as the beacon of brilliance. But spare a thought for Taipei's other monument to the clouds—the Tuntex Sky Tower! Shaped like a rocket ready to fly into space, or a finger pointing to the moon, the tower was completed in 1997 and is 1,140 ft. (347.5 m) tall.

SKY FULL OF STARS

The spectacular Pingxi Sky Lantern Festival is a breathtaking New Year celebration. Along with street carnivals and a firecracker ceremony, more than 200,000 "fire balloons" are let go into the moonlit sky— a stunning sight to see!

FASTER THAN A SPEEDING BULLET

Taiwan's High Speed Rail is a 214 mi. (344 km) railway line that runs from the northern capital city, Taipei, to the southern city of Kaohsiung. Trains whiz across the whole length of the country at a top speed of 186 mph (303 km/h), reaching their destinations in as little as 96 minutes. The train line connects 90 percent of Taiwan's population and is considered one of the fastest in the world.

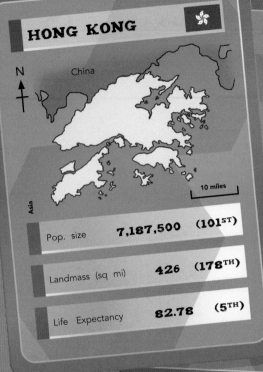

HONG KONG

N

China

Asia

10 miles

Pop. size	7,187,500	(101ST)
Landmass (sq mi)	426	(178TH)
Life Expectancy	82.78	(5TH)

Hong Kong is the King Kong of Asian skylines and the best place in the world to see lots of other people!

Translated as "Fragrant Harbor," Hong Kong is one of the world's most densely populated places.

BUN FESTIVAL

Between April and May, residents of Cheung Chau Island organize a bun festival to celebrate Buddha's birthday. This ancient tradition is intended to keep hungry spirits from eating the island's crops. Locals build a 50 ft. (15 m) mountain of steamed lotus-paste buns. On the final day of the festival, the village's best climbers ascend the tower in order to collect as many buns as possible, an event known as "bun snatching." The higher you go, the better fortune you will have in the coming year!

TRAM RIDE TO THE TOP

Hong Kong's double-decker street trams are famous, but not as famous as the Peak Tram, Asia's first cable railway. It started operating in 1888 and remains one of the steepest and oldest cable railways in the world. Around 11,000 people ride the Peak Tram every day in order to catch a glimpse of Victoria Harbour and one of the greatest skylines on Earth, with the most skyscrapers in the world!

THE SYMPHONY OF LIGHTS

The Symphony of Lights is the world's largest permanent light and sound show, as stated by Guinness World Records. Every night at 8 P.M., more than 40 skyscrapers in the Victoria Harbour skyline light up the night with laser beams, searchlights, and dancing lights, all perfectly timed with dramatic music. The show lasts precisely 13 minutes and is designed to celebrate the energy, spirit, and diversity of Hong Kong's history through five main themes: Awakening, Energy, Heritage, Partnership, and Celebration.

DRAGON RACING

The Hong Kong Dragon Boat Carnival is one of the most exciting boat races in the world. Every year, teams of rowers race along Victoria Harbour, cheered on by thousands of revelers, to pay respect to dragons—the rulers of rivers, lakes, and seas, according to Chinese mythology!

SEE PAGE 50 Where in the world can you see nature's biggest light show?

RUBBER DUCKIES LOST AT SEA

On January 10, 1992, a container ship carrying 28,800 yellow rubber ducks from Hong Kong to the U.S. encountered a violent storm in the North Pacific Ocean. The storm was so bad it forced many of the ship's containers overboard. The ducks were lost at sea! Over the next 20 years, these rubber ducks traveled all around the world, with many ducks ending up on shores as far away as Hawaii, New York, and Great Britain! Thousand of the ducks are still floating around the world's oceans, with many of them having circled the Earth several times.

DO YOU WANT TO BUILD A SNOWMAN?

The Harbin International Ice and Snow Sculpture Festival in northeast China draws more than 800,000 visitors every winter. Each year, the frozen Songhua River is put to good use—it is carved up and turned into a magical ice world, complete with the world's largest ice sculptures.

China is a land of extremes. It's the planet's most populated country and it has the most land borders of all countries on Earth.

Chinese people have been responsible for inventing almost everything, from chopsticks to toilet paper, toothbrushes to teapots, fireworks to umbrellas!

CHINA

N

Mongolia

Beijing

Asia

500 miles

Pop. size	1,357,380,000	(1ST)
Landmass (sq mi)	3,705,407	(4TH)
Life Expectancy	75.15	(79TH)

HEAVEN'S GATE

Heaven's Gate Mountain, located in Hunan province, is a spot-on name. This unbelievable structure is a naturally formed hole in the middle of Tiānmén Mountain. Reaching the top of the mountain is a bit of an epic journey. First, you have to drive around 99 perilous bends on the road up the mountain, and then you have to walk up 999 steps to reach the hole! If that sounds like too much hard work, why not do what skydiver Jeb Corliss did in September 2011? He jumped out of a helicopter and flew straight through the 98 ft. (30 m) wide mountain hole wearing a "wing suit"!

CHINESE NEW YEAR

The most celebrated, and important, time of the year in Chinese culture is New Year. Usually falling between the end of January and the beginning of February, the week-long celebrations are marked by parades, where Chinese people perform the ancient Dragon Dance. Huge brightly colored dragons—often as long as 328 ft. (100 m)—are made out of paper, wood, and cardboard and paraded down the streets in an effort to scare away evil spirits, while firecrackers bang and fireworks whiz.

TERRACOTTA WARRIORS

The first Chinese emperor, Qin Shi Huang, ordered the construction of more than 8,000 terracotta warriors, horses, and chariots to stand in front of his tomb and guard his body after he died. The life-sized clay statues—each with their own unique facial features—date back 2,200 years and took 700,000 workers around 36 years to build.

RAINBOW ROCKS

It isn't just man-made structures that China has to be proud of—our planet has also given the country some awe-inspiring views. The Dānxiá Dìmào rock formation in Gānsù province, also called Rainbow Rocks, is without doubt the most striking example. The unbelievable colors of the rocks are the result of mineral deposits mixing with the red sandstone over a period of 24 million years.

THE WORLD'S GREATEST?

China is a nation of super-shiny skyscrapers, and for a period of three years, from 2011 to 2013, a brand-new one was built roughly every five days! While that's impressive, it's nothing compared to the 13,171 mi. (21,196 km) wall the Chinese constructed in 210 B.C. Built to keep out Mongol and Manchu invaders from the north, the Great Wall of China is the longest man-made structure ever built.

MONGOLIA

N

Russia

Ulaanbaatar

China

Asia

500 miles

Pop. size	2,839,073	(140TH)
Landmass (sq mi)	603,906	(18TH)
Life Expectancy	68.98	(136TH)

From the far-reaching steppe landscape to the vast and (relatively) empty Gobi Desert and spectacular Altai Mountains, Mongolia is not renowned for its urban cities and wild party life.

However, what it lacks in sprawling cities, it makes up for by quite simply being one of the most awe-inspiring places on Earth.

FLAMING CLIFFS

A trip to the Flaming Cliffs in the Gobi Desert will prove illuminating. Here you will see fossilized dinosaur bones and nests of dinosaur eggs imprinted into the surface of the desert floor. Among many of the different species of dinosaur bones found here, the most awesome is the velociraptor, a dino that lived on the planet 75 million years ago. One of the greatest velociraptor fossils was discovered in Mongolia—it was preserved with its right arm stuck firmly between the jaws of a protoceratops. The dinosaurs must both have died during their fight on a sand dune and their bones were preserved exactly as they fell, until they were found in 1971.

Velociraptor

Protoceratops

GOLDEN EAGLE

In Western Mongolia, people practice the 1,200-year-old art of hunting with magnificent golden eagles every day. Mongolians come together to celebrate the ritual at the Golden Eagle Festival in October, at the foot of the Altai Mountains in Bayan-Ölgii. Eagles, and their owners, battle it out for the title of Best Eagle at Hunting Prey and Best Eagle at Locating Its Owner from a Distance.

MONGOLIAN OLYMPICS!

Held every July at Naadam Stadium, the Naadam Festival is Mongolia's very own nomadic equivalent of the Olympics. Players compete in three sports: wrestling, horse racing, and archery. The horse that finishes last in the race is called *bayan khodood*, or "full stomach."

GENGHIS KHAN

Many nations have tried to claim the mighty nomadic warrior Genghis Khan as their own. But it is Mongolia with which the feared leader is most associated. He united the nomadic Mongol tribes in 1206, and conquered much of central Asia and China, creating one of the largest empires in history, around one-fifth of the entire planet! With over 500 wives—and presumably many more children—Genghis is believed to be the direct ancestor of one in every 200 Central Asian men. That's 16 million people!

DEATH WORM

If you touch it, you die. If you see it, you won't be able to outrun it. If it hunts you, you won't escape. The Mongolian death worm, a bright-red deadly worm that's 3.3 ft. (1 m) long, kills its prey with electric shocks from its eyes, lives deep under the Gobi Desert floor, and is one of Asia's cryptic legends. Never photographed, rarely reliably witnessed. . . but feared throughout the country. What do you think?

Fact or fiction?

The Mongolian death worm

SWEET NOT SWEATY!

Research has shown that Koreans lack the ABCC11 gene that produces smelly armpits, and that they have fewer apocrine sweat glands than other races of people in the world. As a result, Koreans are a very nice-smelling group of people, no matter how much they sweat!

MASS GAMES

North Korea's Rungrado 1st of May Stadium is the largest stadium in the world and has more than 150,000 seats. It is here that the Mass Games traditionally take place. Around 100,000 performers take part in a 90-minute display of synchronized gymnastics, acrobatics, dance, and drama.

THE GREAT LEADERS

North Korea's 'Eternal President', the self-proclaimed Great Leader Kim Il-Sung died in 1994 but is still president. Many North Koreans believe that Kim Il-sung and his descendants are deities and deserve to be treated as such. Kim Il-sung's embalmed body now lies in a glass case at the Kumsusan Palace of the Sun, where people can go to pay their respects. His grandson, Kim Jong-un, is now the country's leader, and is revered as a god, too.

Kim Il-sung

NORTH KOREA

Welcome to North Korea, the world's most secretive country. This land exists in self-imposed solitude, and is sometimes referred to as the "Hermit Kingdom" because it is so isolated.

Only around 1,500 Western tourists are allowed to visit each year. But at heart, North Korea is a beautiful country with a long history.

N

China

Asia

100 miles

Pyongyang

South Korea

Pop. size	24,895,480	(49TH)
Landmass (sq mi)	46,540	(98TH)
Life Expectancy	69.81	(133RD)

CHINA

NORTH KOREA

Demilitarized Zone (DMZ)

CIVIL WAR

In 1950, North Korea invaded South Korea. This was the start of the Korean War—a conflict that still persists. Many nations of the world fought on the side of South Korea, while China was on North Korea's side. Following the war, a strip of land 2.5 mi. (4 km) wide and 160 mi. (257 km) long was set up to divide the Korean Peninsula in half. It is known as the Korean Demilitarized Zone (or the DMZ, for short) and is surrounded by each nation's armies on either side, as well as more than one million landmines.

SOUTH KOREA

HOTEL OF DOOM

At the heart of Pyongyang is the 105-story Ryugyong Hotel, dubbed the "Hotel of Doom." Construction began on the hotel in 1987, but was halted for 16 years after the country hit financial problems. The hotel was finally completed in 2011 but hasn't opened yet, making it a striking but slightly sinister silhouette on the Pyongyang skyline.

HEAVEN LAKE

This beautiful lake is found in the crater of a volcano on the border between North Korea and China. One of the world's deepest lakes, it sits at the top of Paekdu Mountain. According to myth, Hwanung, the Korean Lord of Heaven, descended the mountain in 2333 B.C. and founded the original Korean nation, known as Choson.

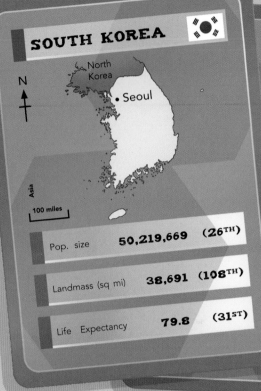

SOUTH KOREA

N

North Korea

• Seoul

Asia

100 miles

Pop. size	50,219,669	(26TH)
Landmass (sq mi)	38,691	(108TH)
Life Expectancy	79.8	(31ST)

South Korea is a land of intense contrasts.

It celebrates the ultra-sleek and modern as well as the ancient and traditional. For every high-tech gadget and gizmo, there is an equally sacred custom and cultural event.

AGE MATTERS!

When babies are born in South Korea, they are already called "one" year old because they are living in their first year of life. On their first birthday, they begin their second year of life, so they are two.

TOILET THEME PARK

The world's first toilet theme park, called the Restroom Cultural Park, is a great place to sit down and think. With a museum shaped like a massive toilet, and a sculpture garden dedicated to people having a poop, this theme park shows the stranger side of South Korean life.

MUD BATH

South Korea's Boryeong Mud Festival, on Daecheon Beach in Chungcheongnam-do, is known as one of the best mud sites in the world. Every July, millions of travelers and nearby residents get into the mud and get dirty. The mud is prized for its minerals, which cleanse the skin—but it's also fun to play in, and there are mud slides, mud showers, and mud pools to splash around in too.

GANGNAM STYLE

The planet's most famous modern South Korean is the charismatic and flamboyant *Gangnam Style* singer, Psy. In 2012, it was voted World's Best Song at the World Music Awards and has been viewed on YouTube more than 2.5 billion times. It is the most watched video of all time. All together now, "Oppa Gangnam Style. . ."

SAMSUNG

SAMSUNG STYLE

The planet these days is ruled by mobile phones. More than seven billion text messages are sent every day across the whole planet—that's one for every person alive! The world's largest smartphone manufacturer, Samsung, is a South Korean company and sells almost 300 million smartphones a year! Amazingly, 98 percent of South Koreans own more than one smartphone.

CHANGING OF THE GUARD

Standing watch over Namdaemun (the Great South Gate), guards in scaly and decorated uniforms protect this fortress wall that has surrounded the capital city of Seoul since the 1390s. The Changing of the Guard ceremony, which happens twice every day, is a colorful and musical event that has occurred for more than 800 years.

FUGU AND FRIES

Japanese people have been eating sushi, raw fish, for thousands of years. It's delicious! The ultimate delicacy on the sushi menu, however, is the fugu, also known as the pufferfish. Chefs who prepare this dish have to expertly cut the fish in the right way to remove all traces of the deadly poison from its skin and guts.

Pufferfish

For a nation that is 70 percent mountains, Japan does a very good job of squeezing a lot of people into it!

Home to origami, ninjas, samurais, bullet trains, sumo wrestlers, geishas, manga comics, and Mount Fuji, Japan means a whole lot more to the world than just the sum of its famous parts. . .

JAPAN

China
North Korea
South Korea
Asia
200 miles
Tokyo
N

Pop. size	127,338,621	(10TH)
Landmass (sq mi)	145,920	(62ND)
Life Expectancy	84.48	(2ND)

HOT SPRING MONKEYS!

"Hell's Valley," a hot spring in the Nagano area, is where Japan's mighty macaque monkeys come to splash around and warm up. The steaming mist and bubbling waters that erupt from the frozen ground make the area a popular destination for the monkeys, which have been seen having snowball fights with one another!

OODLES OF NOODLES

Loudly slurping noodles and soup is acceptable in Japan. Slurpers believe that eating the noodles hot improves their flavor. So Japanese diners don't wait for the noodles to cool down. Slurrrrp!

TSUNDOKU

The Japanese language is fantastic at expressing things that other languages don't have words for. For example, *tsundoku* is a word that means "buying books and never getting around to reading them."

CAT ISLAND

The tiny fishing island of Aoshima has become known as Cat Island. With only 20 people inhabiting the island and more than 150 cats running wild, the people are outnumbered by cats by more than seven to one. . . and counting. The cats were originally brought onto the island to control the mouse population, but now the cat population is getting out of hand!

CHERRY BLOSSOM

Everyone loves the start of spring, but in Japan it's a true time of celebration. When the beautiful cherry trees blossom, it signals the start of Hanami, a festival dedicated to the fleeting beauty of flowers. People picnic under the trees, and there's even a blossom forecast issued by the weather stations to make sure that locals catch the blooms at the best time.

PALAU

N↑

Melekeok

Oceania

20 miles

Pop. size	20,918	(200TH)
Landmass (sq mi)	177	(188TH)
Life Expectancy	72.6	(111TH)

Alii! "Hi!" Floating alone east of the Philippines and directly above Papua New Guinea in the vast North Pacific Ocean lies our next stop—Palau.

Located in an area known as Micronesia, it is made up of more than 250 coral atolls, and is a nation that is as awesome underwater as it is on land.

OMENGAT

When a woman gives birth to her first child, the event is celebrated with a traditional ceremony in Palau called *Omengat*, or the "Hot Bath." Over several days, the woman is rubbed with a mixture of coconut oil and a yellow spice called turmeric, and bathed with hot water and herbs. After several days of this happening, the new mother is rubbed again in the yellow spice mix and then dressed in a traditional grass skirt, jewelry, and flowers, and taken through the village to a feast in her honor.

CHELBACHEB

Palau's Rock Islands, or Chelbacheb, as the locals call them, are funny-looking mushroom islands! These ancient coral reefs sprang up out of the ocean and became islands thousands of years ago.

SWIM TOWARDS THE LIGHT

Jellyfish Lake is home to millions of them—but these are no ordinary jellyfish! These squishy creatures of the sea are the majestic (and friendly!) golden jellyfish. Unlike any jellyfish in other parts of the ocean, golden jellyfish don't just float about in the waves, they instinctively follow the sun as it moves in the sky, causing them to swim back and forth across the lake in the same pattern every day.

THE BIG DROP OFF

Loved by scuba divers all around the world, the Ngemelis Wall, or the Big Drop Off, is a vertical drop of 900 ft. (275 m)—the height of four jumbo jets lying nose to tail on top of each other! The Big Drop Off is home to thousands of fish and colorful coral.

VERY CLAMMY

Palau's Malakai Island has some very clammy residents—giant clams! They can grow larger than 3 ft. (1 m) in diameter, and can live for more than a century. Giant clams are valuable to the Palauan people for their shells, as well as their very rare pearls!

FRUIT-BAT CRAZY!

The Bulmer's fruit bat is the world's largest cave-dwelling bat. It was thought to be long extinct until some were rediscovered in a remote cave in Papua New Guinea in 1975.

SHE SELLS SEASHELLS

As recently as 1933, seashells were the currency of Papua New Guinea!

Sharing the island of New Guinea with Indonesia, Papua New Guinea is one of the least-explored tropical island countries in the world.

This nation is so beautiful it's no wonder more than 7,000 different tribes and millions of exotic birds of paradise continue to live here!

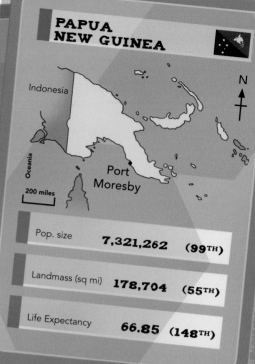

PAPUA NEW GUINEA

Indonesia

Oceania

Port Moresby

200 miles

N

Pop. size	7,321,262	(99TH)
Landmass (sq mi)	178,704	(55TH)
Life Expectancy	66.85	(148TH)

THE ABYSS

Located close to the coast of Papua New Guinea is the deepest and lowest point of the Earth's surface. Known as the Mariana Trench, this canyon is so deep that no light from the sun touches it. It is where some of the world's most alien-like life forms live, including the barreleye fish, the deep-sea dragonfish, the dumbo octopus, and the goblin shark!

Dugong

Goblin shark

SEA COWS

Papua New Guinea's beloved "sea cows," or dugongs, are the country's national mammal. The tails of these large creatures are also the known inspiration of mermaid tales and legends—though that's where the similarities end!

Deep-sea dragonfish

SING SING!

Papua New Guinea has many annual celebrations called "sing sings" that show off its diverse cultural communities. Every year, hundreds of tribes come together to sing traditional songs, share stories and rituals, and dance and dress up in colorful costumes, masks, and headwear.

Barreleye fish

CANNIBALS!

Thought to have had no knowledge of the outside world until the 1970s, the Korowai tribe of New Guinea lives high up among the forest treetops in amazing tree houses. It is thought that the Korowai is the last tribe in the world to still practice cannibalism—the ritual of eating other humans.

Dumbo octopus

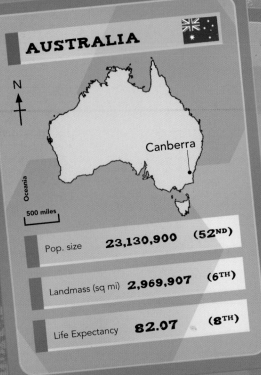

AUSTRALIA

N

500 miles

Oceania

Canberra

Pop. size	23,130,900	(52ND)
Landmass (sq mi)	2,969,907	(6TH)
Life Expectancy	82.07	(8TH)

From the ever-changing color of the ancient monolith Uluru to the neon, underwater paradise of the Great Barrier Reef, it is understandable why Australia is one the most visited nations on Earth.

It is a destination teeming with life as beautiful and colorful as the country itself.

The Australian outback is renowned around the world for being one of the most desolate areas on Earth—it is around 10.3 million sq. mi. (16.5 million km²) of flat, arid land and home to the world's most venomous snake, the inland taipan.

G'DAY AUSTRALIA

Before Australia became known as Australia in 1824, the country was actually called New Holland, after the Dutch Navigator Willem Janzsoon, who first landed on Australian shores in 1606 and decided the land deserved a name. The name "Australia" comes from the Latin term *Terra Australis*, meaning "land of the south."

YOO-HOO ULURU...

The base of Uluru (or Ayers Rock), Australia's famous sandstone, measures 5.8 mi. (9.4 km) and would take you about 3.5 hours to walk around.

BOOMERANG

A boomerang, a wooden weapon used by indigenous Australians for hunting, is a popular Australian icon. In 2005, a boomerang was thrown 1,402 ft. (427.5 m). That's the length of four soccer fields!

RABBITS GALORE!

Until British convicts began settling in Australia, not one bunny had ever set a furry foot in the country. Then one day in 1859, 24 rabbits were released into the wild for hunting purposes. They were never seen again—and Australia's rabbit population went from zero to millions almost overnight. It was the fastest spread ever recorded of any mammal anywhere in the world.

GOOD GRIEF . . . WHAT A REEF!

Larger than the U.K., Holland, and Switzerland combined—and with coral types dating back 20 million years—the Great Barrier Reef is one of the world's most famous natural hotspots and something about which Australia is justly proud. It's the largest reef system in the world and can even be seen from outer space. Around 1,500 species of fish inhabit the reef, and the colorful coral makes it a perfect playground for snorkelers and scuba divers.

ORIGINAL ABORIGINALS

Australia's first peoples, known as Aboriginals, are one of the oldest continuing civilizations in the world. Aboriginal Australians lived in harmony with the natural environment for an estimated 60,000 years before the British settlers came in 1776. Modern Aboriginal Australians have become well-known for their distinct style of artwork, which tells stories about their history.

BLOBFISH

Swimming deep in the seas off New Zealand's coast is the blobfish, officially the world's ugliest animal. If you were to hold it, it would feel like very slippery jelly—its body is almost the same density as water.

New Zealand is like nowhere else on Earth. Tucked away in the Pacific Ocean, it's 1,400 mi. (2,250 km) away from Australia, its nearest neighbor.

Maori people, the original inhabitants of the land, call New Zealand *Aotearoa*, which means, the "land of the long white cloud."

NEW ZEALAND

N

Oceania

200 miles

Wellington

Pop. size	4,470,800	(124TH)
Landmass (sq mi)	104,428	(76TH)
Life Expectancy	80.93	(19TH)

THE DEVIL'S BATH

Dip a toe in the Devil's Bath, a sulphuric crater lake that is one of the strangest places on the planet. Located in the Wai-O-Tapu Thermal Wonderland near Rotorua, the Devil's Bath is so named because the geothermal water bubbles very hot . . . and bright green!

THE HAKA

Made world-famous by the New Zealand All Blacks Rugby team, the *haka* is the traditional Maori dance. The *haka* is not a war cry, as people think. It is, in fact, a dance designed to show the fitness and power of the Maori warriors.

START

x6

x2

SEA MARBLES

Scattered along Koekohe Beach are the Moeraki Boulders, strange marble-shaped rocks emerging from the sand, as if thrown there by alien civilizations from space. The boulders date back at least 60 million years. But how did they get there?

ARACHNOCAMPA LUMINOSA!

The Waitomo Caves may be located deep underground on the North Island, but in the darkness the ceilings light up as bright as a starry night, thanks to thousands of the bright blue glow-worm, *Arachnocampa luminosa*, a species that radiates luminescent light and is unique to New Zealand.

SAY HI WITH A HONGI

Like a *kunik*, an Inuit's kiss, a *hongi* is a traditional Maori greeting in New Zealand. Press your nose and forehead to another person's—much friendlier than a handshake. Give it a try today!

VANUATU

N

Oceania

Port Vila

100 miles

Pop. size	252,763	(182ND)
Landmass (sq mi)	4,706	(161ST)
Life Expectancy	72.72	(110TH)

Meaning "land eternal," Vanuatu is part of the Pacific island chain called Melanesia.

With a heritage thousands of years old, Vanuatu's original inhabitants have left a massive footprint on this Y-shaped archipelago that stretches over more than 80 islands.

RING OF FIRE

Mount Yasur is one of the islands' many volcanoes. It's thought to be the world's most accessible active volcano—you can walk right up and look straight down into its fiery belly. It erupts, shooting fire and brimstone into the air, several times an hour.

BIRTH OF BUNGEE

The land-diving ritual known as *nagol* is performed by the men from Pentecost Island. This is bungee jumping's older brother, and it's one of the biggest adrenalin thrills in the world. Men from the village perform the land dive each year, leaping from tall wooden towers with vines tied around their ankles.

UNDERWATER POST OFFICE

Put on your snorkel and flippers and swim down to the world's only underwater post office! Located off Hideaway Island, the post office is 10 ft. (3 m) underwater, and a place where you can send waterproof postcards to anywhere in the world.

VANUATU POST

LAP LAP

The national dish of Vanuatu is "lap lap"—a cake made from shaved cassava (a root vegetable), wild local cabbage, and coconut, all wrapped in a banana leaf. It tastes both sweet and savory!

FLY, FOX, FLY!

The Vanuatu flying fox is not actually a fox that can zoom through the air. It is, in fact, a megabat—*Pteropus anetianus*—one of the largest fruit-bat species in the world.

Pteropus anetianus

TOKA CEREMONY

Held every four years, the Toka is Tanna Island's largest cultural tradition, and Vanuatu's most celebrated festivity. The native Melanesian villagers come together and dance the Toka dance—a colorful and highly energetic dance with much chanting, singing, and foot stomping. The fun lasts all day and night.

TOMOKO WAR CANOES

The Tomoko war canoes are an important part of the Solomon Islands' history. Warriors would paddle across the water in their highly decorated canoes and fight enemies on nearby islands. The warriors carried out head-hunting, a ritual where an enemy's head was chopped off and then preserved as a trophy!

The Solomon Islands may have a small landmass and just two seasons, dry and rainy, but everything else about the islands is incredibly diverse and BIG.

Underwater, the Solomon Islands have submerged, violent volcanoes erupting into the sea, hot springs, and spooky shipwrecks.

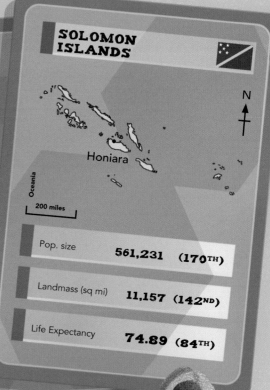

SOLOMON ISLANDS

Honiara

Oceania

200 miles

N

Pop. size	561,231	(170TH)
Landmass (sq mi)	11,157	(142ND)
Life Expectancy	74.89	(84TH)

ANCIENT TRIBES

Nearly all of the residents of the Solomon Islands are Melanesians, the original inhabitants of the area. A genetic mutation—unique to Melanesian nations—causes the growth of striking blonde hair!

SKULL ISLAND

One of the most sacred areas of the Solomon Islands is Skull Island, near the Vona Vona Lagoon. The island contains a wooden shrine filled with the skulls of deceased chiefs and famous Melanesian warriors, and is protected every hour of the day.

ARE'ARE PEOPLE

The Are'are people, from the island of Malaita, are world famous for their panpipe music and their special bond with bamboo. This type of spherical wood is vital to creating the instruments, which have been handcrafted for generations, and are made pitch perfect every time.

VOLCANO CHICKEN

The islands are home to megapodes—big chicken-like birds that use underground volcanic heat to warm their eggs in the sand. The megapode digs a hole about 34 in. (90 cm) deep—three times the height of this book!—and buries its eggs. When the egg hatches, the baby chick must dig its way out all by itself!

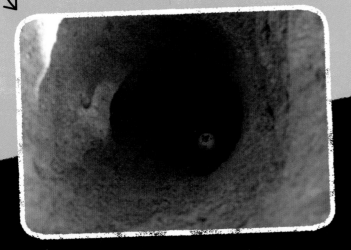

CAVE OF THE CUSTOM SHARK

Residents of Munda village speak of a Solomon Islands' legend—the Cave of the Custom Shark. It is said that each local village has a shark to protect it, and the sharks live in this cave. The cave is also home to pygmy seahorses, the smallest type of seahorse on the planet!

NAURU

N ↑

Oceania

Yaren (de facto)

1 mile

Pop. size	10,051	(201ST)
Landmass (sq mi)	8	(201ST)
Life Expectancy	66.4	(149TH)

The smallest island country in the world, Nauru is a tiny green dot in the vast blue waters of the Pacific Ocean.

Located between Micronesian states Palau and Kiribati, it's right on top of the equator, so Nauru spends 365 days a year as a sunny island paradise.

Fried chicken

PLEASANT ISLAND
It was British Captain John Fearn who was the first European to set foot on the island, in 1798. He named it Pleasant Island, a tribute to the island's geographical features as well as the friendliness of the Nauruan people.

A SMALL LARGE NATION
Nauru's population numbers just 10,051 people. A whopping 95 percent are thought to be overweight, and Nauru is often regarded as the "fattest country on Earth." This dilemma arose when Western culture arrived—with its unhealthy food. The nation's most popular meal is fried chicken and Coca-Cola.

BABY JOY
Due to a population decline at the start of the 20th century, the race of Nauruan people was close to extinction. To try to avert the crisis, a population target of 1,500 was announced, and the birth of the baby that met this figure was celebrated in 1932. The country now holds a major festival every year on October 26 to celebrate the birth of Eidagaruwo, the angam ("celebration") baby.

EKAWADA
Ekawada string figures are a popular Nauruan custom. These complex string patterns—known to children around the world as "cat's cradles"—are passed down through families, and tell traditional stories.

Disused phosphate-processing plant, a common sight on Nauru

NODDY HUNTING
Nauru's traditional "sport" is catching noddy birds at sunset, the time the birds return to the island after a day of catching fish at sea. Using recordings of the noddy's call, the hunters wait for them to fly past and then catch them in nets! The birds are killed, plucked, and cooked, and supposedly taste like slightly fishy chicken.

PHOSPHATE BOOM!
In the 1980s, Nauru was considered the second-richest nation on Earth, after the precious mineral phosphorus was discovered on the island. Phosphorus was deposited on Nauru by thousands of years of birds' pooping on the land. It is used in fertilizers—vital to keeping the world's food crops healthy. Nauru's, and the world's, phosphorus supply is almost exhausted.

MICRONESIAN GAMES

Competitors from the five Micronesian nations—Federated States of Micronesia, Kiribati, Nauru, Palau, and Marshall Islands—take part every four years in their own Olympic-style Games. In 2014, the Federated States of Micronesia hosted the competition, with sports including basketball, beach volleyball, wrestling, and swimming. There were also other tropical sports such as coconut-tree climbing, spear fishing, and canoeing!

Logo for Micronesian Games 2014

The Federated States of Micronesia is composed of over 600 islands.

Together, the country spans over 1 million sq. mi. (2.6 million km²) of Pacific Ocean from the most westerly state of Yap to the most easterly of Kosrae. But the overall landmass is only the size of Singapore!

FEDERATED STATES OF MICRONESIA

N

Palikir
Yap
Chuuk
Pohnpei
Kosrae
Oceania
300 miles

Pop. size	103,549	(189TH)
Landmass (sq mi)	271	(185TH)
Life Expectancy	72.35	(114TH)

Chuukese love-stick

STONE MONEY

Centuries ago, people from Yap didn't have money to pay for things. Instead, they used *rai*—large discs carved out of limestone with holes in the middle—as their currency. Most of these *rai* were so big and heavy that they were impossible to lift and move, so they rarely actually changed hands, but everyone on the island understood who owned them.

A POKE OF LOVE

The Chuukese love-stick is a local traditional custom once used for courtship. Young men would carve an identical pattern onto two wooden love-sticks. The man would wear the shorter stick in his hair, and the long stick would be used to poke through the wall of the hut where the girl he loved lived! If the girl recognized the love-stick's design and liked its owner, she would pull on the end of the stick. If she didn't, she'd push it away!

SHIP GRAVEYARD

The world's largest battleship graveyard—more than 60 massive warships and 200 planes!—lies at the bottom of Chuuk Lagoon. In 1944, over a period of three days, these Japanese war machines were sunk during a giant battle with the U.S. Air Force. Many of the shipwrecks still contain their cargo, including tanks, bullets, bombs, and bulldozers. The graveyard, now a scuba diving site, also contains the skeletons of those who died. Spooky!

1940s' car submerged in Chuuk Lagoon

NAN MADOL

On the island of Pohnpei lies a ruined city that's centuries old. Nan Madol used to be home to Micronesian nobles and royals hundreds of years ago. This amazing site is made up of 92 tiny man-made islands. It's the only city in the world built on top of coral reefs and connected by twisting canals, and it's often called "the Venice of the Pacific" because of this.

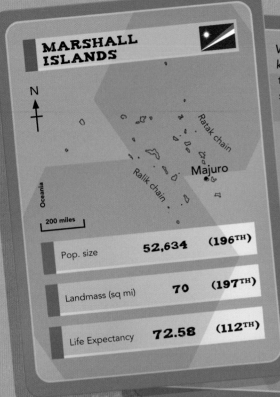

MARSHALL ISLANDS

N ↑

Ratak chain

Majuro

Ralik chain

Oceania

200 miles

Pop. size	52,634	(196TH)
Landmass (sq mi)	70	(197TH)
Life Expectancy	72.58	(112TH)

When it comes to knowing what makes the Marshall Islands stand out from every other country in the world, all you need to know is the word "atoll," meaning a ring-shaped reef or island. The place has loads of them—29 in fact!

But that's not all—this tropical paradise has an explosive history . . .

BIKINI MANIA

The word "atoll" was coined by the world-famous naturalist Charles Darwin, the man who gave the world the theory of evolution. But the most famous atoll, Bikini Atoll, gave its name to another world-famous creation—the bikini! In the mid-1940s, Bikini Island and Bikini Atoll made global headlines when the U.S. military continued nuclear testing of hydrogen bombs. A few days later, French swimsuit designer Louis Réard named his new beachwear after Bikini Atoll, hoping it would blow the world away just as much as the bombs did!

CASTLE BRAVO

On March 1, 1954, Operation Castle Bravo, the U.S. military's largest-ever detonation of a nuclear bomb, occurred at Bikini Atoll, along with 67 other nuclear-weapon blasts. In the 1950s, the Marshall Islands were considered the most contaminated place in the world, with many Marshall Islanders experiencing radioactive fallout for decades afterwards.

COCONUT CRABS

Coconut crabs are the largest type of crab in the world and roam the Marshall Islands like kings. Fully grown, they can measure up to a whopping 3 ft. (1 m). These crabby creatures can climb coconut trees, where they knock the coconuts off and use their sharp pincers to crack them open and eat them.

SUNSET AND SUNRISE

The Marshall Islands are in fact two island chains that sit back to back to one another. The westerly string of islands is called the Ralik Chain, and the easterly group of islands is called the Ratak Chain. In Marshallese, ratak means "sunrise" and ralik means "sunset."

TUVALU—DO YOU?

Tuvalu isn't just one big blob of land. It's nine separate islands. One of the island names below is false—can you guess which?

1. Funafeti
2. Nanumea
3. Nui
4. Nukufetau
5. Nukulaelae
6. Vaitupu
7. Nanonanoa
8. Nanumanga
9. Niulakita
10. Niutao

Answer: 7 is false

TE ANO

Literally translated as "the ball," *te ano* is the national sport of Tuvalu. A bit like volleyball, the game consists of two teams facing each other on a *malae* (playing field), and throwing the ball at each other, trying not to let it touch the ground. The only person allowed to catch the ball is called a *tino pukepuke*.

Midway between Hawaii and Australia, Tuvalu is the heart of the South Pacific Ocean.

Being no bigger than a village, this quiet and unspoiled island nation has a word that sums it up perfectly: *fifilemu* (peaceful).

TUVALU

N

Oceania

100 miles

♦ Funafuti

Pop. size	9,876	(201ST)
Landmass (sq mi)	10	(200TH)
Life Expectancy	65.81	(150TH)

NUTS ABOUT COCO

Due to the abundance of salt water and poor soil, Tuvalu is only able to grow one major food crop—coconuts! This hairy ball of food is an iconic symbol of Tuvaluan life and many residents have created inventive ways to use it in everyday life. The husks are used for brushes, ropes, and mattresses, the flesh can be used for coconut oil, milk, and candy, the leaves are used to make baskets, the trunks are used to make canoes and furniture, and the roots can be used as a mouthwash as well as a toothbrush!

HOUSE UNDER THE SEA

The Fire Caves of Nanumanga is a spooky submerged cave off the coast of Nanumanga, Tuvalu. A local Tuvaluan legend spoke of a "large house under the sea," and one day in 1986 two scuba divers went looking for it! What they found was evidence of human life and their use of fire. The discovery was historic; it showed that a gigantic rise in sea level wiped out all traces of humans in the region 4,000 years ago.

A DANCE FATELE

A traditional Tuvaluan dance and song performance is called a *fatele*, and is performed by girls wearing grass skirts and colorful decorations. They sway elegantly to the *pehe anamau* (ancient songs) while singers chant in harmony.

WWW.TV

Tuvalu is lucky enough to have .tv as its national internet domain name. It's allowed the tiny nation to earn millions by selling web addresses with the super-recognizable ending!

16 FT.

BELOW SEA LEVEL

GLOBAL WARMING

Tuvalu is one of the most low-lying countries on the planet. Most of the islands surrounding Tuvalu are about 16 ft. (5 m) below sea level. The nation is thought to be one of the first that will disappear completely if the sea levels continue to rise dramatically as the result of global warming.

FIJI

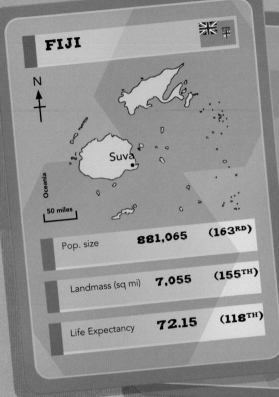

N

Oceania

Suva

50 miles

Pop. size	**881,065**	**(163RD)**
Landmass (sq mi)	**7,055**	**(155TH)**
Life Expectancy	**72.15**	**(118TH)**

Fiji is well known throughout the world for being a tropical island haven, and it's popular with vacationers from across the globe.

The nation is an icon of the Pacific islands of Melanesia, loved for its friendly people, fruit, fire walking, and rare Fijian monkey-faced bats. Made up of 332 islands, Fiji is fantastic!

RAINBOW REEF

Many marine biologists believe that all life on the planet began in the Western Pacific Ocean, near Fiji. That's hard to deny at the Somosomo (Fijian for "good water") Strait, home to the Rainbow Reef, considered one of the most vibrant underwater worlds. It's a place where reef sharks, manta rays, and clownfish all share the same house.

All the colors of the rainbow!

DON'T READ IF HUNGRY

In 1867, an English missionary called Thomas Baker was killed and eaten by a Fijian tribe after he accidentally touched the head of the village chief—an act of war at that time. He was knocked out with a rock, boiled, and then eaten by the tribe. Only one of his shoes was not eaten and it can be viewed at the Fiji Museum.

Boiled shoe, anyone?

THE MEKE

The traditional Fijian dance is known as the *meke*. Through the spirit of the song and the dance, the performers tell the story of Fijian culture, history, and legends. Performed by men and women (but never together), the *meke* is performed by dancers wearing flowing grass skirts.

WORLD-CLASS WAVE

Thought of as one of the best places in the world to surf, Cloudbreak is a wave that is sacred to the Fijian people. Occurring a mile out to sea from the island of Tavarua, Cloudbreak is a unique wave that is "owned" by the Tavarua surf resort; the resort regulates the number of surfers on the reef that causes the wave (so as not to harm it) and pays the local chief for the right to surf the wave!

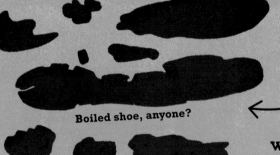

First king of Fiji

SERU EPENISA CAKOBAU

Fiji's most feared chief was Seru Epenisa Cakobau, a warlord who became the first king of Fiji when he united the many warring Fijian tribes under his control. Until 1854, Cakobau was a cannibal who would boil and eat his enemies after defeating them in battle.

WHAT DAY IS IT?

The 180th meridian, or the International Date Line, is a theoretical line that divides the world into two hemispheres, East and West. This line passes right through the middle of the Fijian island of Taveuni. There is even a spot on Taveuni where you can jump forward and back in time between today and

FAMILY VALUES

Tongan society is guided by four core values.

1) **Fefaka'apa'apa'aki** (mutual respect)
2) **Feveitokai'aki** (sharing and cooperation)
3) **Lototoo** (humility and generosity)
4) **Tauhi vaha'a** (loyalty and commitment)

Made up of 160 islands, Tonga is a country where time has stood still.

One of the few nations in the world never to be colonized by a foreign power, Tonga is a pure Polynesian paradise that has continued to enjoy its own culture, traditions, and ways of life for almost 3,000 years.

TONGA

N

Oceania

100 miles

Nuku'alofa

Pop. size	105,323 (188TH)
Landmass (sq mi)	288 (183RD)
Life Expectancy	75.82 (69TH)

RECORD-BREAKING ROYALTY

The world's heaviest monarch to ever squash the throne was Tonga's King Taufa'ahau Tupou IV. In the 1970s, the king was labeled the Fat King. He weighed 440 lb. (200 kg)—twice the weight of an average king! He ruled Tonga for 41 years.

LAKALAKA TIME!

Tonga's revered traditional dance is the *lakalaka*, performed by both men and women, sometimes in groups of several hundred. Dancers sway their arms and legs and wear a feather headpiece called a *tekiteki*.

DRESSED FOR SUCCESS

Worn by both men, women, and Tongan royalty, the nation's everyday traditional dress is called *ta'ovala*—a mat made out of leaves woven together from a Pandanus tree and worn around the waist.

MAMMOTH MIGRATION

The longest migration of any mammal on Earth is the one achieved by the majestic humpback whale. Their 5,000 mi. (8,000 km) journey from Antarctica ends in Tonga, in the warm waters of Vava'u, where the 53 ft. (16 m) long whales give birth to their calves and younger whales breach—a playtime ritual of throwing their entire body out of the water and crashing back into the sea!

GONE FISHING

Some of Tonga's pigs have a taste for seafood! You might find them snuffling about in the waves, looking for tasty shellfish. Locals say that their pork tastes salty because of the pigs' fishy diet!

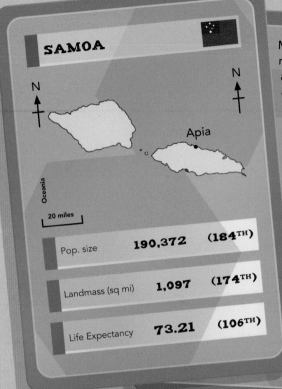

SAMOA

Oceania

20 miles

N

N

Apia

Pop. size	190,372	(184TH)
Landmass (sq mi)	1,097	(174TH)
Life Expectancy	73.21	(106TH)

Made up of two main islands, Savai'i and Upolu, as well as seven smaller islands, Samoa is the second-largest Polynesian nation.

Famous for its traditional way of life, known as *Fa'a Samoa*, or the Samoan Way, as well as its enticing dancing, the country is on a planet all of its own, a place where time just disappears . . .

BACK TO THE FUTURE

In 2011, Samoa moved its position on the International Date Line to the east, so that the country would lie west of the date line—a change that would align it with the Australian business day. By doing so, the country went to bed on Thursday, December 29, and woke up on Saturday, December 31—Friday, December 30, disappeared completely!

29 DEC

?

31 DEC

BLOWHOLES!

Take a trip to Taga and watch the locals throw coconuts into the Alofaaga Blowholes. When the ocean waves hit the holes in the lava rock on the shore, the water pressure propels the coconuts high into the air!

DIVE IN!

The main island of Upolu is the nation's coolest place to take a 98 ft. (30 m) dive! To Sua Ocean Trench in the Lotofaga village is one big electric-blue swimming hole that looks too tempting not to jump in.

EPIC FALES

Samoa's traditional houses are known as *fales*. These oval structures have thatched roofs and no walls, and can sleep up to 20 people—plenty of room for the *aiga* (a large Samoan family) to rest their heads.

IT'S NOT CRICKET

Samoa's national sport looks a lot like cricket but has a lot more dancing. *Kilikiti* players pitch and field a ball using a three-sided Samoan war club called the *lapalapa*. Often when a ball is caught, and a player is out, a celebratory *fia-fia* (happy) dance follows!

SAMOAN SLAP DANCE

Known by the locals as *fa'ataupati*, this is a percussive dance that is performed only by Samoan men. The dance originated in the 1900s when mosquitoes invaded the land. The dance represents the slapping of mosquitoes off the dancers' bodies and is now an iconic part of Samoan culture.

Lapalapa ➡

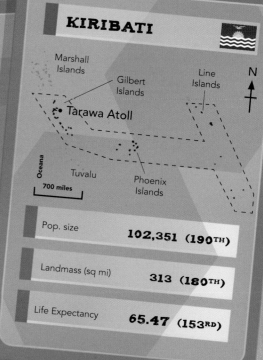

KIRIBATI

Lying across the equator like an outstretched sleepy sunbather, the 33 islands that make up Kiribati are unspoiled, idyllic, and laid-back.

These islanders live their lives according to the tides, and boats are the main form of transport.

Marshall Islands
Gilbert Islands
Line Islands
N
Tarawa Atoll
Oceana
700 miles
Tuvalu
Phoenix Islands

Pop. size	102,351 (190TH)
Landmass (sq mi)	313 (180TH)
Life Expectancy	65.47 (153RD)

FIRST PLACE ON EARTH

Kiribati stretches out over 313 sq. mi. (811 km²). Its westernmost point, Kiritimati (Christmas Island)—the world's largest coral atoll—is the first place on Earth to celebrate New Year. When the clock strikes midnight in Kiritimati, it's 5 A.M. in New York. Last of all to celebrate is American Samoa, 23 hours after Kiritimati.

BOKIKOKIKO

The Kiritimati reed warbler is a little bird found only on tiny Christmas Island in Kiribati. It's known as the bokikokiko because of the chirruping sound it makes.

Bokikokiko (Kiritimati reed warbler)

SERIOUSLY SPIKY

Kiribati warriors in the 17th and 18th centuries were a force to be reckoned with. Armor made from coconut fiber was common, and sharp weapons studded with shark teeth were often wielded.

The most eye-catching part of the outfit, however, was the helmet, which was made from a poisonous and spiny pufferfish. Ouch!

PRONUNCIATION

How do you pronounce *Kiribati*?
Clue: It's not **C)**

A) Kirry-bat-tea
B) Kira-bas
C) Keira-Knight-ly
D) Kie-ra-b at-tie

Answer: B

THE BIRDIE DANCE

Dance on Kiribati is an important part of daily life and culture. The movement of the dancers reflects the movement of the frigate bird—a national symbol of peace. Dancers keep their arms open, and often move their heads suddenly from side to side.

TAHITI AND FRENCH POLYNESIA

Marquesas Islands
Tuamotu Islands
Society Islands
Papeete (Tahiti)
Oceania
Austral Islands
Gambier Islands
250 miles
N

Pop. size	276,831	(181ST)
Landmass (sq mi)	1,609	(172ND)
Life Expectancy	76.79	(55TH)

Paradise on Earth. Heaven. Just two names used to describe the exotic Tahiti and French Polynesia, with their amazing black-sand beaches, black pearls, and fragrant flowers.

Made up of 130 islands and atolls, the area covered by Tahiti and French Polynesia is roughly the same size as the whole of Europe!

TATTOO TIME
The word "tattoo" originated in French Polynesia. Tattoos have long been considered signs of beauty in Polynesian culture, and in ancient times were ceremoniously applied to the body when reaching adolescence. The English word "tattoo" comes from the Tahitian word *tatau*.

THE YOUNG ONES
Around a quarter of the whole population of Tahiti and French Polynesia is under 14 years old.

MUSEUM OF THE BLACK PEARL
The world's only museum dedicated to pearls can be found on Tahiti, home of the highly prized black pearl. Tahitian black pearls are more than 100 times rarer than their paler cousins, and are used to create some of the world's most beautiful jewelry.

Tahitian black pearls

RECORD-BREAKING ART
In 2015 a painting of two Tahitian girls by French artist Paul Gauguin called *Nafaa Faa Ipoipo* (When Will You Marry?) became the most expensive piece of art ever sold, reaching $300 million! In the 1890s the famous artist—known for his post-impressionist style—relocated to Tahiti, settling in the village of Puna'auia.

FLOWER POWER
The Tiare flower is the national symbol of Tahiti. Both men and women wear these flowers, as a necklace or a crown, or behind the ear. You wear a Tiare flower on your left ear if you're taken and on your right ear to indicate you're available.

THE TRAVEL BOOK

Published in September 2015
by Lonely Planet Publications Pty Ltd.
ABN 36 005 607 983
www.lonelyplanetkids.com
ISBN 978 1 74360 774 9
© Lonely Planet 2015
Printed in Singapore

Publishing Director Piers Pickard
Commissioning Editor Jen Feroze
Designer Sally Bond
In-house Senior Designer Andy Mansfield
Illustrator Maggie Li
Author Malcolm Croft
Print production Nigel Longuet and Larissa Frost

Thanks to Sarah Bailey, Joe Bindloss, Claire Clewley, Tim Cook, Laura Crawford, Jennifer Dixon, Megan Eaves, Helen Elfer, Gemma Graham, Alexander Howard, Ruth Martin, Nick Mee, Ma Sovaida Morgan, Lorna Parkes, Mina Patria, Matt Phillips, Christopher Pitts, Sarah Reid, Samantha Russell-Tulip, James Smart, Lyahna Spencer, Anna Tyler, Branislava Vladisavljevic, Tasmin Waby, Steve West, Dora Whitaker, Clifton Wilkinson.

LONELY PLANET OFFICES

Australia
90 Maribymong St, Footscray, Victoria, 3011, Australia
Phone 03 8379 8000
Email talk2us@lonelyplanet.com.au

USA
150 Linden St, Oakland, CA 94607
Phone 510 250 6400
Email info@lonelyplanet.com

UK
240 Blackfriars Road, 6th Floor, London SE1 8NW
Phone 020 3771 5100
Email go@lonelyplanet.co.uk

INDEX

In the alphabetical list below, each country's page number appears in bold, followed by the country's coordinates (the letter and number combination) corresponding to the map's grid.

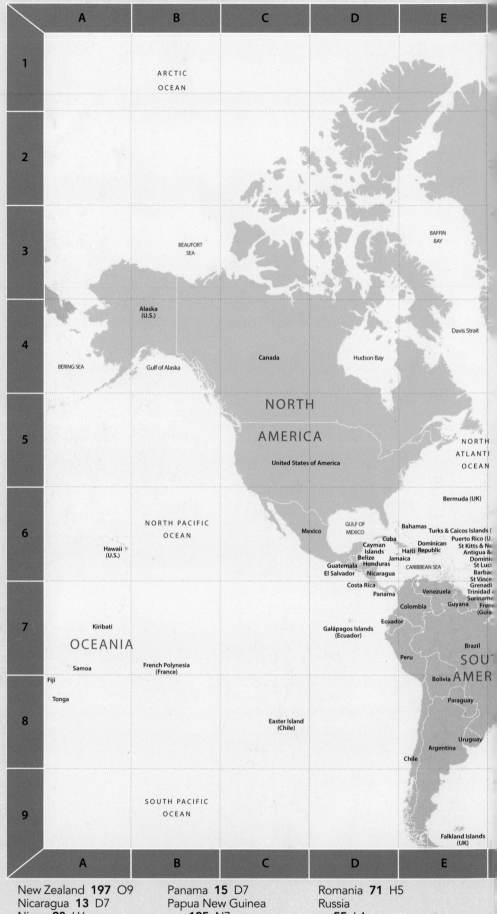